The National Parks Index 1916-2016

Revised to Include the Actions of the
114th Congress ending December 31, 2015

Produced by the Office of Communications
and the Office of Legislative and Congressional Affairs
National Park Service

U.S. Department of the Interior
Washington, D.C.

FOREWORD

2016 marks the 100th anniversary of the National Park Service—a defining moment to reflect on and celebrate our accomplishments as we embark on a new century of stewardship and public engagement.

America has changed dramatically since the birth of the National Park Service in 1916. The agency's roots lie in the parks' majestic, often isolated natural wonders and in places that exemplify our cultural heritage, but our reach now extends to places difficult to imagine 100 years ago — urban centers, rural landscapes, deep oceans, and night skies.

In our second century, we recommit to our core mission, providing exemplary stewardship and public enjoyment of the very special places in our care. We will also continue to support communities through community assistance programs and to create jobs, strengthen local economies, and support ecosystem services. We will use the collective power of the parks, our historic preservation programs, and community assistance programs to protect, preserve, and share the places that tell the American story in the next century.

Of course, all of this cannot be done without the efforts of our dedicated employees, volunteers, and partners. I express my sincere thanks to each and every one of them for their support and passion for the NPS mission entrusted to us by the American people.

Jonathan B. Jarvis
Director

About this Book
This index is a complete administrative listing of the National Park System's areas and related areas. It has been revised to reflect congressional actions. The entries, grouped by state, include administrative addresses and phone numbers, dates of authorization and establishment, boundary change dates, acreages, website addresses, and brief statements explaining the areas' national significance. This book is not intended as a guide for park visitors. There is no information regarding campgrounds, trails, visitor services, hours, etc. Those needing such information can visit each area's web site, accessible through the National Park Service home page: www.nps.gov.

The Mission of the National Park Service
The National Park Service preserves unimpaired the natural and cultural resources and values of the National Park System for the enjoyment, education, and inspiration of this and future generations. The National Park Service cooperates with partners to extend the benefits of natural and cultural resource conservation and outdoor recreation throughout this country and the world.

For sale by the Superintendent of Documents, U.S. Government Publishing Office
Internet: bookstore.gpo.gov   Phone: toll free (866) 512-1800;   DC area (202) 512-1800
Fax: (202) 512-2104 Mail: Stop IDCC, Washington, DC 20402-0001

ISBN 978-0-16-093209-0

CONTENTS

Part 1

Introduction

Grand Canyon National Park

Lincoln Memorial

On August 25, 1916, President Woodrow Wilson signed the act creating the National Park Service, a new federal bureau in the Department of the Interior responsible for protecting the 35 national parks and monuments then managed by the department and those yet to be established. This "Organic Act" states that "the Service thus established shall promote and regulate the use of the Federal areas known as national parks, monuments and reservations . . . by such means and measures as conform to the fundamental purpose of the said parks, monuments and reservations, which purpose is to conserve the scenery and the natural and historic objects and the wild life therein and to provide for the enjoyment of the same in such manner and by such means as will leave them unimpaired for the enjoyment of future generations."

The National Park Service strives to meet those original goals, while filling other roles as well: guardian of our diverse cultural and recreational resources; environmental advocate; world leader in the parks and preservation community; and pioneer in the drive to protect America's open space.

The National Park System comprises 409 areas covering over 84 million acres in 50 States, the District of Columbia, American Samoa, Guam, Puerto Rico, Saipan, and the Virgin Islands. These areas are of such national significance as to justify special recognition and protection in accordance with various acts of Congress.

By the Act of March 1, 1872, Congress established Yellowstone National Park in the Territories of Montana and Wyoming "as a public park or pleasuring-ground for the benefit and enjoyment of the people" and placed it "under exclusive control of the Secretary of the Interior." The founding of Yellowstone National Park began a worldwide national park movement. Today over 100 nations contain some 100,000 national parks or equivalent preserves.

In the years following the establishment of Yellowstone, the United States authorized additional national parks and monuments, most of them carved from the federal lands of the West. These, also, were administered by the Department of the Interior, while other monuments and natural and historical areas were administered as separate units by the War Department and the Forest Service of the Department of Agriculture. No single agency provided unified management of the varied federal parklands.

An Executive Order in 1933 transferred 56 national monuments and military sites from the Forest Service and the War Department to the National Park Service. This action was a major step in the development of today's truly national system of parks—a system that includes areas of historical, scenic, cultural, and scientific importance.

Congress declared in the General Authorities Act of 1970 "that the National Park System, which began with the establishment of Yellowstone National Park in 1872, has since grown to include superlative natural, historic, and recreation areas in every region . . . and that it is the purpose of this Act to include all such areas in the System. . . ."

Additions to the National Park System are now generally made through acts of Congress, and national parks can be created only through such acts. But the president has authority, under the Antiquities Act of 1906, to proclaim national monuments on lands already under federal jurisdiction. The Secretary of the Interior is usually asked by Congress for recommendations on proposed additions to the System. The Secretary is counseled by the National Park System Advisory Board, composed of private citizens, which advises on possible additions to the System and policies for its management.

Nomenclature of Park System Areas

The diversity of the parks is reflected in the variety of titles given to them. These include such designations as national park, national preserve, national monument, national memorial, national historic site, national seashore, and national battlefield park.

Although some titles are self-explanatory, others have been used in many different ways. For example, the title "national monument" has been given to natural reservations, historic military fortifications, prehistoric ruins, fossil sites, and to the Statue of Liberty.

In recent years, both Congress and the National Park Service have attempted to simplify the nomenclature and to establish basic criteria for use of the different official titles. Brief definitions of the most common titles follow.

Areas added to the National Park System for their natural values are expanses or features of land or water of great scenic and scientific quality and are usually designated as national parks, monuments, preserves, seashores, lakeshores, or riverways. Such areas contain one or more distinctive attributes like forest, grassland, tundra, desert, estuary, or river systems; they may contain windows on the past for a view of geological history; they may contain imposing landforms like mountains, mesas, thermal areas, and caverns; and they may be habitats of abundant or rare wildlife and plantlife.

Generally, a **national park** contains a variety of resources and encompasses large land or water areas to help provide adequate protection of the resources.

A **national monument** is intended to preserve at least one nationally significant resource. It is usually smaller than a national park and lacks its diversity of attractions.

In 1974, Big Cypress and Big Thicket were authorized as the first **national preserves**. This category is established primarily for the protection of certain resources. Activities like hunting and fishing or the extraction of minerals and fuels may be permitted if they do not jeopardize the natural values. **National reserves** are similar to the preserves. Management may be transferred to local or state authorities. The first reserve, City of Rocks, was established in 1988.

Preserving shoreline areas and off-shore islands, the **national lakeshores** and **national seashores** focus on the preservation of natural values while at the same time providing water-oriented recreation. Although national lakeshores can be established on any natural freshwater lake, the existing four are all located on the Great Lakes. The national seashores are on the Atlantic, Gulf, and Pacific coasts.

National rivers and **wild and scenic riverways** preserve free-flowing streams and their immediate environment with at least one outstandingly remarkable natural, cultural, or recreational value. They must flow naturally without major alteration of the waterway by dams, diversion, or otherwise alteration. Besides protecting and enhancing rivers, these areas provide opportunities for outdoor activities like hiking, canoeing, and hunting.

National scenic trails are generally long-distance footpaths winding through areas of natural beauty. **National historic trails**

recognize original trails or routes of travel of national historical significance.

Although best known for its great scenic parks, over half the areas of the National Park System preserve places and commemorate persons, events, and activities important in the nation's history. These range from archeological sites associated with prehistoric Indian civilizations to sites related to the lives of modern Americans. Historical areas are customarily preserved or restored to reflect their appearance during the period of their greatest historical significance.

In recent years, **national historic site** has been the title most commonly applied by Congress in authorizing the addition of such areas to the National Park System. A wide variety of titles—**national military park, national battlefield park, national battlefield site**, and **national battlefield**—has been used for areas associated with American military history. But other areas like **national monuments** and **national historical parks** may include features associated with military history. **National historical parks** are commonly areas of greater physical extent and complexity than national historic sites. The lone **international historic site** refers to a site relevant to both U.S. and Canadian history.

The title **national memorial** is most often used for areas that are primarily commemorative. They need not be sites or structures historically associated with their subjects. For example, the home of Abraham Lincoln in Springfield, Ill., is a national historic site, but the Lincoln Memorial in the District of Columbia is a national memorial.

Several areas whose titles do not include the words "national memorial" are nevertheless classified as memorials. These are Franklin Delano Roosevelt Memorial, Korean War Veterans Memorial, Lincoln Memorial, Lyndon Baines Johnson Memorial Grove, Theodore Roosevelt Island, Thomas Jefferson Memorial, Vietnam Veterans Memorial, Washington Monument, and World War II Memorial in the District of Columbia; Jefferson National Expansion Memorial in Missouri; Perry's Victory in Ohio; and Arlington House in Virginia.

Originally, **national recreation areas** in the park system were units surrounding reservoirs impounded by dams built by other federal agencies. The National Park Service manages many of these areas under cooperative agreements. The concept of recreational areas has grown to encompass other lands and waters set aside for recreational use by acts of Congress and now includes major areas in urban centers. There are also national recreation areas outside the National Park System that are administered by the Forest Service, U.S. Department of Agriculture.

National parkways encompass ribbons of land flanking roadways and offer an opportunity for driving through areas of scenic interest. They are not designed for high speed travel. Besides the four areas set aside as parkways, other units of the National Park System include parkways within their boundaries.

One area of the National Park System has been set aside primarily as a site for the **performing arts**. This is Wolf Trap National Park for the Performing Arts, Virginia, America's first such national park. Two historical areas, Ford's Theatre National Historic Site, in Washington, D.C., and Chamizal National Memorial, Texas, also provide facilities for the performing arts.

Designation of Wilderness Areas

In the Wilderness Act of 1964 Congress directed certain federal agencies, including the National Park Service, to study lands they administer for their suitability for inclusion in the National Wilderness Preservation System. Congress has now designated **wilderness areas** in 47 units of the National Park System. Wilderness designation does not remove these lands from the parks but ensures they are managed to retain their "primeval character and influence, without permanent improvements or human habitation." There are also 38 wilderness study areas under National Park Service management. Of these areas, 19 were formally transmitted for Congressional action over the last 35 years.

The Act provides that "there shall be no commercial enterprise and no permanent road within any wilderness area . . . and (except for emergency uses) no temporary road, no use of motor vehicles, motorized equipment or motor boats, no landing of aircraft, no other form of mechanical transport, and no structure or installation." Wilderness areas are open to hiking and, in some cases, horseback riding, primitive camping, and other nonmechanical recreation. The Wilderness Act recognizes that wilderness "may also contain ecological, geological, or other features of scientific, educational, scenic, or historical value." Wilderness embodies spiritual, artistic, therapeutic, cultural, and other important values.

Wilderness holds exciting prospects for future management of National Park Service lands. Because wilderness exists on lands of the National Park System, National Forest System, National Wildlife Refuge System, and Bureau of Land Management, it offers a common statutory basis for interagency cooperation in ecosystem management. Only the Wilderness Act mandates preservation of natural processes, making wilderness areas ideal protected core areas for ecosystems, just as national parks often provide core protection for biosphere reserves and world heritage sites. As such, wilderness areas provide important benchmark areas for scientific research and monitoring.

Growing demand for wilderness experience makes sophisticated, sensitive wilderness management essential. The National Park Service believes that wilderness management is the highest form of stewardship it can provide for the public lands in its care.

Parks in the Nation's Capital

Washington, D.C., has a unique park system. Most public parks are administered by the federal government through the National Capital Region of the National Park Service.

National Capital Region has inherited duties originally assigned to three Federal Commissioners appointed by President George Washington in 1790. The city's parks were administered by a variety of federal agencies until this responsibility was assigned to the National Park Service under the Reorganization Act of 1933. Most city parklands are included in the federal holdings, although the District of Columbia also operates parks, playgrounds, and recreational facilities. National Capital Region also administers National Park System units in Maryland, Virginia, and West Virginia.

Related Areas

Besides the National Park System, five area designations—Authorized Areas, Affiliated Areas, National Heritage Areas, the National Wild and Scenic Rivers System, and the National Trails System—are linked in importance and purpose to areas managed by the National Park Service. These areas are not all units of the National Park System, yet they preserve important segments of the nation's heritage. They are listed in Part 3 of this book.

Regional Offices

Alaska Region
National Park Service
240 West 5th Avenue
Anchorage, AK 99501
907-644-3510

Intermountain Region
National Park Service
12795 Alameda Parkway
Denver, CO 80225
303-969-2500

Midwest Region
National Park Service
601 Riverfront Drive
Omaha, NE 68102
402-661-1736

National Capital Region
National Park Service
1100 Ohio Drive SW
Washington, DC 20242
202-619-7000

Northeast Region
National Park Service
U.S. Custom House
200 Chestnut Street, Fifth Floor
Philadelphia, PA 19106
215-597-7013

Pacific West Region
National Park Service
333 Bush Street, suite 350
San Francisco, CA 94104-2628
415-623-2100

Southeast Region
National Park Service
100 Alabama Street SW
1924 Building
Atlanta, GA 30303
404-507-5600

For more information call the National Park Service Office of Public Affairs: 202-208-6843 or visit www.nps.gov.

Two national park areas in the lower 48 states have adjoining national preserves that are separate units of the National Park System but are managed jointly. They are: Great Sand Dunes and Craters of the Moon.

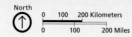

North

| 0 | 100 | 200 Kilometers |
| 0 | 100 | 200 Miles |

Noatak

Cape Krusenstern

Bering Land Bridge

Kobuk Valley

Gates of the Arctic

ALASKA

Yukon-Charley Rivers

Denali

Wrangell-St. Elias

Lake Clark

Alagnak

Kenai Fjords

Klondike Gold Rush

Katmai

Glacier Bay

Aniakchak

Sitka

Seven national park areas in Alaska have adjoining national preserves that are separate units of the National Park System but are managed jointly. They are: Aniakchak, Denali, Gates of the Arctic, Glacier Bay, Katmai, Lake Clark, and Wrangell-St. Elias.

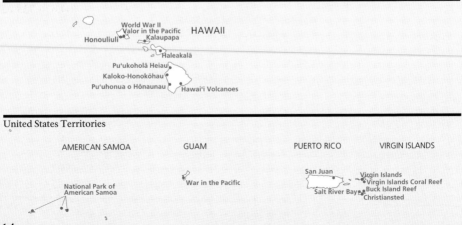

World War II
Valor in the Pacific   HAWAII
Honouliuli   Kalaupapa

Haleakalā

Pu'ukoholā Heiau

Kaloko-Honokōhau

Pu'uhonua o Hōnaunau   Hawai'i Volcanoes

United States Territories

AMERICAN SAMOA   GUAM   PUERTO RICO   VIRGIN ISLANDS

San Juan   Virgin Islands
Virgin Islands Coral Reef
War in the Pacific   Buck Island Reef
Salt River Bay   Christiansted

National Park of
American Samoa

Classification	Number	Acreage
National Battlefield, National Battlefield Park, National Military Park, and National Battlefield Site	25	73,368.23
National Historical Park, National Historic Site, and International Historic Site	129	223,036.40
National Lakeshore	4	229,170.54
National Memorial	30	10,735.13
National Monument	80	2,028,142.61
National Park	59	52,202,282.86
National Parkway	4	179,088.15
National Preserve and National Reserve	21	24,317,862.67
National Recreation Area	18	3,704,876.57
National River[1] and National Wild and Scenic River and Riverway[2]	15	764,953.88
National Scenic Trail	3	246,967.92
National Seashore	10	596,931.79
Other Designations[3]	11	38,907.10
Totals	**409**	**84,616,323.85**

[1] National Park System units only.

[2] National Park System units and components of the National Wild and Scenic Rivers System.

[3] Includes White House, National Mall, and other areas.

Part 2

Listing of National Park System Areas by State

Wright Brothers National Memorial

Alabama

**Horseshoe Bend
National Military Park**
11288 Horseshoe Bend Road
Daviston, AL 36256
256-234-7111
www.nps.gov/hobe

On March 27, 1814, at the "horseshoe bend" on the Tallapoosa River, Gen. Andrew Jackson's forces broke the power of the Upper Creek Indian Confederacy and opened large parts of Alabama and Georgia to settlement.
Authorized July 25, 1956.
Acreage—2,040.00, all Federal.

**Little River Canyon
National Preserve**
4322 Little River Trace NE,
Suite 100
Fort Payne, AL 35967-9300
256-845-9605
www.nps.gov/liri

The preserve protects the natural, recreational, and cultural resources of the Little River Canyon of northeast Alabama. A variety of rock expanses, benches, and bluffs creates a unique environment for several threatened and endangered species and for recreational pursuits, including kayaking and rock climbing. Hunting, fishing, and trapping are permitted.
Authorized Oct. 24, 1992.
Acreage—15,288.37 Federal: 11,081.72 Nonfederal: 4,206.65

**Natchez Trace
National Scenic Trail**
(See Mississippi)

Natchez Trace Parkway
(See Mississippi)

**Russell Cave
National Monument**
3729 County Road 98
Bridgeport, AL 35740-9770
205-495-2672
www.nps.gov/ruca

An almost continuous archeological record of human habitation from at least 9000 B.C.E. to about 1650 C.E.—Transitional Paleo to Mississippian cultural periods—is revealed in this cave.
Proclaimed May 11, 1961.
Acreage—310.45, all Federal.

**Tuskegee Airmen
National Historic Site**
c/o Tuskegee Institute
National Historic Site
PO Drawer 10
Tuskegee Institute, AL
36087-0010
334-724-0922
www.nps.gov/tuai

This site preserves the airfield, historic hangar, and other buildings at Moton Field, where African-American pilots known as the Tuskegee Airmen received their initial flight training during World War II.
Established Nov. 6, 1998.
Acreage—89.69 Federal: 44.71 Nonfederal: 44.98.

**Tuskegee Institute
National Historic Site**
P.O. Drawer 10
Tuskegee Institute, AL
36087-0010
334-727-3200
www.nps.gov/tuin

Booker T. Washington founded this college for African Americans in 1881. Preserved here are the brick buildings the students constructed themselves, Washington's home, and the George Washington Carver Museum, which serves as the visitor center. The college is still an active institution that owns most of the property within the national historic site.
Authorized Oct. 26, 1974.
Acreage—57.92 Federal: 8.92 Nonfederal: 49.

Alaska

Alagnak Wild River
1000 Silver Street, Bldg.603
PO Box 245
King Salmon, AK 99613
907-246-3305
www.nps.gov/alag

The Alagnak River flows from Kukaklek Lake in Katmai National Preserve and offers 67 miles of outstanding whitewater floating, scenery, recreation, historic, cultural and natural values. The river is also noted for abundant wildlife and sport fishing for five species of salmon. Established Dec. 2, 1980. Length: 67 miles.
Acreage—30,664.79 Federal: 26,417.85
Nonfederal: 4,246.94.

Aniakchak
National Monument and
Aniakchak
National Preserve
1000 Silver Street, Bldg.603
PO Box 245
King Salmon, AK 99613
907-246-3305
www.nps.gov/ania

The Aniakchak Caldera, covering some 30 square miles, is one of the great dry calderas in the world. Located in the volcanically active Aleutian Mountains, the Aniakchak last erupted in 1931. The crater includes lava flows, cinder cones, and explosion pits, as well as Surprise Lake, source of the Aniakchak River, which cascades through a 1,500-foot gash in the crater wall. NO FEDERAL FACILITIES.
Proclaimed Aniakchak National Monument Dec. 1, 1978; established as a national monument and national preserve Dec. 2, 1980.
*Acreage—**National monument: 137,176.00, all Federal.***
National preserve: 464,117.93 Federal: 458,809.35
Nonfederal: 5,308.58.

Bering Land Bridge
National Preserve
PO Box 220
Nome, AK 99762-0220
907-443-2522
www.nps.gov/bela

Located on the Seward Peninsula, the preserve is a remnant of the land bridge that once connected Asia with North America over 13,000 years ago. Paleontological and archeological resources abound; large populations of migratory birds nest here. Ash explosion craters and lava flows, rare in the Arctic, are present. LIMITED FEDERAL FACILITIES.
Proclaimed a national monument Dec. 1, 1978; established as a national preserve Dec. 2, 1980.
Acreage—2,697,391.01 Federal: 2,632,508.00
Nonfederal: 64,883.01

Cape Krusenstern
National Monument
PO Box 1029
Kotzebue, AK 99752-0029
907-442-3890
www.nps.gov/cakr

Archeological sites located along a succession of 114 lateral beach ridges illustrate Eskimo communities of every known cultural period in arctic Alaska, dating back some 4,000 years. Nearly pristine barrier islands, lagoons, and beaches provide habitat for fish, marine mammals, and migratory birds while allowing legal harvest by local subsistence users. LIMITED FEDERAL FACILITIES.
Proclaimed Dec. 1, 1978. Boundary change: Dec. 2, 1980.
Acreage—649,096.15 Federal: 627,190.67
Nonfederal: 21,905.48.

Denali National Park and **Denali National Preserve**
PO Box 9
McKinley Park, AK 99755-0009
907-683-2253
www.nps.gov/dena

The park contains North America's highest mountain, 20,310-foot Denali. Large glaciers of the Alaska Range, caribou, Dall sheep, moose, grizzly bears, and timber wolves are highlights of this national park and preserve.

Established as Mt. McKinley National Park Feb. 26, 1917. Separate Denali National Monument proclaimed Dec. 1, 1978. Both incorporated into and established as Denali National Park and Denali National Preserve Dec. 2, 1980. Wilderness designated Dec. 2, 1980. Other boundary changes: Jan. 30, 1922; March 19, 1932. Designated a Biosphere Reserve 1976.

*Acreage—**National park:** 4,740,911.16 Federal: 4,732,650.51 Nonfederal: 8,260.65. Wilderness area: 1,900,000. **National preserve:** 1,334,117.80 Federal: 1,304,241.97 Nonfederal: 29,875.83.*

Gates of the Arctic National Park and **Gates of the Arctic National Preserve**
4175 Geist Road
Fairbanks, AK 99709
907-457-5752
www.nps.gov/gaar

Lying north of the Arctic Circle, the park and preserve include part of the Central Brooks Range, the northernmost extension of the Rocky Mountains. Often called the greatest wilderness in North America, these NPS units are characterized by jagged peaks, gentle arctic valleys, wild rivers, and many lakes. With adjacent Kobuk Valley National Park and Noatak National Preserve, they form one of the largest park areas in the world.

Proclaimed Gates of the Arctic National Monument Dec. 1, 1978; established as a national park and national preserve Dec. 2, 1980. Wilderness designated Dec. 2, 1980. Designated a Biosphere Reserve (portion) 1984.

*Acreage—**National park:** 7,523,897.45 Federal: 7,359,650.20 Nonfederal: 164,247.25. **National preserve:** 948,608.07 Federal: 948,203.00 Nonfederal: 405.07.*

Glacier Bay National Park and **Glacier Bay National Preserve**
PO Box 140
Gustavus, AK 99826-0140
907-697-2232
www.nps.gov/glba

Covering 3.3 million acres of rugged mountains, dynamic glaciers, temperate rainforests, wild coastlines, and deep sheltered fjords, Glacier Bay is a highlight of Alaska's Inside Passage offering limitless opportunities for adventure and inspiration.

Proclaimed Glacier Bay National Monument Feb. 26, 1925; established as a national park and national preserve Dec. 2, 1980. Boundary changes: April 18, 1939; March 31, 1955; December 1, 1978. Wilderness designated Dec. 2, 1980. Designated a Biosphere Reserve 1986. Designated a World Heritage site Dec, 14, 1992.

*Acreage—**National park:** 3,223,383.43 Federal: 3,222,284.20 Nonfederal: 1,099.23 Wilderness area: 2,770,000. **National preserve:** 58,406.00, all Federal.*

Katmai National Park and
Katmai National Preserve
PO Box 7
King Salmon, AK 99613-0007
907-246-3305
www.nps.gov/katm

Variety marks this vast land: lakes, forests, mountains, and marshlands abound in wildlife. The Alaska brown bear, the world's largest carnivore, thrives here, feeding on red salmon that spawn in the lakes and streams. Wild rivers and renowned sport fishing add to the attractions of this subarctic environment. Here, in 1912, Novarupta Volcano erupted violently, forming the ash-filled "Valley of Ten Thousand Smokes" where steam rose from countless fumaroles.
Proclaimed Katmai National Monument Sept. 24, 1918; established as national park and national preserve Dec. 2, 1980. Boundary changes: April 24, 1931; Aug. 4, 1942; Jan. 20, 1969; Dec. 1, 1978; Dec. 2, 1980. Wilderness designated Dec. 2, 1980.
Acreage—National park: 3,674,368.02 Federal: 3,611,403.12 Nonfederal: 62,964.90 Wilderness area: 3,473,000. National preserve: 418,698.80 Federal: 333,400.98 Nonfederal: 85,297.82.

**Kenai Fjords
National Park**
PO Box 1727
Seward, AK 99664-1727
907-422-0500
www.nps.gov/kefj

The park preserves the 800-square-mile Harding Icefield, the largest icefield solely contained within the United States, its outflowing glaciers, and coastal fjords and islands in their natural state. Here a rich, varied rainforest is home to tens of thousands of breeding seabirds, and adjoining marine waters support a multitude of sea lions, sea otters, and seals. The visitor center is located in Seward.
Proclaimed a national monument Dec. 1, 1978; established as a national park Dec. 2, 1980.
Acreage—669.983.65 Federal: 603,129.86 Nonfederal: 66,853.79.

**Klondike Gold Rush
National Historical Park**
PO Box 517
Skagway, AK 99840-0517
907-983-2921
www.nps.gov/klgo
(See also Washington)

Historic buildings and exhibits in Skagway, the Chilkoot Trail, and portions of the White Pass Trail, all prominent in the 1898 gold rush, are included in the park. The National Park Service has restored more than 20 Gold Rush era buildings in downtown Skagway that house a visitor center, a Junior Ranger activity center, an international trail center operated in conjunction with Parks Canada, several museums, administrative offices, and businesses that lease space from the Federal government.
Authorized June 30, 1976.
Acreage—12,996.49 Federal: 3,420.00 Nonfederal: 9,576.49.

**Kobuk Valley
National Park**
PO Box 1029
Kotzebue, AK 99752-1029
907-442-3890
www.nps.gov/kova

This remote park embraces the central Kobuk River valley, north of the Arctic Circle. At the northern-most extent of the boreal forest, the park protects several rivers, designated wilderness, the Great Kobuk Sand Dunes, and archeological resources such as Onion Portage. An array of wildlife are legally harvested by subsistence users, including caribou, grizzlies, wolves, and waterfowl. LIMITED FEDERAL FACILITIES.
Proclaimed a national monument Dec. 1, 1978; established as a national park Dec. 2, 1980. Wilderness designated Dec. 2, 1980.
Acreage—1,750,716.16 Federal: 1,713,938.48 Nonfederal: 36,777.68. Wilderness area: 190,000.

**Lake Clark National Park
and Lake Clark
National Preserve**
240 W. 5th Ave., Suite 236
Anchorage, AK 99501
907-644-3810
www.nps.gov/lacl

Located in the heart of the Chigmit mountains, the park and preserve contain great geologic diversity, including jagged peaks, granite spires, and two symmetrical active volcanoes. Over a score of glacially carved lakes rim the mountain mass. Lake Clark, over 40 miles long, is the largest lake here and also the headwaters for red salmon spawning.
Proclaimed Lake Clark National Monument Dec. 1, 1978; established as a national park and national preserve Dec. 2, 1980. Wilderness designated Dec. 2, 1980.
Acreage—National park: 2,619,836.49 Federal: 2,481,439.42 Nonfederal: 138,397.07 Wilderness area: 2,470,000. National preserve: 1,410,293.68 Federal: 1,259,128.14 Nonfederal: 151,165.54.

Noatak National Preserve
PO Box 1029
Kotzebue, AK 99752-0129
907-442-3890
www.nps.gov/noat

The Noatak River basin is the largest untrammeled mountain-ringed river basin in the nation. The preserve is a transition zone and migration route for plants and animals between subarctic and arctic environments. It is specially designated as a place for scientific study of the archeological, plant and wildlife resources that it protects. LIMITED FEDERAL FACILITIES.
Proclaimed a national monument Dec. 1, 1978; established as a national preserve Dec. 2, 1980. Wilderness designated Dec. 2, 1980. Designated a Biosphere Reserve 1976.
Acreage—6,587,071.39 Federal: 6,549,227.93 Nonfederal: 37,843.46. Wilderness area: 5,800,000.

**Sitka
National Historical Park**
106 Metlakatla Street
Sitka, AK 99835-7665
907-747-0110
www.nps.gov/sitk

The site of the 1804 fort and battle that marked the last major Tlingit Indian resistance to Russian colonization is preserved here. Tlingit totem poles and crafts are exhibited. The Russian Bishop's House, built in 1842, is the oldest intact piece of Russian-American architecture.
Proclaimed a national monument March 23, 1910; redesignated Oct. 18, 1972. Boundary changes: Feb. 25, 1952; Oct. 18, 1972.
Acreage—116.16 Federal: 109.89 Nonfederal: 6.27.

**World War II
Valor in the Pacific
National Monument**
(Also in Hawaii and
California)

This monument comprises nine historic sites representing various aspects of World War II history in the Pacific. Five sites are in the Pearl Harbor area: the USS Arizona Memorial and visitor center; the USS Utah Memorial; the USS Oklahoma Memorial; the six chief petty officer bungalows on Ford Island; and mooring quays F6, F7, and F8, which constituted part of Battleship Row. Three sites are located in Alaska's Aleutian Islands: the crash site of a consolidated B-24D liberator bomber on Atka Island, the Kiska Island site of Imperial Japan's occupation that began in June 1942; and Attu Island, the site of the only land battle fought in North America during World War II. The last of the nine designations is the Tule Lake Segregation Center National Historic Landmark and nearby Camp Tule Lake in California—both of which housed Japanese Americans relocated from the west coast of the United States.
Proclaimed Dec. 5, 2008.
Acreage—59.03 Federal: 56.66 Nonfederal: 2.37.

Wrangell-St. Elias National Park and **Wrangell-St. Elias National Preserve**
PO Box 439
Copper Center, AK 99573
907-822-5234
www.nps.gov/wrst

The Chugach, Wrangell, St. Elias, and Alaska mountain ranges converge here in what is often referred to as the "mountain kingdom of North America." The national park is the largest unit of the National Park System. The park and preserve include the continent's largest assemblage of glaciers and the greatest collection of peaks above 16,000 feet, including Mount St. Elias. At 18,008 feet it is the second highest peak in the United States.

Proclaimed Wrangell-St. Elias National Monument Dec. 1, 1978; established as a national park and national preserve Dec. 2, 1980. Wilderness designated Dec. 2, 1980. Designated a World Heritage Site Oct. 24, 1979.

*Acreage—**National park:** 8,323,146.48 Federal: 7,951,154.03 Nonfederal: 371,992.45   **National preserve:** 4,852,644.52 Federal: 4,322,529.88 Nonfederal: 530,114.64 Wilderness area: 8,700,000.*

Yukon-Charley Rivers National Preserve
4175 Geist Road
Fairbanks, AK 99709
907-457-5752
www.nps.gov/yuch

Located along the Canadian border in central Alaska, the preserve protects 128 miles of the 1,900-mile Yukon River and the entire Charley River basin. Old cabins and relics are reminders of the importance of the Yukon River during the 1898 gold rush. The Charley, an 88-mile wild river, is considered by many to be the most spectacular river in Alaska. LIMITED FEDERAL FACILITIES.

Proclaimed Yukon-Charley National Monument Dec. 1, 1978; established as a national preserve Dec. 2, 1980.

Acreage—2,526,512.44 Federal: 2,195,546.98 Nonfederal: 330,965.46.

American Samoa

National Park of American Samoa
MHJ Building, 2nd Floor
Pago Pago AS, 96799
684-633-7082
www.nps.gov/npsa

Paleotropical rain forests, coral reefs, and beaches on three volcanic islands in the South Pacific are home to a variety of ocean life, birds, and two species of fruit bats-the only native mammals. Also, experience 3,000-year-old Samoan culture and its traditions. Overnights in villages are encouraged.

Authorized Oct. 31, 1988; 50-year lease signed Sept. 9, 1993.

Acreage—8,256.67, all Nonfederal. Water area: 2,500.

Arizona

Canyon de Chelly National Monument
PO Box 588
Chinle, AZ 86503-0588
928-674-5500
www.nps.gov/cach

Located on Navajo trust land and having a resident community, Canyon de Chelly is unique among national park units. The National Park Service, Navajo Nation, and canyon community work in conjunction to manage park resources and enable traditional and contemporary lifeways. Canyon de Chelly National Monument preserves one of the longest, continually inhabited locations by American Indian communities in the United States, spanning at least 5,000 years. Tséyi', the place within the rock, sustains a living community connected to a landscape of great historical and spiritual significance. It is essential to the traditional lives and cultural identity of many native peoples.
Authorized Feb. 14, 1931; proclaimed April 1, 1931. Boundary change: March 1, 1933
Acreage—83,840.00, all Nonfederal.

Casa Grande Ruins National Monument
1100 Ruins Drive
Coolidge, AZ 85228-3200
520-723-3172
www.nps.gov/cagr

This multi-storied, earthen-walled structure surrounded by the remains of smaller buildings and a compound wall was constructed by the Hohokam, who farmed the Gila Valley in the early 1200s. Casa Grande was abandoned by the mid-1400s.
Authorized as Casa Grande Ruin Reservation March 2, 1889; proclaimed June 22, 1892; redesignated Aug. 3, 1918. Boundary changes: Dec. 10, 1909; June 7, 1926.
Acreage—472.50, all Federal.

Chiricahua National Monument
12856 E. Rhyolite Creek Rd.
Willcox, AZ 85643-9737
520-824-3560
www.nps.gov/chir

The rock formations here were created millions of years ago by volcanic activity, resulting in a landscape of rare beauty. Faraway Ranch, a cattle ranch/guest ranch, has been restored. Proclaimed April 18, 1924; transferred from U.S. Forest Service, Aug. 10, 1933. Boundary changes: June 10, 1938; Nov. 10, 1978; Aug. 28, 1984; Dec. 2015. Wilderness designated Oct. 20, 1976; Aug. 28, 1984.
Acreage—12,024.73 Federal: 12,022.38 Nonfederal: 2.35. Wilderness area: 10,290.

Coronado National Memorial
4101 East Montezuma Canyon Road
Hereford, AZ 85615-9376
520-366-5515
www.nps.gov/coro

In a natural setting on the Mexican border, the memorial commemorates the first organized expedition into the Southwest led by Francisco Vasquez de Coronado in 1540 and affirms the ties that bind the United States to Mexico and Spain.
Authorized as International Memorial Aug. 18, 1941; redesignated July 9, 1952; established Nov. 5, 1952. Boundary changes: Sept. 2, 1960; Nov. 10, 1978.
Acreage—4,830.22 Federal: 4,828.22 Nonfederal: 2.00.

Fort Bowie National Historic Site
3327 S. Old Fort Bowie Road
Bowie, AZ 85605-0158
520-847-2500
www.nps.gov/fobo

Established in 1862, the fort was the focal point of military operations against the Chiricahua Apache. The site also preserves part of the Butterfield Overland Mail Route.
Authorized Aug. 30, 1964; established July 29, 1972.
Acreage—999.45, all Federal.

**Glen Canyon
National Recreation Area**
Glen Canyon National Recreation Area
PO Box 1507
Page, AZ 86040-1507
928-608-6200
www.nps.gov/glca
(Also in Utah)

The area encompasses over a million acres of the most rugged canyon country on the Colorado Plateau. Lake Powell stretches 186 miles behind Glen Canyon Dam; its 1,960 miles of shore- line provide water-recreation activities.
Administered by the National Park Service in collaboration with several agencies. Established Oct. 27, 1972. Boundary changes: Jan. 3, 1975; July 1, 2003.
Acreage—1,254,116.62 Federal: 1,239,763.84 Nonfederal: 14,352.78.

**Grand Canyon
National Park**
PO Box 129
Grand Canyon, AZ 86023-0129
928-638-7888
www.nps.gov/grca

Grand Canyon National Park encompasses 277 miles of the Colorado River and adjacent uplands, from the southern terminus of Glen Canyon National Recreation Area to the eastern boundary of Lake Mead National Recreation Area. Formations illustrate periods of geological history. Proclaimed as Grand Canyon Forest Reserve Feb. 20, 1893; Grand Canyon Game Preserve proclaimed Nov. 28, 1906; Grand Canyon National Monument proclaimed Jan. 11, 1908; national park established Feb. 26, 1919; transferred from U.S. Forest Service, Aug. 15, 1919. Boundary changes: Feb. 25, 1927; March 7, 1928. A separate Grand Can- yon National Monument proclaimed Dec. 22, 1932. Boundary change: April 4, 1940. Marble Canyon National Monument proclaimed Jan. 20, 1969. Three units and portions of Glen Canyon and Lake Mead national recreation areas combined with additional lands as a national park Jan. 3, 1975. Designated a World Heritage Site Oct. 26, 1979.
Acreage—1,201,647.03 Federal: 1,180,650.85 Nonfederal: 20,996.18.

**Hohokam Pima
National Monument**
c/o Casa Grande Ruins
National Monument
1100 Ruins Drive
Coolidge, AZ 85228-3200
520-723-3172
www.nps.gov/pima

Preserved here are the archeological remains of the Hohokam culture. *Hohokam* is a Pima Indian word meaning "those who have gone." NOT OPEN TO THE PUBLIC.
Authorized Oct. 21, 1972.
Acreage—1,690.00, all Nonfederal.

**Hubbell Trading Post
National Historic Site**
PO Box 150
Ganado, AZ 86505-0150
928-755-3475
www.nps.gov/hutr

The squeaky wooden floor greets you as you enter the oldest operating trading post on the Navajo Nation. When your eyes adjust to the dim light in the "bullpen" you find you've just entered a mercantile. Little changed since it was sold to the National Park Service in 1967, Hubbell is the oldest continuously operated trading post on the Navajo Reservation. Authorized Aug. 28, 1965.
Acreage—160.09, all Federal.

Lake Mead National Recreation Area
601 Nevada Way
Boulder City, NV 89005-2426
702-293-8990
www.nps.gov/lake
(Also in Nevada)

A premier inland water recreation area in the west and the first national recreation area established by an act of Congress. Lake Mead, formed by Hoover Dam, and Lake Mohave, by Davis Dam, provide 290 square miles of water on which to boat, fish, swim, ski, sail and sun. Nearly 87 percent of the 1.5-million-acre park is land, containing a wealth of natural and cultural resources, including nine wilderness areas, the convergence of three of America's deserts and 1,347 recorded archaeological sites. Administered under cooperative agreements with Bureau of Reclamation, Oct. 13, 1936, and July 18, 1947. Name changed from Boulder Dam Recreation Area Aug. 11, 1947. Established Oct. 8, 1964. Boundary change: Jan. 3, 1975.
Acreage—1,495,805.53 Federal: 1,470,913.26 (of which 4,488.47 are administered by Bureau of Reclamation) Nonfederal: 24,892.27 Land area: 1,314,516.39 Water area: 186,700.

Montezuma Castle National Monument
PO Box 219
Camp Verde, AZ 86322-0219
928-567-5276
www.nps.gov/moca

Built in the 1100s and 1200s, this five-story, 20-room cliff dwelling is one of the best preserved in the United States. Included is Montezuma Well, a collapsed limestone sinkhole that contains invertebrates found nowhere else in the world. Proclaimed Dec. 8, 1906. Boundary changes: Feb. 23, 1937; Oct. 19, 1943; April 4, 1947; June 23, 1959; Nov. 10, 1978, Dec. 19, 2003.
Acreage—1,015.52 Federal: 998.69 Nonfederal: 16.83.

Navajo National Monument
HC 71, Box 3
Tonalea, AZ 86044-9704
928-672-2700
www.nps.gov/nava

Perched in remote, breathtakingly hued canyons of unparalleled beauty, three remarkably preserved sanctuaries built into cliff faces are here: Betatakin, Keet Seel, and Inscription House (closed to the public due to its fragility). These ancient Puebloan sites speak on a human level to all who visit, and provide an experience beyond time and words.
Proclaimed March 20, 1909. Boundary change: March 14, 1912. Headquarters is on 244.59 acres of tribal land adjacent to the Betatakin section; used by agreement of May 1962. A right-of-way of 4.59 acres was granted to the National Park Service in 1977.
Acreage—360.00, all Federal.

Organ Pipe Cactus National Monument
10 Organ Pipe Drive
Ajo, AZ 85321-9626
520-387-6849
www.nps.gov/orpi

Sonoran Desert plants and animals found nowhere else in the United States are protected here as are a number of historic and prehistoric National Register and eligible cultural resources.
Proclaimed April 13, 1937. Wilderness designated Nov. 10, 1978. Designated a Biosphere Reserve 1976.
Acreage—330,688.86 Federal: 329,365.29 Nonfederal: 1,323.57. Wilderness area: 312,600.

Petrified Forest National Park
PO Box 2217
Petrified Forest, AZ 86028
928-524-6228
www.nps.gov/pefo

Featured are petrified logs composed of multicolored quartz; shortgrass prairie; part of the Painted Desert; and archeological, paleontological, historic, and cultural resources.
Proclaimed a national monument Dec. 8, 1906; redesignated Dec. 9, 1962. Boundary changes: July 31, 1911; Nov. 14, 1930; Nov. 30, 1931; Sept. 23, 1932; March 28, 1958, Dec. 3, 2004. Wilderness designated Oct. 23, 1970.
Acreage—221,415.74 Federal: 139,219.94 Nonfederal: 82,195.80 Wilderness area: 50,260.

**Pipe Spring
National Monument**
HC 65, Box 5
Fredonia, AZ 86022
928-643-7105
www.nps.gov/pisp

The springs have sustained hundreds of years of cultural occupation. Ancestral Puebloan and Southern Paiute cultures depended on the site, followed by strategic Mormon outpost and ranching enterprises. Historic structures associated with the 1870 – 1923 outpost and ranching operations remain. Proclaimed May 31, 1923.
Acreage—40.00, all Federal.

Saguaro National Park
3693 South Old
Spanish Trail
Tucson, AZ 85730-5601
520-733-5100
www.nps.gov/sagu

A large wilderness park with two districts that bracket the City of Tucson and one million residents provides a unique opportunity to engage urban dwellers. Giant saguaro cacti, unique to the Sonoran Desert, cover the valley floor and rise into the neighboring mountains. Five biotic life zones are represented, from desert to ponderosa pine forest.
Proclaimed a national monument March 1, 1933; transferred from U.S. Forest Service, Aug. 10, 1933; redesignated Oct. 4, 1994. Boundary changes: Nov. 15, 1961; Oct. 21, 1976; June 19, 1991; Oct. 4, 1994. Wilderness designated Oct. 20, 1976.
Acreage—91,442.42 Federal: 87,526.07 Nonfederal: 3,916.35. Wilderness area: 70,905.

**Sunset Crater Volcano
National Monument**
6400 N. Highway 89
Flagstaff, AZ 86004
928-526-0502
www.nps.gov/sucr

This volcanic cinder cone with summit crater was formed just before 1100. Its upper part is colored as if by a sunset.
Proclaimed Sunset Crater National Monument May 26, 1930; transferred from U.S. Forest Service, Aug. 10, 1933; renamed Nov. 16, 1990.
Acreage—3,040.00, all Federal.

**Tonto
National Monument**
HC 02, Box 4602
Roosevelt, AZ 85545
928-467-2241
www.nps.gov/tont

The Salado Phenomena, 700 years ago, blended ideas of neighboring Native American cultures to emerge a unique and vibrant society. Tonto National Monument showcases two Salado-style cliff dwellings. Colorful pottery, woven cotton cloth, and other artifacts tell a story of people living and using resources from the northern Sonoran Desert from 1250 to 1450 CE.
Proclaimed Dec. 19, 1907; transferred from U.S. Forest Service, Aug. 10, 1933. Boundary change: April 1, 1937.
Acreage—1,120.00, all Federal.

**Tumacacori
National Historical Park**
PO Box 67
Tumacacori, AZ 85640-0067
520-398-2341
www.nps.gov/tuma

The park protects the ruins of three Spanish missions: San José de Tumacácori, San Cayetano de Calabazas, and Los Santos Ángeles de Guevavi. These missions serve as a doorway into the rich and complex blending of cultures within the Santa Cruz River Valley from the 17th century to today. The Juan Bautista de Anza National Historic Trail runs through a mile of rare riparian habitat within the Tumacácori unit.
Proclaimed a national monument Sept. 15, 1908; redesignated Aug. 6, 1990. Boundary changes: April 28, 1959; Nov. 10, 1978; Aug. 6, 1990, Aug. 21, 2002.
Acreage—360.32 Federal: 357.74 Nonfederal: 2.58.

**Tuzigoot
National Monument**
PO Box 219
Camp Verde, AZ 86322-0219
928-567-5276
www.nps.gov/tuzi

Ruins of a large Indian pueblo that flourished in the Verde Valley between 1100 and 1450 have been excavated here.
Proclaimed July 25, 1939. Boundary changes: Nov. 10, 1978; Sept. 15, 2005.
Acreage—811.89 Federal: 381.53 Nonfederal: 430.36.

Walnut Canyon
National Monument
6400 N. Highway 89
Flagstaff, AZ 86004
928-526-3367
www.nps.gov/waca

These cliff dwellings were built in shallow caves under ledges of limestone by the Northern Sinagua people about 800 years ago.
Proclaimed Nov. 30, 1915; transferred from U.S. Forest Service, Aug. 10, 1933. Boundary changes: Sept. 24, 1938; Nov. 12, 1996.
Acreage—3,529.26 Federal: 3,251.42 Nonfederal: 277.84.

Wupatki
National Monument
6400 N. Highway 89
Flagstaff, AZ 86004
928-679-2365
www.nps.gov/wupa

Red sandstone pueblos built by farming Ancestral Puebloan people between 1120 and 1250 are preserved here.
Proclaimed Dec. 9, 1924. Boundary changes: July 9, 1937; Jan. 22, 1941; Aug. 10, 1961; Nov. 12, 1996.
Acreage—35,422.13, all Federal.

Arkansas

Arkansas Post
National Memorial
1741 Old Post Road
Gillett, AR 72055-9707
870-548-2207
www.nps.gov/arpo

The park commemorates key events that occurred on site and nearby: the first semi-permanent European settlement in the Lower Mississippi Valley (1686); a Revolutionary War skirmish (1783); the first territorial capital of Arkansas (1819–1821); and the Civil War Battle of Arkansas Post (1863).
Authorized July 6, 1960. Boundary change: Nov. 14, 1997.
Acreage—757.51 Federal: 663.91 Nonfederal: 93.60.

Buffalo National River
402 North Walnut
Suite 136
Harrison, AR 72601-1173
870-365-2700
www.nps.gov/buff

The Buffalo River winds its way through the Arkansas Ozarks, past towering bluffs and numerous springs, caves, and waterfalls. The river's lower 135 miles and adjacent lands, including 3 wilderness areas, were designated the nation's first national river in 1972 and provide the setting for plentiful recreational and educational opportunities, including canoeing, hiking, and exploring a 19th century mining town.
Authorized March 1, 1972. Wilderness designated Nov. 10, 1978.
Acreage—94,293.31 Federal: 91,813.09 Nonfederal: 2,480.22. Wilderness Area: 36,000.

Fort Smith
National Historic Site
PO Box 1406
Fort Smith, AR 72902-1406
479-783-3961
www.nps.gov/fosm
(Also in Oklahoma)

From the establishment of the first Fort Smith on December 25, 1817, to the final days of Judge Isaac C. Parker's jurisdiction over Indian Territory in 1896, the park preserves almost 80 years of history related to Federal Indian policy. Included are compelling stories of two frontier forts, the tragic Trail of Tears, and the historic jail and federal courthouse of Judge Parker. It is also a site on the Trail of Tears National Historic Trail.
Authorized Sept. 13, 1961. Boundary change: Oct. 21, 1976.
Acreage—75.00 Federal: 37.96 Nonfederal: 37.04.

Fordyce Bathhouse, Hot Springs National Park

Hot Springs National Park
101 Reserve Street
Hot Springs, AR 71901-4195
501-623-2824
www.nps.gov/hosp

The 47 hot springs, numerous hiking trails, and scenic drives are located in the forested Ouachita Mountains. Eight historically and architecturally significant bathhouses compose Bathhouse Row, a National Historic Landmark District. Thermal bathing continues today.
Established as Hot Springs Reservation April 20, 1832; dedicated to public use as a park June 16, 1880; redesignated March 4, 1921. Boundary changes: June 22, 1892; July 14, 1892; Feb. 21, 1903; May 23, 1906; Sept. 18, 1922; June 5, 1924; June 25, 1930; Feb. 14, 1931; June 15, 1936; June 24, 1938; Aug. 10, 1939; Aug. 24, 1954; Aug. 18, 1958; Sept. 21, 1959; Aug. 2, 1993.
Acreage—5,549.10 Federal: 4,958.60 Nonfederal: 590.50.

Little Rock Central High School National Historic Site
2120 Daisy Bates Drive
Little Rock, AR 72202-5212
501-374-1957
www.nps.gov/chsc

Little Rock Central High School National Historic Site serves to provide interpretation and education commemorating the struggle to desegregate Central High School, and the role of these events as a catalyst for the Civil Rights Movement. The site emphasizes the stories of citizens exercising their fundamental human rights in pursuance of justice and equality in a land of promise and democracy that remain as valid today as they were in 1957; and preserves and protects the tangible and intangible (emotional and social) resources associated with those stories.
Established Nov. 6, 1998.
Acreage—27.28 Federal: 2.22 Nonfederal: 25.06.

Pea Ridge National Military Park
15930 U.S. Hwy 62 East
Garfield, AR 72732
479-451-8122
www.nps.gov/peri

The victory here on March 7–8, 1862, in one of the major battles of the Civil War west of the Mississippi, allowed the Union to maintain control of Missouri, thus assisting the strategic Mississippi campaign. Among the Confederate troops at Pea Ridge were about 1,000 Cherokee and Choctaw-Chickasaw Indians.
Authorized July 20, 1956.
Acreage—4,300.35 Federal: 4,278.75 Nonfederal: 21.60.

President William Jefferson Clinton Birthplace Home National Historic Site
117 S. Hervey Street
Hope, AR 71801
870-777-4455
www.nps.gov/wicl

On August 19, 1946, Virginia Blythe gave birth to her son, William Jefferson Blythe, III. Named for his father who died before he was born, he grew up to become William Jefferson Clinton – the 42nd president of the United States. In this house, he learned many of the early lessons that defined his life and his presidency.
Authorized March 30, 2009. Established Dec. 14, 2010. *Acreage – 0.68, all Federal.*

California

Cabrillo National Monument
1800 Cabrillo Memorial Drive
San Diego, CA 92106-3601
619-557-5450
www.nps.gov/cabr

Juan Rodriguez Cabrillo, Iberian explorer who claimed this coast for Spain in 1542, is memorialized here. Old Point Loma Lighthouse is restored to its most active period—the 1880s. Remnants of World War II coastal defense batteries dot the landscape. Gray whales migrate offshore in winter. Intertidal habitats are among the most sensitive in the world.
Proclaimed Oct. 14, 1913; transferred from War Dept. Aug. 10, 1933. Boundary changes: Feb. 2, 1959; Sept. 28, 1974; July 3, 2000.
Acreage—159.94, all Federal.

César E. Chávez National Monument
29700 Woodford-Tehachapi Road
Keene, CA 93531
661-823-6134
www.nps.gov/cech

Widely recognized as the most important Latino leader in the United States during the twentieth century, César E. Chávez led farm workers and supporters in the establishment of the century's first permanent agricultural union. His leadership brought sustained international attention to the plight of the U.S. farm workers, and secured for them higher wages and safer working conditions.
Proclaimed Oct. 8, 2012.
Acreage – 116.56 Federal: 10.50 Nonfederal: 106.06.

Channel Islands National Park
1901 Spinnaker Drive
Ventura, CA 93001-4354
805-658-5700
www.nps.gov/chis

The park consists of five islands off southern California: San Miguel, Santa Rosa, Santa Cruz, Anacapa, and Santa Barbara, including the surrounding one nautical mile of marine waters. Nesting sea birds, sea lion rookeries, and unique plants inhabit the area. Archaeological evidence of substantial populations of Native Americans. Anacapa, Santa Rosa, and Santa Barbara are administered by the National Park Service; Santa Cruz Island is administered by the National Park Service and The Nature Conservancy; is owned by the U.S. Navy and administered by the National Park Service.
Proclaimed a national monument April 26, 1938; redesignated March 5, 1980. Boundary changes: June 10, 1949; May 15, 1978; Oct. 25, 1978. Designated a Biosphere Reserve 1976.
Acreage—249,561.00 Federal: 79,018.62 Nonfederal: 170,542.38.

Death Valley National Park
PO Box 579
Death Valley, CA 92328-0579
760-786-3200
www.nps.gov/deva
(Also in Nevada)

The largest national park in the lower 48 states, this desert park contains mountain ranges, sand dunes, dry lake playas, and many desert springs. It is the lowest point in North America and holds the record for the hottest temperature ever recorded. The area includes Scotty's Castle, a Spanish Mediterranean mansion containing many innovative design features for its time (1930s), the grandiose home of a famous prospector, and other features remnants of gold and borax mining. The Nevada section is home to the Devils Hole pupfish, a tiny desert fish protected endemic to this underground habitat.
Proclaimed a national monument Feb. 11, 1933; redesignated as a national park Oct. 31, 1994. Boundary changes: March 26, 1937; Jan. 17, 1952; Oct. 31, 1994. Designated a Biosphere Reserve 1984. Wilderness designated Oct. 31, 1994.
Acreage—3,373,063.14 Federal: 3,321,159.32 Nonfederal: 51,903.82.

Devils Postpile
National Monument
PO Box 3999
Mammoth Lakes, CA 93546
760-934-2289
www.nps.gov/depo

Preserves and protects the glacially exposed columns of the Devils Postpile, the scenic Rainbow Falls, and the wilderness landscape of the upper Middle Fork San Joaquin River in the Sierra Nevada for scientific value, public interest, and inspiration. Hot lava cooled and cracked some 100,000 years ago to form basalt columns 40 to 60 feet high resembling a giant pipe organ. The John Muir Trail and Pacific Crest National Scenic Trail traverse the monument.
Proclaimed July 6, 1911; transferred from U.S. Forest Service, Aug. 10, 1933.
Acreage—800.19, all Federal. Wilderness area: 750.

Eugene O'Neill
National Historic Site
PO Box 280
Danville, CA 94526-0280
925-838-0249
www.nps.gov/euon

Tao House was built for playwright Eugene O'Neill, who lived here from 1937 to 1944. "The Iceman Cometh" and "Long Day's Journey Into Night" were written here.
Authorized Oct. 12, 1976.
Acreage—13.19, all Federal.

Fort Point
National Historic Site
Fort Mason, Building 201
San Francisco, CA 94123
415-556-1693
www.nps.gov/fopo

This classic brick and granite mid-1800s coastal fort is the only one of its style on the west coast of the United States.
Established Oct. 16, 1970.
Acreage—29.00, all Federal.

Golden Gate
National Recreation Area
Fort Mason, Building 201
San Francisco, CA 94123
415-561-4700
www.nps.gov/goga

The park spans San Francisco, Marin and San Mateo counties, and includes ocean beaches, lagoons, former military properties, Nike missile sites, Fort Mason, Alcatraz Island, more than 100 miles of trails, and the most threatened and endangered species in the NPS.
Established Oct. 27, 1972. Boundary changes: Dec. 26, 1974; Nov. 10, 1978; Sept. 8, 1980; Dec. 28, 1980; June 9, 1992; Oct. 24, 2000; Dec. 20, 2005. Designated a Biosphere Reserve 1988.
Acreage—82,026.51 Federal: 57,378.91 Nonfederal: 24,647.60.

John Muir
National Historic Site
4202 Alhambra Avenue
Martinez, CA 94553-3883
925-228-8860
www.nps.gov/jomu

The park preserves and protects the home and portions of the Alhambra Valley agricultural estate where John Muir lived, worked, and is buried, to memorialize and connect people with Muir's global legacy as an influential naturalist, writer, and champion for protecting national parks and wild lands.
Authorized Aug. 31, 1964. Boundary changes: Oct. 31, 1988; Oct. 30, 2004.
Acreage—344.14 Federal: 338.30 Nonfederal: 5.84.

Joshua Tree
National Park
74485 National Park Drive
Twentynine Palms, CA 92277
760-367-5500
www.nps.gov/jotr

A representative stand of Joshua trees and a great variety of plants and animals exist in this desert region.
Proclaimed a national monument Aug. 10, 1936; redesignated Oct. 31, 1994. Boundary changes: Sept. 25, 1950; June 30, 1961; Oct. 31, 1994. Wilderness designated Oct. 20, 1976. Designated a Biosphere Reserve 1984.
Acreage—790,635.74 Federal: 779,188.51 Nonfederal: 11,447.23. Wilderness area: 429,690.

**Kings Canyon
National Park**
47050 Generals Highway
Three Rivers, CA 93271-9651
559-565-3341
www.nps.gov/seki

Two enormous canyons of the Kings River and the summit peaks of the High Sierra dominate this mountain wilderness. Established as General Grant National Park Oct. 1, 1890; renamed and enlarged March 4, 1940. Other boundary changes: June 21, 1940; Aug. 14, 1958; Aug. 6, 1965. Wilderness designated Sept. 28, 1984. Designated a Biosphere Reserve 1976.
Acreage—461,901.20 Federal: 461,846.05 Nonfederal: 55.15. Wilderness area: 456,552.

**Lassen Volcanic
National Park**
PO Box 100
Mineral, CA 96063-0100
530-595-4444
www.nps.gov/lavo

Lassen Peak erupted intermittently from 1914 to 1917. All four types of volcanoes; thermal features steaming fumaroles, mudpots, sulfurous vents, boiling springs and pools are found in the park.
Proclaimed as Lassen Peak and Cinder Cone National Monuments May 6, 1907; made part of Lassen Volcanic National Park when established Aug. 9, 1916. Boundary changes: April 26, 1928; May 21, 1928; Jan. 19, 1929; April 19, 1930; July 3, 1930; Aug. 10, 1961; April 11, 1972. Wilderness designated Oct. 19, 1972.
Acreage—106,589.02 Federal: 106,448.11 Nonfederal: 140.91.Wilderness area: 78,982.

**Lava Beds
National Monument**
1 Indian Wells Headquarters
Tulelake, CA 96134-8216
530-667-2282
www.nps.gov/labe

Volcanic activity spewed forth molten rock and lava here, creating an incredibly rugged landscape—a natural fortress used by American Indians in the Modoc Indian War, 1872–73. Proclaimed Nov. 21, 1925; transferred from U.S. Forest Service Aug. 10, 1933. Boundary changes: April 27, 1951; Oct. 26, 1974; Jan. 26, 2011. Wilderness designated Oct. 13, 1972.
Acreage—46,692.42, all Federal. Wilderness area: 28,460.

**Manzanar
National Historic Site**
PO Box 426
Independence, CA 93526-0426
760-878-2194
www.nps.gov/manz

Located in the Owens Valley of eastern California, the site protects and interprets the historical, cultural, and natural resources associated with the relocation and internment of Japanese Americans during World War II. Authorized March 3, 1992.
Acreage—813.81, all Federal.

Mojave National Preserve
2701 Barstow Road
Barstow, CA 92311
760-252-6100
www.nps.gov/moja

The third largest park site outside Alaska, Mojave National Preserve protects the fragile habitat of the desert tortoise and other wildlife, vast open spaces little changed by man, and historic mining, ranching, and railroad scenes such as the Kelso railroad depot. A sense of adventure and personal discovery enhance a visit to this minimally developed area. Authorized Oct. 31, 1994.
Acreage—1,542,741.90 Federal: 1,478,953.51 Nonfederal: 63,788.39.

**Muir Woods
National Monument**
Mill Valley, CA 94941-2696
415-388-2596
www.nps.gov/muwo

This virgin stand of coastal redwoods was named for John Muir, writer and conservationist. Proclaimed Jan. 9, 1908. Boundary changes: Sept. 22, 1921; April 5, 1935; June 26, 1951; Sept. 8, 1959; April 11, 1972.
Acreage—553.55 Federal: 522.98 Nonfederal: 30.57.

American kestrel . . .

Skunk . . .

Jackrabbit . . .

Pinnacles
National Park
5000 Highway 146
Paicines, CA 95043-9770
831-389-4485
www.nps.gov/pinn

Spirelike rock formations 500 to 1,200 feet high, with caves and a variety of volcanic features, rise above the smooth contours of the surrounding countryside.
Proclaimed a national monument Jan. 16, 1908; redesignated as national park Jan. 10, 2013. Boundary changes: May 7, 1923; July 2, 1924; April 13, 1931; July 11, 1933; Dec. 5, 1941; Oct. 20, 1976; Jan. 11, 2000. Wilderness designated Oct. 20, 1976.
Acreage—26,685.73 Federal: 26,634.29 Nonfederal: 51.44. Wilderness area: 16,048.

Point Reyes
National Seashore
Point Reyes, CA 94956-9799
415-464-5100
www.nps.gov/pore

This peninsula near San Francisco is noted for its long beaches backed by tall cliffs, lagoons and esteros, forested ridges, and offshore bird and sea lion colonies. The park contains a historic ranching area.
Authorized Sept. 13, 1962; established Oct. 20, 1972. Boundary changes: Dec. 26, 1974; Nov. 10, 1978; March 5, 1980. Wilderness designated Oct. 18, 1976. Designated a Biosphere Reserve 1988.
Acreage—71,055.41 Federal: 65,234.35 Nonfederal: 5,821.06. Land area: 53,883.98. Wilderness area: 25,370.

Port Chicago Naval
Magazine National
Memorial
4202 Alhambra Ave.
Martinez, CA 94553
925-228-8860 x.0
www.nps.gov/poch

This memorial preserves the site of the deadliest home front disaster of World War II, honoring those who lost their lives or were affected by the munitions explosion on July 17, 1944. The disaster and its aftermath illuminated the issues of segregation and revealed inequality in the military. Today the memorial serves as a springboard for exploring social justice in our society. Authorized Oct. 28, 1992. Established Oct. 28, 2009.
Acreage—5.00, all Federal.

Chuckwalla . . .   Desert kit fox . . . all residents of Joshua Tree.

Redwood National Park
1111 Second Street
Crescent City, CA 95531-4198
707-464-6101
www.nps.gov/redw

Coastal redwood forests with virgin groves of ancient trees, including the world's tallest, thrive in the foggy and temperate climate. The park includes 40 miles of scenic Pacific coastline. Established Oct. 2, 1968. Boundary change: March 27, 1978 and Dec. 5, 2005. Designated a World Heritage Site Sept. 2, 1980. Designated a Biosphere Reserve 1983.
Acreage—138,999.37 Federal: 77,746.46 Nonfederal: 61,252.91.

Rosie the Riveter/ World War II Home Front National Historical Park
1401 Marina Way South
Suite C
Richmond, CA 94804
510-232-5050
www.nps.gov/rori

Commemorates the contributions of those who supported World War II: workers, including women and minorities, in the war industries and those who stayed stateside and recycled, collected, saved and sacrificed. The shipyards, day care centers, first managed-health-care hospital, war worker housing, and a liberty ship built in the shipyards are included in the park. Sites open to the public include the Rosie the Riveter Memorial and additional memorials along the Bay Trail through former shipyards.
Authorized and established Oct. 24, 2000.
Acreage—145.19, all Nonfederal.

San Francisco Maritime National Historical Park
2 Marina Blvd. Bldg. E
Fort Mason Center
San Francisco, CA 94123-1382
415-561-7000
www.nps.gov/safr

A fleet of historic vessels at Hyde Street Pier commemorating the achievements of seafaring Americans; a small craft collection; a maritime research center; a maritime museum; a visitor center, and the WPA-era Aquatic Park historic district are highlights of this waterfront park.
Established June 27, 1988.
Acreage—49.86 Federal: 30.03 Nonfederal: 19.83.

**Santa Monica Mountains
National Recreation Area**
401 West Hillcrest Drive
Thousand Oaks, CA 91360
805-370-2301
www.nps.gov/samo

This recreation area near Los Angeles offers rugged mountains, a coastline with sandy beaches and rocky shores, chaparral-blanketed canyons with abundant wildlife, and the 67-mile Backbone Trail. The area preserves the rare Mediterranean ecosystem while also protecting historical sites like Paramount Ranch and the Satwiwa Native American Indian Cultural Center.
Established Nov. 10, 1978. Boundary change: Oct. 9, 2002.
Acreage—156,669.93 Federal: 23,410.89 Nonfederal: 133,259.04.

Sequoia National Park
47050 Generals Highway
Three Rivers, CA 93271
559-565-3341
www.nps.gov/seki

Great groves of giant sequoias, the world's largest living things, Mineral King Valley, and Mount Whitney, the highest mountain in the U.S. outside of Alaska, are spectacular attractions here in the High Sierra.
Established Sept. 25, 1890. Boundary changes: Oct. 1, 1890; July 3, 1926; Dec. 21, 1943; July 21, 1949; Oct. 19, 1951; Aug. 14, 1958; Nov. 10, 1978. Wilderness designated Sept. 28, 1984. Designated a Biosphere Reserve 1976.
Acreage—404,062.63 Federal: 403,908.67 Nonfederal: 153.96. Wilderness area: 356,855.

**Whiskeytown-Shasta-
Trinity
National Recreation Area**
PO Box 188
Whiskeytown, CA 96095
530-242-3400
www.nps.gov/whis

Whiskeytown Unit, with its scenic mountains and large reservoir, provides a multitude of outdoor recreation opportunities and preserves historic sites that highlight the dramatic effects of the Gold Rush. The Shasta and Trinity Units are administered by the U.S. Forest Service.
Authorized Nov. 8, 1965; established Oct. 21, 1972.
Acreage—42,503.25 Federal: 42,463.116 Nonfederal: 40.09.

**World War II
Valor in the Pacific
National Monument**
1845 Wasp Boulevard
#176
Honolulu, HI 95818
808-422-3399
www.nps.gov/valr
(Also in Hawaii and
Alaska)

This monument comprises nine historic sites representing various aspects of World War II history in the Pacific. Five sites are in the Pearl Harbor area: the USS Arizona Memorial and visitor center; the USS Utah Memorial; the USS Oklahoma Memorial; the six chief petty officer bungalows on Ford Island; and mooring quays F6, F7, and F8, which constituted part of Battleship Row. Three sites are located in Alaska's Aleutian Islands: the crash site of a consolidated B-24D liberator bomber on Atka Island, the Kiska Island site of Imperial Japan's occupation that began in June 1942; and Attu Island, the site of the only land battle fought in North America during World War II. The last of the nine designations is the Tule Lake Segregation Center National Historic Landmark and nearby Camp Tule Lake in California—both of which housed Japanese Americans relocated from the west coast of the United States.
Proclaimed Dec. 5, 2008.
Acreage—59.03 Federal: 56.66 Nonfederal: 2.37.

Yosemite National Park

Yosemite National Park
PO Box 577
Yosemite National Park, CA
95389-0577
209-372-0200
www.nps.gov/yose

Granite peaks and domes rise high above broad meadows in the heart of the Sierra Nevada; groves of giant sequoias dwarf other trees and tiny wildflowers; and mountains, lakes, and waterfalls, including the nation's highest, are found here.
Yosemite Valley and Mariposa Big Tree Grove granted to State of California June 30, 1864; established as a national park Oct. 1, 1890; Federal government accepted lands returned by state June 11, 1906. Boundary changes: Feb. 7, 1905; June 11, 1906; Dec. 19, 1913; May 28, 1928; April 14, 1930; Feb. 14, 1931; Aug. 13, 1932; July 9, 1937. El Portal site authorized Sept. 2, 1958. Wilderness designated Sept. 28, 1984. Designated a World Heritage Site Oct. 31, 1984.
Acreage—761,347.50 (does not include 1,397.99 acres composing El Portal administrative site, adjacent to park)
Federal: 759,620.05 Nonfederal: 1,727.45 Wilderness area: 677,600.

Colorado

Bent's Old Fort National Historic Site
35110 Highway 194 East
La Junta, CO 81050-9523
719-383-5010
www.nps.gov/beol

The fort, now completely reconstructed on its original footprint, was an important fur trading post on the Santa Fe Trail between 1833 and 1849, where Indians and trappers exchanged furs for trade goods.
Authorized June 3, 1960. Boundary change: Nov. 10, 1978.
Acreage—798.80 Federal: 735.60 Nonfederal: 63.20.

Black Canyon of the Gunnison National Park
102 Elk Creek
Gunnison, CO 81230
970-641-2337
www.nps.gov/blca

Over the past two million years, the Gunnison River, along with the forces of weathering, has sculpted this vertical wilderness of rock, water, and sky. The Painted Wall, a sheer drop of 2,250 feet, is the highest cliff in Colorado.
Proclaimed a national monument March 2, 1933; redesignated as a national park Oct. 21, 1999. Boundary changes: May 16, 1938; Oct. 28, 1939; April 13, 1960; July 13, 1984; Oct. 21, 1999; Nov. 11, 2003. Wilderness designated Oct. 20, 1976; Oct. 21, 1999.
Acreage—30,749.75 Federal: 30,637.25 Nonfederal: 112.50 Wilderness area: 15,599.

Colorado National Monument
1750 Rim Rock Drive
Fruita, CO 81521-0001
970-858-3617
www.nps.gov/colm

Sheer-walled canyons, towering monoliths, soaring arches, unusual formations, dinosaur fossils, and remains of prehistoric Indian cultures reflect the environment and history of this colorful sandstone country.
Proclaimed May 24, 1911. Boundary changes: March 3, 1933; Aug. 7, 1959; Oct. 21, 1976; Nov. 10, 1978.
Acreage—20,536.39 Federal: 20,533.93 Nonfederal: 2.46.

Curecanti National Recreation Area
102 Elk Creek
Gunnison, CO 81230
970-641-2337
www.nps.gov/cure

Curecanti National Recreation Area is a series of three reservoirs along the once-wild Gunnison River. The reservoirs that make up Curecanti today are a destination for water-based recreation high in the Rocky Mountains.
Administered under cooperative agreement with the Bureau of Reclamation, Feb. 11, 1965.
Acreage—43,094.72, all Federal.

Dinosaur National Monument
4545 E. Highway 40
Dinosaur, CO 81610-9724
970-374-3000
www.nps.gov/dino
(Also in Utah)

The monument provides a remarkable window onto the Late Jurassic world of dinosaurs, as well as displaying the most complete geological record of any national park unit. The exceptionally diverse communities of plants and animals and thousands of years of human history in the monument result from its geographic locations at the hub of five major biophysical regions, including the lower 46 miles of the Yampa River, which is the last remaining large, free-flowing river in the entire Colorado River system
Proclaimed Oct. 4, 1915. Boundary changes: July 14, 1938; Sept. 8, 1960; Feb. 21, 1963; Oct. 9, 1964; Nov. 10, 1978.
Acreage—210,281.92 Federal: 205,685.51 Nonfederal: 4,596.41.

Florissant Fossil Beds National Monument
PO Box 185
Florissant, CO 80816-0185
719-748-3253
www.nps.gov/flfo

Beneath a grassy mountain valley in central Colorado lies one of the richest and most diverse fossil deposits in the world. Petrified redwood stumps up to 14 feet wide and thousands of detailed fossils of insects and plants reveal the story of a very different, prehistoric Colorado of 34 million years ago.
Authorized Aug. 20, 1969.
Acreage—5,998.09 Federal: 5,992.32 Nonfederal: 5.77.

Great Sand Dunes National Park and Great Sand Dunes National Preserve
11500 Highway 150
Mosca, CO 81146-9798
719-378-6300
www.nps.gov/grsa

The tallest in North America, these dunes developed as southwesterly winds blew ancient alluvial sediments from the San Luis Valley toward the Sangre de Cristo Mountains. The preserve, containing the entire surface watershed and primary topographic features interacting with the Great Sand Dunes, ranges in elevation from 8,000 to over 13,000 feet and includes life zones from desert to alpine tundra.
Proclaimed a national monument March 17, 1932. Boundary changes: March 12, 1946; June 7, 1956; Nov. 10, 1978. Boundary change/redesignation as a national park and national preserve Nov. 22, 2000. Established Sept. 24, 2004. Wilderness designated Oct. 20, 1976; Aug. 13, 1993.
Acreage—National Park: 107,301.87 Federal: 94,687.84
Nonfederal: 12,614.03
National Preserve: 41,686.00, all Federal
Wilderness area: 75,225.

Hovenweep National Monument
McElmo Route
Cortez, CO 81321-8901
970-562-4282
www.nps.gov/hove
(Also in Utah)

The park protects Ancestral Puebloan towers, pueblos, and cliff dwellings spread over 26 miles on the Utah-Colorado border.
Proclaimed March 2, 1923. Boundary changes: April 26, 1951; Nov. 20, 1952; April 6, 1956. Designated an International Dark Sky Park 2014.
Acreage—784.93, all Federal.

Mesa Verde National Park
PO Box 8
Mesa Verde National Park, CO 81330-0008
970-529-4465
www.nps.gov/meve

These world-famous cliff dwellings and other works of the Ancestral Puebloan people are the most notable and best preserved in the United States.
Established June 29, 1906. Boundary changes: June 30, 1913; May 27, 1932; Dec. 23, 1963; Dec. 26, 2007. Wilderness designated Oct. 20, 1976. Designated a World Heritage Site Sept. 6, 1978.
Acreage—52,485.17 Federal: 52,253.29 Nonfederal: 231.88 Wilderness area: 8,100.

Rocky Mountain National Park
1000 Highway 36
Estes Park, CO 80517-8397
970-586-1206
www.nps.gov/romo

The park's rich scenery, typifying the massive grandeur of the Rocky Mountains, is accessible by Trail Ridge Road, which crosses the Continental Divide. Numerous peaks towering over 13,000 feet shadow wildlife and wildflowers in these 415 square miles of the Rockies.
Established Jan. 26, 1915. Boundary changes: Feb. 14, 1917; Sept. 18, 1922; June 2, 1924; Feb. 24, 1925; June 9, 1926; July 17, 1930; Jan. 11, 1932; March 5, 1936; Aug. 24, 1949; June 27, 1950; April 21, 1959; Sept. 23, 1960; Oct. 26, 1974; Dec. 22, 1980; Nov. 29, 1989. Wilderness transferred Dec. 22, 1980. Designated a Biosphere Reserve 1976.
Acreage—265,795.20 Federal: 265,425.84 Nonfederal: 369.36. Wilderness area: 2,917.

Sand Creek Massacre National Historic Site
PO Box 249
Eads, CO 81036
719-438-5916
www.nps.gov/sand

On November 29, 1864, U.S. soldiers attacked a peaceful Cheyenne and Arapaho encampment along Sand Creek. Over 200 Indians were killed; mostly women, children, or the elderly. The Sand Creek Massacre profoundly influenced U.S.-Indian relations and changed Cheyenne and Arapaho history, society and culture. The site preserves the cultural and natural landscape and enhances public understanding of the tragedy. Authorized Nov. 7, 2000; established Apr. 23, 2007.
Acreage—12,583.34 Federal: 2,385.43 Nonfederal: 10,197.91.

Yucca House National Monument
c/o Mesa Verde
National Park
PO Box 8
Mesa Verde National
Park, CO 81330-0008
970-529-4465
www.nps.gov/yuho

Ruins of these large prehistoric Indian pueblos are as yet unexcavated. NO FEDERAL FACILITIES.
Proclaimed Dec. 19, 1919. Boundary change: Nov. 12, 1996.
Acreage—33.87, all Federal.

Connecticut

Appalachian National Scenic Trail
(See Maine)

Weir Farm National Historic Site
735 Nod Hill Road
Wilton, CT 06897-1309
203-834-1896
www.nps.gov/wefa

Artists intentionally designed Weir Farm National Historic Site so that everyone can experience the power of light and color. Escape to the only national park dedicated to American painting and rediscover the beauty of the world. Authorized Oct. 31, 1990. Boundary change: Nov. 10, 1998.
Acreage—74.20 Federal: 68.05 Nonfederal: 6.15.

Delaware

First State National Historical Park
c/o New Castle Court House Museum
211 Delaware Street
New Castle, DE 19720
202-824-3560
www.nps.gov/frst
(Also in Pennsylvania)

Famous as the First State to ratify the Constitution, Delaware was born out of a conflict among three world powers for dominance of the Delaware Valley. From this beginning, the region developed a distinct character that tolerated diversity in religion and national origin and valued independence. First State National Historical Park includes sites associated with the state's Colonial history, including the New Castle Court House Museum and the Green in New Castle, the Green in Dover, and the Woodlawn Tract at Brandywine Hundred. Proclaimed as a national monument Mar. 25, 2013; Redesignated as a national historical park Dec. 19, 2014.
Acreage – 1,155.04 Federal: 1,110.67 Nonfederal: 44.37.

District of Columbia

Carter G. Woodson Home National Historic Site
c/o Mary McLeod Bethune Council House NHS
1318 Vermont Avenue, NW
Washington, DC 20005-3607
202-673-2402
www.nps.gov/cawo

Dr. Woodson lived in this house at 1538 9th Street, NW, in Washington, D.C., from 1915 until his death in 1950. He directed operations of the Association for the Study of African American Life and History while pursuing his own studies of African American history. After his death, the home served as the association's national headquarters until the early 1970s. NOT OPEN TO THE PUBLIC.
Authorized Dec. 19, 2003, established Feb. 27, 2006.
Acreage—0.15, all Federal.

Chesapeake and Ohio Canal National Historical Park
1850 Dual Highway, Ste. 100
Hagerstown, MD 21740
301-714-2201
www.nps.gov/choh
(Also in Maryland and West Virginia)

The park follows the route of the 184.5-mile canal along the Potomac River between Washington, D.C., and Cumberland, Maryland. The canal was built between 1828 and 1850. Placed under National Park Service Sept. 23, 1938; upper canal proclaimed a national monument Jan. 18, 1961; established as a national historical park Jan. 8, 1971. Boundary change: Nov. 10, 1978.
Acreage—19,612.37 Federal: 14,465.19 Nonfederal: 5,147.18

Constitution Gardens
c/o National Mall and Memorial Parks
900 Ohio Drive, SW
Washington, DC 20242-0004
202-426-6841
www.nps.gov/coga

This 40-acre park was constructed during the American Revolution Bicentennial in 1976. On an island in the lake is a memorial to the 56 Signers of the Declaration of Independence. Authorized Aug. 1, 1974; dedicated May 27, 1978.
Acreage—39.23, all Federal.

**Ford's Theatre
National Historic Site**
c/o National Mall and
Memorial Parks
900 Ohio Drive, SW
Washington, DC 20242-0004
202-426-6924
www.nps.gov/foth

On April 14, 1865, President Abraham Lincoln was shot while attending a play at 511 10th Street, NW. He died across the street the following morning at the William Petersen House, also part of the park. The museum beneath the theater contains objects associated with the life and death of President Lincoln.

Act of April 7, 1866, provided for purchase of Ford's Theatre by the federal government; designation changed to Lincoln Museum Feb. 12, 1932; redesignated Ford's Theatre (Lincoln Museum) April 14, 1965. House Where Lincoln Died authorized June 11, 1896. Both areas transferred from Office of Public Buildings and Public Parks of the National Capital Aug. 10, 1933; combined as Ford's Theatre National Historic Site June 23, 1970. Boundary change: June 23, 1970.
Acreage—0.30, all Federal.

**Franklin Delano
Roosevelt Memorial**
c/o National Mall and
Memorial Parks
900 Ohio Drive, SW
Washington, DC 20242-0004
202-426-6841
www.nps.gov/frde

Located along the cherry tree walk on the Tidal Basin near the National Mall, this memorial designed by Lawrence Halprin is dedicated to President Franklin Roosevelt and his times. Twelve years of American history are traced through a sequence of four outdoor rooms—each devoted to one of FDR's four terms in office. Sculptures inspired by photographs depict the 32nd president and First Lady Eleanor Roosevelt, and quotes from Roosevelt's presidency are carved throughout the memorial's granite walls.

Authorized Sept. 5, 1959; dedicated May 2, 1997.
Acreage—8.14, all Federal.

**Frederick Douglass
National Historic Site**
1411 W Street, SE
Washington, DC 20020-4813
202-426-5961
www.nps.gov/frdo

From 1877 to 1895 this was the home of the nation's leading African American spokesman. Among other achievements, he was U.S. minister to Haiti in 1889.

Authorized as Frederick Douglass Home Sept. 5, 1962; redesignated as a national historic site Feb. 12, 1988.
Acreage—8.57, all Federal.

**George Washington
Memorial Parkway**
Turkey Run Park
McLean, VA 22101-0001
703-289-2500
www.nps.gov/gwmp
(Also in Maryland and
Virginia)

The parkway, developed as a memorial to the first U.S. president, preserves the natural scenery along the Potomac River. It connects historic sites from Mount Vernon, where George Washington lived, past the Nation's Capital, which he founded, to the Great Falls of the Potomac, where he demonstrated his skill as an engineer.

Authorized May 29, 1930; transferred from Office of Public Buildings and Public Parks of the National Capital Aug. 10, 1933. On Nov. 28, 1989, the road in Maryland was renamed the Clara Barton Parkway. Boundary changes: May 13, 1947; Oct. 10, 1965; Oct. 21, 1976.
Acreage—7,035.22 Federal: 6,803.99 Nonfederal: 231.23.

**Korean War Veterans
Memorial**
c/o National Mall and
Memorial Parks
900 Ohio Drive, SW
Washington, DC 20242-0004
202-426-6841
www.nps.gov/kowa

Southeast of the Lincoln Memorial, this grouping of 19 statues of infantry soldiers by sculptor Frank Gaylord stand before a polished granite wall bearing the images of more than 1,789,000 American soldiers, sailors, airmen and Marines who fought in the defense of South Korea from 1950 to 1953.

Authorized October 28, 1986; dedicated July 27, 1995.
Acreage—1.56, all Federal.

Lincoln Memorial

c/o National Mall and
Memorial Parks
900 Ohio Drive, SW
Washington, DC 20242-0004
202-426-6841
www.nps.gov/linc

Architect Henry Bacon designed this neoclassical tribute to Abraham Lincoln, 16th president of the United States. The 19-foot-high marble statue of Lincoln by sculptor Daniel Chester French dominates the memorial, and the Gettysburg Address and Lincoln's Second Inaugural Address are engraved on the north and south interior walls.
Authorized Feb. 9, 1911; dedicated May 30, 1922; transferred from Office of Public Buildings and Public Parks of the National Capital Aug. 10, 1933.
Acreage—7.29, all Federal.

Lyndon Baines Johnson Memorial Grove on the Potomac

c/o George Washington
Memorial Parkway
Turkey Run Park
McLean, VA 22101-0001
703-289-2500
www.nps.gov/lydo

A living memorial to the 36th president, the park overlooks the Potomac River vista of the Capital. The design features 500 white pines and inscriptions on Texas granite.
Authorized Dec. 28, 1973; dedicated Sept. 27, 1974.
Acreage—17.00, all Federal.

Martin Luther King Jr. Memorial

c/o National Mall and
Memorial Parks
900 Ohio Drive, SW
Washington, DC 20242-0004
202-426-6841
www.nps.gov/mlkm

The memorial honors Dr. Martin Luther King's contributions as a leader of the modern Civil Rights movement. The figure of Dr. King serves as the forward element of the Stone of Hope, detached from the Mountain of Despair to reflect victory borne from disappointment. A wall of 16 quotes, presenting Dr. King's ideals of hope, democracy and love, flanks the Mountain of Despair and encircles the Stone of Hope.
Authorized November 12, 1996, dedicated August 28, 2011.
Acreage – 2.74, all Federal.

Mary McLeod Bethune Council House National Historic Site

1318 Vermont Avenue, NW
Washington, DC 20005-3607
202-673-2402
www.nps.gov/mamc

This was the headquarters of the National Council of Negro Women, established by Mary McLeod Bethune in 1935. It commemorates Bethune's leadership in the black women's rights movement from 1943 to 1949.
Designated Oct. 15, 1982; National Park Service administration authorized Dec. 11, 1991.
Acreage—0.07, all Federal.

National Capital Parks - East

1900 Anacostia Drive, SE
Washington, DC 20020
202-690-5185
www.nps.gov/nace
(Also in Maryland)

A unit consisting of several natural resource and recreational park sites located in southeast Washington within the Anacostia River watershed. Authorized in 1932, Anacostia Park, site of the 1932 "Bonus March," is 1,200 acres stretching the length of the Anacostia River. The southern portion is a multi-use recreational park with shoreline and river access, ball fields, tennis courts, swimming pool, roller skating pavilion, riverwalk trail, and picnic areas. The northern section contains Kenilworth Park and Aquatic Gardens which is the only NPS park dedicated to cultivating water-loving plants. A 12-acre sanctuary featuring ponds filled with a variety of water lilies, lotus, and other aquatic species surrounded by 70 acres of freshwater tidal wetlands with boardwalk river trail. Both park sites support a large variety of birds and wildlife.
Transferred from Office of Public Buildings and Public Parks of the National Capital Aug. 10, 1933.
Acreage—8,693.37 Federal: 8,462.47 Nonfederal: 230.90.

National Mall and Memorial Parks
900 Ohio Drive, SW
Washington, DC 20242-0004
202-485-9880
www.nps.gov/nama

The park system of the Nation's Capital comprises parks, parkways, and reservations in the District of Columbia, including such properties as the Battleground National Cemetery, President's Parks (Lafayette Park north of the White House and the Ellipse south of the White House), a variety of military fortifications, and green areas. Includes the National Mall, a landscaped park extending from the Capitol to the Washington Monument, defined as a principal axis in the L'Enfant Plan for the city of Washington.
National Mall authorized on July 16, 1790. National Mall and park areas transferred from the Office of Public Buildings and Public Parks of the National Capital Aug. 10, 1933.
Acreage—155.84, all Federal.

Pennsylvania Avenue National Historic Site
c/o National Mall and Memorial Parks
900 Ohio Drive, SW
Washington, DC 20242-0004
202-426-6841
www.nps.gov/paav

Pennsylvania Avenue, linking the Capitol to the White House, serves as America's Main Street, providing a setting for parades and cultural activities. The site is composed of parks, plazas, sculpture and memorials adjacent to the avenue, including John Marshall Park, the United States Navy Memorial, and Freedom Plaza.
Designated Sept. 30, 1965. Boundary change April 26,1996.
Acreage—17.61 Federal: 16.43 Nonfederal: 1.18.

Potomac Heritage National Scenic Trail
(See Maryland)

Rock Creek Park
3545 Williamsburg La., NW
Washington, DC 20008-1207
202-895-6004
www.nps.gov/rocr

One of the largest natural urban parks in the United States, this wooded preserve also contains a range of historic and recreational features in the midst of Washington, D.C.
Authorized Sept. 27, 1890; transferred from Office of Public Buildings and Public Parks of the National Capital Aug. 10, 1933.
Acreage—1,755.21, all Federal.

Theodore Roosevelt Island
c/o George Washington Memorial Parkway
Turkey Run Park
McLean, VA 22101-0001
703-289-2500
www.nps.gov/this

On this wooded island sanctuary in the Potomac River, trails lead to an imposing statue of Roosevelt, the conservation-minded 26th president, by Paul Manship. His tenets on nature, manhood, youth, and the state are inscribed on tablets.
Authorized May 21, 1932; transferred from Office of Public Buildings and Public Parks of the National Capital Aug. 10, 1933; memorial dedicated Oct. 27, 1967.
Acreage—88.50, all Federal.

Thomas Jefferson Memorial
c/o National Mall and Memorial Parks
900 Ohio Drive, SW
Washington, DC 20242-0004
202-485-9880
www.nps.gov/thje

Thomas Jefferson was the primary author of the Declaration of Independence, America's first Secretary of State, and president from 1801 to 1809. Architect John Russell Pope designed this circular, colonnaded structure in an adaptation of the neoclassical style brought into use in this country by Jefferson.
Authorized June 26, 1934; dedicated April 13, 1943.
Acreage—18.36, all Federal.

Vietnam Veterans Memorial

c/o National Mall and
Memorial Parks
900 Ohio Drive, SW
Washington, DC 20242-0004
202-485-9880
www.nps.gov/vive

Located near the Lincoln Memorial at the west end of Constitution Gardens, the polished black granite wall is inscribed with the names of over 58,300 persons who gave their lives in the Vietnam War or remain missing. The memorial was designed by Maya Ying Lin. The site also includes a bronze statue of three Vietnam war servicemen sculpted by Frederick Hart. as well as the Vietnam Women's Memorial, by Glenna Goodacre, dedicated to American women who served in the Vietnam War.
Authorized July 1, 1980; dedicated Nov. 13, 1982.
Acreage—2.18, all Federal.

Washington Monument

c/o National Mall and
Memorial Parks
900 Ohio Drive, SW
Washington, DC 20242-0004
202-485-9880
www.nps.gov/wamo

The dominating feature of the Nation's Capital skyline, this 555-foot obelisk honors the country's first president, George Washington. The architect-designer was Robert Mills, but Lt. Col. Thomas Casey of the U.S. Army Corps of Engineers redesigned and completed the monument.
Authorized Jan. 31, 1848; dedicated Feb. 21, 1885; transferred from Office of Public Buildings and Public Parks of the National Capital Aug. 10, 1933.
Acreage—106.01, all Federal.

White House

c/o National Capital Region
1100 Ohio Drive, SW
Washington, DC 20242-0001
202-619-6344
www.nps.gov/whho

The White House has been the residence and office of U.S. presidents since November 1800, and it symbolizes the presidency. The cornerstone was laid Oct. 13, 1792, on the site selected by George Washington and included in the L'Enfant Plan; renovations were made 1949–52.
Transferred Aug. 10, 1933, to National Park Service, the legal successor of three Federal Commissioners appointed by the president under the act of July 16, 1790, who directed initial construction. Their authority developed through acts of May 1, 1802; April 29, 1816; March 3, 1849; March 2, 1867; July 1, 1898; Feb. 26, 1925; March 3, 1933; and Executive Order of June 10, 1933. Under act of Sept. 22, 1961, "the White House . . . shall be administered pursuant to the act of August 25, 1916" and supplementary and amendatory acts.
Acreage—18.07, all Federal.

World War I Memorial

c/o National Mall and
Memorial Parks
900 Ohio Drive, SW
Washington, DC 20242-0004
202-426-6841
www.nps.gov/nama

Sited at Pershing Park on Pennsylvania Avenue and scheduled for dedication in 2018, the World War I Memorial will honor the 4.7 million Americans who served in the Great War, including the 116,516 who gave their lives.
Redesignation of Pershing Park Dec. 19, 2014.
Acreage—1.39, all Federal.

World War II Memorial

c/o National Mall and
Memorial Parks
900 Ohio Drive, SW
Washington, DC 20242-0004
202-426-6841
www.nps.gov/wwii

The memorial honors the 16 million Americans who served during World War II, along with the millions who supported them on the home front during a time of unprecedented national unity. A wall contains 4,000 gold stars symbolizing the over 400,000 Americans who died during the war. Architect Friedrich St. Florian designed the memorial.
Authorized May 25, 1993; dedicated May 29, 2004.
Acreage—7.50, all Federal.

Florida

**Big Cypress
National Preserve**
HCR 61, Box 110
Ochopee, FL 34141
239-695-2000
www.nps.gov/bicy

This large area protects the watershed for the threatened ecosystem of South Florida. Subtropical plant and animal life abounds in a park that is home to endangered species like the Florida panther and the red-cockaded woodpecker. Authorized Oct. 11, 1974. Boundary change: April 29, 1988. *Acreage—720,564.01 Federal: 677,275.67 Nonfederal: 43,288.34.*

Biscayne National Park
9700 SW 328 Street
Homestead, FL 33033-5634
305-230-1140
www.nps.gov/bisc

Subtropical islands form a north-south chain, with Biscayne Bay on the west and the Atlantic Ocean on the east. The park protects the longest stretch of mangrove forest on Florida's east coast, the clear, shallow waters of Biscayne Bay, the northernmost Florida Keys, part of the world's third-longest reef tract and 10,000 years of human history. Authorized as a national monument Oct. 18, 1968; redesignated as a national park and enlarged June 28, 1980. Boundary change: Oct. 26, 1974. *Acreage—172,971.11 Federal: 171,002.81 Nonfederal: 1,968.30. Land area: 4,446.23.*

**Canaveral
National Seashore**
212 S. Washington Ave.
Titusville, FL 32796
321-267-1110
www.nps.gov/cana

Twenty-five miles of undeveloped barrier island preserve the natural beach, dune, marsh, and lagoon habitats for many species of birds. The Kennedy Space Center occupies the southern end of the island and temporary closures are possible due to launch-related activities. Established Jan. 3, 1975. *Acreage—57,661.69 Federal: 57,647.69 Nonfederal: 14.00.*

**Castillo de San Marcos
National Monument**
1 Castillo Drive South
St. Augustine, FL 32084-3699
904-829-6506
www.nps.gov/casa

Construction of the oldest masonry fort in the continental United States was started in 1672 by the Spanish to protect St. Augustine, the first permanent settlement by Europeans in the continental United States, 1565. The floor plan is the result of modernization work done in the 1700s. Proclaimed Fort Marion National Monument Oct. 15, 1924; transferred from the War Dept. Aug. 10, 1933; renamed June 5, 1942. Boundary changes: June 29, 1936; July 5, 1960; Dec. 23, 2004. *Acreage—19.38 Federal: 19.31 Nonfederal: 0.07.*

**De Soto National
Memorial**
PO Box 15390
Bradenton, FL 34280-5390
941-792-0458
www.nps.gov/deso

The park commemorates the landing of Spanish explorer Hernando de Soto in Florida in 1539 and the first extensive organized exploration by Europeans of what is now the southern United States. Authorized March 11, 1948. Boundary change: Sept. 8, 1960. *Acreage—30.00 Federal: 24.78 Nonfederal: 5.22.*

**Dry Tortugas
National Park**
c/o Everglades National Park
40001 State Road 9336
Homestead, FL 33034-6733
305-242-7700
www.nps.gov/drto

Fort Jefferson was built 1846–66 to help control the Florida Straits. It is the largest all-masonry fortification in the Western world. The bird refuge and marine life are notable features. Proclaimed Fort Jefferson National Monument Jan. 4, 1935; renamed and redesignated as a national park Oct. 26, 1992. *Acreage—64,701.22 Federal: 61,481.22 Nonfederal: 3,220.00 Land area: 39.28.*

Everglades National Park

40001 State Road 9336
Homestead, FL 33034-6733
305-242-7700
www.nps.gov/ever

This largest remaining subtropical wilderness in the contiguous United States has extensive fresh water and salt water areas, open sawgrass prairies, and mangrove forests. Abundant wildlife includes rare and colorful birds.
Authorized May 30, 1934; established Dec. 6, 1947. Boundary changes: July 2, 1958; Sept. 14, 1959; Sept. 2, 1960; Sept. 12, 1964; Oct. 17, 1969; Dec. 13, 1989; Dec. 23, 2004. Wilderness designated Nov. 10, 1978. Designated a Biosphere Reserve 1976. Designated a World Heritage Site Oct. 24, 1979.
Acreage—1,508,975.57 Federal: 1,508,243.04 Nonfederal: 732.53 Wilderness area: 1,296,500 Water area: 625,000.

Fort Caroline National Memorial

12713 Fort Caroline Road
Jacksonville, FL 32225-1240
904-641-7155
www.nps.gov/timu

Two centuries of French and Spanish colonial rivalry in North America began here with the establishment of a French Huguenot settlement, 1564–65.
Authorized Sept. 21, 1950. Boundary changes: April 11, 1972; Nov. 10, 1978; Nov. 19, 1979.
Acreage—138.39 Federal: 133.15 Nonfederal: 5.24.

Fort Matanzas National Monument

c/o Castillo de San Marcos
National Monument
1 Castillo Drive South
St. Augustine, FL 32084-3699
904-471-0116
www.nps.gov/foma

This Spanish fort was built, 1740–42, to warn St. Augustine of British or other enemy approach from the south.
Proclaimed Oct. 15, 1924; transferred from War Dept. Aug. 10, 1933. Boundary changes: Jan. 9, 1935; March 24, 1948; Nov. 22, 2000.
Acreage—300.11 Federal: 298.51 Nonfederal: 1.60

Gulf Islands National Seashore

1801 Gulf Breeze Parkway
Gulf Breeze, FL 32561-5000
850-934-2600
www.nps.gov/guis
(Also in Mississippi)

Offshore islands have sparkling white sand beaches, historic fortifications, and nature trails. Mainland features of this unit, which is located near Pensacola, include the Naval Live Oaks Reservation, beaches, and military forts. All areas in Florida are accessible by car.
Authorized Jan. 8, 1971. Boundary change: Nov. 10, 1978.
Acreage—138,305.52 Federal: 99,779.27 Nonfederal: 38,526.25. Land area: 19,445.46.

Timucuan Ecological and Historic Preserve

13165 Mt. Pleasant Road
Jacksonville, FL 32225-1227
904-641-7155
www.nps.gov/timu

Named for the American Indians who lived here for over 3,000 years, the preserve encompasses Atlantic coastal marshes, islands, tidal creeks, and the estuaries of the St. Johns and Nassau rivers. Besides traces of Indian life, remains of Spanish, French, and English colonial ventures can be found, as well as plantation life and military activities in the 1800s.
Authorized Feb. 16, 1988. Boundary change: Oct. 5, 2004.
Acreage—46,262.67 Federal: 8,863.31 Nonfederal: 37,399.36

Georgia

**Andersonville
National Historic Site**
496 Cemetery Road
Andersonville, GA 31711-
9707
229-924-0343
www.nps.gov/ande

Located in rural Georgia, this park protects the original site of the Civil War prisoner of war camp used from 1864-1865. The site includes the National Prisoner of War Museum, which is dedicated to the stories of all American POWs, and Andersonville National Cemetery. The cemetery began as the burial grounds for almost 13,000 Union POWs, but continues as an active national cemetery. There are over 21,000 interments of soldiers and dependents within the cemetery to date. Authorized Oct. 16, 1970.
Acreage—515.61 Federal: 500.88 Nonfederal: 14.73.

**Appalachian
National Scenic Trail**
(See Maine)

**Chattahoochee River
National Recreation Area**
1978 Island Ford Parkway
Atlanta, GA 30350-3400
678-538-1200
www.nps.gov/chat

An ecological oasis at the intersection of the southern Piedmont and Appalachian mountain habitats, the park spans a 48-mile stretch of the Chattahoochee River and offers abundant opportunities for recreation, solitude, and respite from the urban surroundings. Cultural resources along the Chattahoochee River represent the continuum of human interaction over the past 10,000 years that is reflected in archeological sites, historic structures, and cultural landscapes that owe their locations to the abundant natural features and diverse ecological habitats of the river corridor.
Established Aug. 15, 1978. Boundary change: Oct. 30, 1984.
Acreage—9,798.07 Federal: 5,072.45 Nonfederal: 4,725.62.

**Chickamauga and
Chattanooga
National Military Park**
PO Box 2128
Fort Oglethorpe, GA 30742-
0128
706-866-9241
www.nps.gov/chch
(Also in Tennessee)

A major Confederate victory on Chickamauga Creek in Georgia, Sept. 18–20, 1863, was countered by Union victories at Orchard Knob, Lookout Mountain, and Missionary Ridge in Chattanooga, Tenn., Nov. 23–25, 1863. This was the first national military park.
Established Aug. 19, 1890; transferred from War Dept. Aug. 10, 1933. Boundary changes: Aug. 9, 1939; March 5, 1942; June 24, 1948; Feb. 24, 2003.
Acreage—9,077.57 Federal: 8,987.06 Nonfederal: 90.51.

**Cumberland Island
National Seashore**
101 Wheeler Street
St Marys, GA 31558
912-882-4335
www.nps.gov/cuis

Magnificent and unspoiled beaches and dunes, marshes, and freshwater lakes, along with historic sites, make up the largest of Georgia's Golden Isles. Accessible by tour boat only.
Established Oct. 23, 1972. Boundary changes: Nov. 10, 1978; Dec. 8, 2004. Wilderness designated Sept. 8, 1982. Designated a Biosphere Reserve 1986.
Acreage—36,346.83 Federal: 19,524.92 Nonfederal: 16,821.91 Land area: 26,153.10 Wilderness area: 8,840.

**Fort Frederica
National Monument**
Route 9, Box 286-C
St. Simons Island, GA
31522-9710
912-638-3639
www.nps.gov/fofr

Gen. James E. Oglethorpe built this British town and fort in 1736–48 during the Anglo-Spanish struggle for control of what is now the southeastern United States.
Authorized May 26, 1936. Boundary changes: Sept. 20, 1950; May 16, 1958; July 3, 1984; Nov. 30, 2004.
Acreage—284.49 Federal: 283.20 Nonfederal: 1.29.

Fort Pulaski National Monument
PO Box 30757
Savannah, GA 31410-0757
912-786-5787
www.nps.gov/fopu

Fort Pulaski took 18 years and 25 million bricks to build, but in 30 hours, new, experimental rifled cannon tore great, gaping holes in its walls, forcing the Confederate garrison to surrender in 1862. The strategy of warfare and the role of fortifications were changed forever.
Proclaimed Oct. 15, 1924; transferred from War Dept. Aug. 10, 1933. Boundary changes: June 26, 1936; May 25, 1959.
Acreage—5,623.10 Federal: 5,365.13 Nonfederal: 257.97.

Jimmy Carter National Historic Site
300 N. Bond Street
Plains, GA 31780-0392
229-824-4104
www.nps.gov/jica

The rural southern culture of Plains, Ga., had a large influence in molding the character and in shaping the political policies of the 39th president of the United States. The site includes President Carter's residence and boyhood home. Plains High School serves as the park visitor center. The railroad depot, which served as campaign headquarters during the 1976 election, houses additional exhibits. The area surrounding the residence is under the protection of the Secret Service, and no attempt should be made to enter.
Authorized Dec. 23, 1987.
Acreage—72.21 Federal: 47.54 Nonfederal: 24.67.

Kennesaw Mountain National Battlefield Park
905 Kennesaw
Mountain Drive
Kennesaw, GA 30152
770-427-4686
www.nps.gov/kemo

Eleven miles of Union and Confederate earthworks are preserved within the park. These earthworks mark the sites of the battles of Kolb's Farm, June 22, 1864, and Kennesaw Mountain, June 27, 1864. Gen. William T. Sherman's southward advance was temporarily halted here by Gen. Joseph T. Johnston and the stalwart defense of his Confederates.
Authorized as a national battlefield site Feb. 8, 1917; transferred from War Dept. Aug. 10, 1933; redesignated as a national battlefield park June 26, 1935. Boundary change: Aug. 9, 1939.
Acreage—2,894.29 Federal: 2,887.92 Nonfederal: 6.37.

Martin Luther King, Jr., National Historic Site
450 Auburn Avenue, NE
Atlanta, GA 30312-0526
404-331-5190
www.nps.gov/malu

The birthplace, church, and grave of Dr. Martin Luther King, Jr., civil rights leader, compose this park. The park visitor center has exhibits and films on Dr. King. The surrounding 68.19-acre preservation district includes Sweet Auburn, the economic and cultural center of Atlanta's African American community during most of the 1900s.
Established Oct. 10, 1980. Boundary change: Oct. 5, 2004.
Acreage—38.70 Federal: 13.62 Nonfederal: 25.08.

Ocmulgee National Monument
1207 Emery Highway
Macon, GA 31217-4399
478-752-8257
www.nps.gov/ocmu

Traces of 12,000 years of Southeastern culture from Ice Age Indians to the historic Creek Confederacy are preserved here. The park includes many artifacts and the massive temple mounds of a Mississippian Indian ceremonial complex that thrived here between 900 and 1100.
Authorized June 14, 1934. Established December 23, 1936. Boundary changes: June 13, 1941; July 9, 1991.
Acreage—703.70 Federal: 701.54 Nonfederal: 2.16.

Guam

War in the Pacific
National Historical Park
135 Murray Blvd, Suite 100
Hagatna, GU 96910
671-477-7278
www.nps.gov/wapa

The 1944 recapture of Guam by American forces during World World II is interpreted at seven units on this island, from the summit of Mt. Tenjo (1,033 ft.) to the submerged war relics on the offshore coral reefs (132 feet deep). Authorized Aug. 18, 1978.
Acreage—2,030.65 Federal: 958.25 Nonfederal: 1,072.40 Water area: 1,002.

Hawaii

Haleakalā National Park
PO Box 369
Makawao, Maui, HI 96768-0369
808-572-4400
www.nps.gov/hale

A variety of areas, from the summit to the ocean, protect fragile native Hawaiian ecosystems, rare and endangered species, and cultural sites.
Established as a part of Hawaii National Park Aug. 1, 1916; renamed Sept. 13, 1960. Boundary changes: Feb. 12, 1927; Jan. 10, 1969; Oct. 21, 1976. Wilderness designated Oct. 20, 1976. Designated a Biosphere Reserve 1980.
Acreage—33,264.62 Federal: 33,264.47 Nonfederal: 0.15. Wilderness area: 19,270.

Hawai'i Volcanoes
National Park
PO Box 52
Hawai'i National Park, HI 96718-0052
808-985-6000
www.nps.gov/havo

Erupting volcanoes, rare and endangered plant and animal communities, and prehistoric sites are special features of the park.
Established as part of Hawaii National Park Aug. 1, 1916; renamed Sept. 22, 1961. Boundary changes: May 1, 1922; April 11, 1928; June 20, 1938; Dec. 3, 1940; July 1, 1961; Nov. 10, 1978; Nov. 12, 1998; July 3, 2003. Wilderness designated Nov. 10, 1978. Designated a Biosphere Reserve 1980. Designated a World Heritage Site Dec. 10, 1987.
Acreage—323,431.38, all Federal. Wilderness area: 130,950.

Honouliuli National
Monument
300 Ala Moana Boulevard
Honolulu, HI 96850
808-725-6149
www.nps.gov/hono

Honouliuli National Monument tells the history of internment and martial law in Hawai'i during World War II. Honouliuli is a place to reflect on wartime experiences and recommit ourselves to the pursuit of freedom and justice. Proclaimed Feb. 24, 2015.
Acreage 154.46 Federal: 123.02 Nonfederal: 31.44.

Kalaupapa
National Historical Park
PO Box 2222
Kalaupapa, HI 96742-2222
808-567-6802
www.nps.gov/kala

This park contains the site of the Moloka'i Hansen's disease (leprosy) settlement (1866–1969), areas relating to early settlement, and habitats for rare and endangered species. Authorized Dec. 22, 1980.
Acreage—10,778.88 Federal: 22.88 Nonfederal: 10,756.00 Water area: 2,000.

Kaloko-Honokōhau
National Historical Park
73-4786 Kanalani Street, #14
Kailua Kona, HI 96740-2608
808-329-6881
www.nps.gov/kaho

This was the site of important Hawaiian settlements before the arrival of European explorers. It includes coastal areas, two large fishponds, and other archeological remnants. The park preserves the native culture of Hawaii.
Established Nov. 10, 1978.
Acreage—1,163.05 Federal: 615.90 Nonfederal: 547.15.

**Pu'uhonua o Hōnaunau
National Historical Park**
PO Box 129
Honaunau, HI 96726-0129
808-328-2326
www.nps.gov/puho

Until 1819, vanquished Hawaiian warriors, noncombatants, and kapu breakers could escape death by reaching this sacred ground. The park includes ancient house sites, royal fishponds, coconut groves, and spectacular shore scenery.
Authorized as City of Refuge National Historical Park July 26, 1955; renamed Nov. 10, 1978. Boundary change: Dec. 16, 2002.
Acreage—419.80, all Federal.

**Pu'ukoholā Heiau
National Historic Site**
PO Box 44340
Kawaihae, HI 96743-4340
808-882-7218
www.nps.gov/puhe

Ruins of Pu'ukoholā Heiau ("Temple on the Hill of the Whale"), built in 1791 by King Kamehameha the Great during his rise to power, are preserved.
Authorized Aug. 17, 1972.
Acreage—86.24 Federal: 60.95 Nonfederal: 25.29.

**World War II Valor
in the Pacific
National Monument**
Pearl Harbor
1 Arizona Memorial Place
Honolulu, HI 96818-3145
808-422-2771
www.nps.gov/valr
(Also in Alaska and California)

This monument comprises nine historic sites representing various aspects of World War II history in the Pacific. Five sites are in the Pearl Harbor area: the USS *Arizona* Memorial and visitor center; the USS *Utah* Memorial; the USS *Oklahoma* Memorial; the six chief petty officer bungalows on Ford Island; and mooring quays F6, F7, and F8, which constituted part of Battleship Row. Three sites are located in Alaska's Aleutian Islands: the crash site of a consolidated B-24D liberator bomber on Atka Island, the Kiska Island site of Imperial Japan's occupation that began in June 1942; and Attu Island, the site of the only land battle fought in North America during World War II. The last of the nine designations is the Tule Lake Segregation Center National Historic Landmark and nearby Camp Tule Lake in California, both of which housed Japanese Americans relocated from the west coast of the United States.
Proclaimed Dec. 5, 2008.
Acreage—59.03 Federal: 56.66 Nonfederal: 2.37.

Idaho

**City of Rocks
National Reserve**
PO Box 169
Almo, ID 83312-0169
208-824-5901
www.nps.gov/ciro

Scenic granite spires and sculptured rock formations dominate this landscape. Remnants of the California Trail are still visible in the area. Recreational opportunities include rock climbing, hiking, and camping. LIMITED FACILITIES.
Authorized Nov. 18, 1988. Administered cooperatively by the National Park Service and the Idaho Department of Parks and Recreation.
Acreage—14,407.19 Federal: 9,680.28 Nonfederal: 4,726.91.

**Craters of the Moon
National Monument** and
**Craters of the Moon
National Preserve**
PO Box 29
Arco, ID 83213-0029
208-527-3257
www.nps.gov/crmo

15,000 to 2,000 year-old lava flows produced a "weird" and harsh landscape of steep cinder cones, unforgiving rocks, and lava tube caves. Twisted, splattered lava, steep-sided cinder cones, tubelike caves, and lava flows 2,100 years old produce an amazing landscape. Administered cooperatively by the National Park Service and the Bureau of Land Management.
Proclaimed May 2, 1924. Boundary changes: July 23, 1928; July 9, 1930; June 5, 1936; July 18, 1941; Nov. 19, 1962; Nov. 9, 2000. Wilderness designated Oct. 23, 1970. Designated a national preserve Aug. 21, 2002.
Acreage—464,303.97, all Federal. Wilderness area: 43,243.

Hagerman Fossil Beds
National Monument
221 North State Street
PO Box 570
Hagerman, ID 83332-0570
208-993-4100
www.nps.gov/hafo

Extraordinary fossils from the Pliocene Epoch, 3.5 million years ago, are covered in sediment from the Snake River Plain. The Hagerman Horse Quarry, a National Natural Landmark, and over 200 fossilized plant and animal species are here. LIMITED FEDERAL FACILITIES.
Authorized Nov. 18, 1988.
Acreage—4,351.15 Federal: 4,334.65 Nonfederal: 16.50.

Minidoka
National Historic Site
221 North State Street
PO Box 570
Hagerman, ID 83332
208-837-4793
www.nps.gov/miin
(Also in Washington)

The history and cultural resources associated with the relocation and internment of Japanese Americans during World War II are interpreted here. UNDER DEVELOPMENT. Includes Bainbridge Island Japanese American Exclusion Memorial in Washington.
Proclaimed Jan. 17, 2001; redesignated a national historic site May 8, 2008.
Acreage—396.30 Federal: 388.30 Nonfederal: 8.00.

Nez Perce
National Historical Park
36063 U.S. Highway 95
Spalding, ID 83540-9715
208-843-7001
www.nps.gov/nepe
(Also in Montana, Oregon, and Washington)

The park's 38 sites, spreading across Idaho, Washington, Oregon, and Montana, commemorate the Nez Perce. Six sites are owned and managed by the National Park Service at Spalding, Canoe Camp, Buffalo Eddy, East Kamiah, White Bird Battlefield, and Big Hole National Battlefield.
Authorized May 15, 1965. Boundary change: Oct. 30, 1992.
Acreage—4,564.93 Federal: 3,858.63 Nonfederal: 706.30.

Yellowstone National Park
(See Wyoming)

Illinois

Lincoln Home
National Historic Site
413 S. Eighth Street
Springfield, IL 62701-1905
217-492-4241
www.nps.gov/liho

Abraham Lincoln resided in this house for 17 years before he became president. The surrounding historic district preserves the 1860s environment in which the Lincoln family lived.
Authorized Aug. 18, 1971.
Acreage—12.24 Federal: 12.03 Nonfederal: 0.21.

Pullman National
Monument
11111 S. Forrestville Avenue
Chicago, IL 60628
773-660-2341
www.nps.gov/pull

George Pullman created an integrated manufacturing complex and residential community south of Chicago in the 1880s, with the intention of retaining skilled workers for his varied rail cars assembled there. The town of Pullman's design and architecture still resonate with today's urban planners. The name "Pullman" globally became synonymous with luxurious rail car travel, partly due to the exceptional rail car staff's service as well as the opulent interior furnishings and finishes. Worker opportunities were created for a wide variety of Euro-American immigrants and recently emancipated southern slaves. The Pullman company reflected many of America's labor issues over the century of its operation. Nationally significant issues occurred with both the 1894 strike that sparked the federalization of the Labor Day holiday and establishment of the first recognized African-American labor union in 1937.
Proclaimed Feb. 19, 2015.
Acreage – 0.40, all Federal.

Pullman National Monument

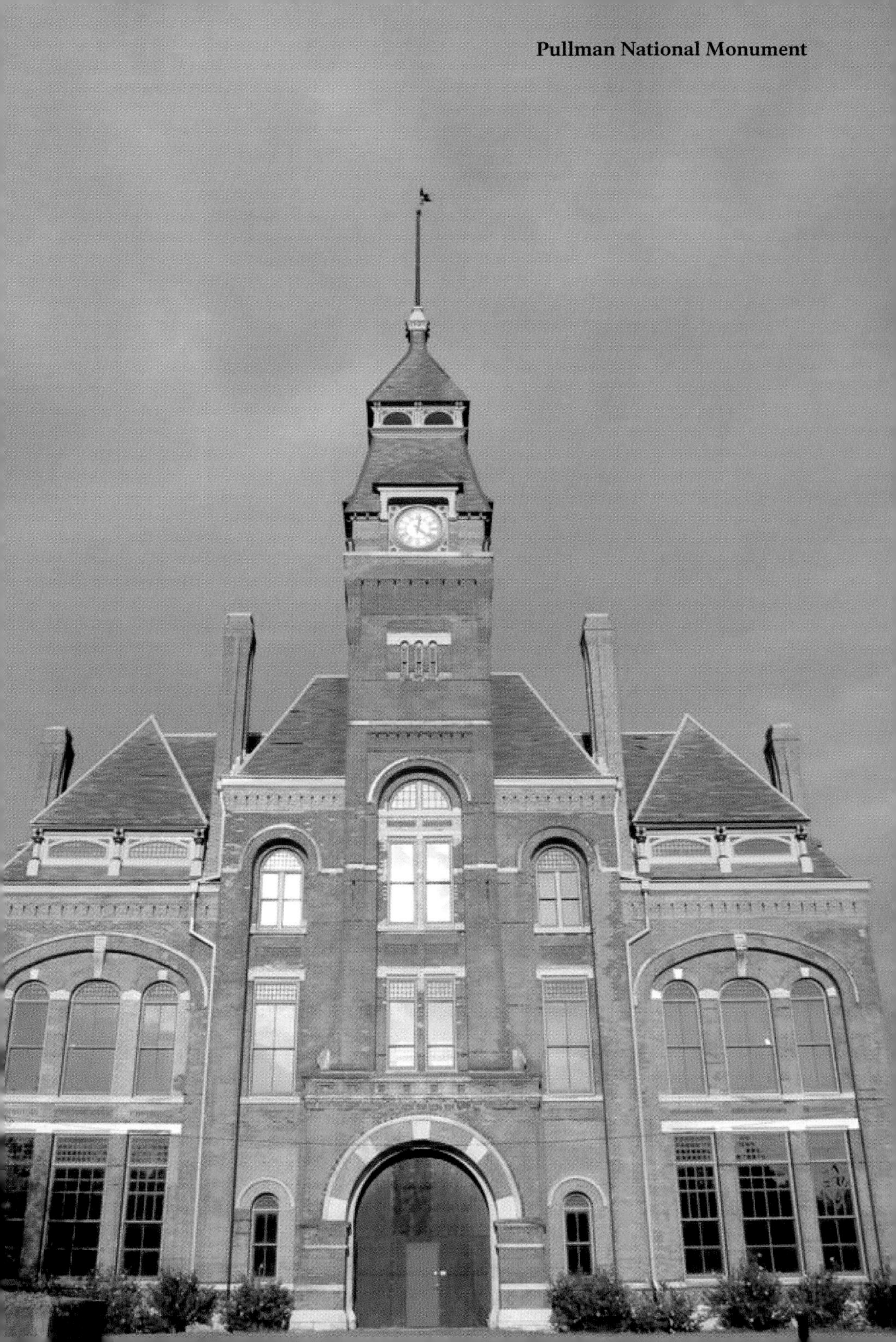

NPS/©LAURENCE PARENT

Indiana

George Rogers Clark National Historical Park
401 S. Second Street
Vincennes, IN 47591-1001
812-882-1776
www.nps.gov/gero

This site commemorates the capture of Fort Sackville from the British by Lieutenant Colonel George Rogers Clark on Feb. 25, 1779, and the subsequent settlement of the region north of the Ohio River. A classical memorial building with seven large murals and a Hermon MacNeil statue of Lieutenant Colonel Clark stands near the former location of the fort. Authorized July 23, 1966.
Acreage—26.17 Federal: 25.30 Nonfederal: 0.87.

Indiana Dunes National Lakeshore
1100 N. Mineral Springs Rd.
Porter, IN 46304-1299
219-395-8585
www.nps.gov/indu

Beaches, dunes, bogs, marshes, swamps, and prairie remnants grace the southern shore of Lake Michigan in this park, which encompasses four National Natural Landmarks. An 1822 homestead, 1900s family farm, and houses originally exhibited at the 1933 Chicago World's Fair accent the historic landscape.
Authorized Nov. 5, 1966. Boundary changes: Oct. 18, 1976; Dec. 28, 1980; Oct. 29, 1986; Oct. 23, 1992.
Acreage—15,347.13 Federal: 11,040.90 Nonfederal: 4,306.23.

Lincoln Boyhood National Memorial
3027 E. South Street
Lincoln City, IN 47552-1816
812-937-4541
www.nps.gov/

Abraham Lincoln lived on this southern Indiana farm from 1816 to 1830. During that time, he grew from a 7-year-old boy to a 21-year-old man. His mother, Nancy Hanks Lincoln, is buried here.
Authorized Feb. 19, 1962.
Acreage—199.65 Federal: 185.68 Nonfederal: 14.28.

Iowa

Effigy Mounds National Monument
151 Highway 76
Harpers Ferry, IA 52146-7519
563-873-3491
www.nps.gov/efmo

The monument preserves 206 American Indian mound sites built along the Mississippi River between 450 B.C.E. and 1300, including 31 effigy mounds in the shapes of birds and bears. These mounds are examples of a significant phase of mound-building culture, commemorating the passing of

loved ones and the sacred beliefs of these ancient peoples. Proclaimed Oct. 25, 1949. Boundary changes: May 27, 1961; Oct. 31, 1983, Oct. 19, 2000.
Acreage—2,526.39, all Federal.

Herbert Hoover
National Historic Site
110 Parkside Drive
West Branch, IA 52358-0607
319-643-2541
www.nps.gov/heho

The site commemorates the life of the 31st U.S. president. The site includes the cottage where Hoover was born, a blacksmith shop, the first West Branch schoolhouse, the Friends Meetinghouse where the Hoover family worshipped, the Hoover Presidential Library-Museum, and the graves of President and Mrs. Hoover.
Authorized Aug. 12, 1965.
Acreage—186.80 Federal: 181.11 Nonfederal: 5.69

Kansas

Brown v. Board of
Education
National Historic Site
1515 SE Monroe Street
Topeka, KS 66612-1143
785-354-4273
www.nps.gov/brvb

The 1954 landmark Supreme Court decision in *Oliver L. Brown, et. al. v. the Topeka Board of Education, et. al.* concluded that "separate educational facilities are inherently unequal," effectively ending legal racial segregation in the public schools of this country. That decision is commemorated at the former Monroe Elementary School, one of four segregated schools for African American children in Topeka.
Established Oct. 26, 1992.
Acreage—1.85, all Federal.

Fort Larned
National Historic Site
1767 KS Highway 156
Larned, KS 67550-9321
620-285-6911
www.nps.gov/fols

In 1859, Fort Larned was established along the Santa Fe Trail. It was deactivated in 1878 after the railroads replaced the trail. Troops stationed here escorted mail coaches, protected wagon trains, and patrolled the region. Throughout 1860s, the fort served as an Agency for the Indian Bureau and was a key military base of operations during the Indian War of 1867-69. Fort Larned survives as one of the best and most authentic examples of a frontier military post.
Authorized Aug. 31, 1964.
Acreage—718.39 Federal: 679.66 Nonfederal: 38.73.

Fort Scott
National Historic Site
PO Box 918
Old Fort Boulevard
Fort Scott, KS 66701-0918
620-223-0310
www.nps.gov/fosc

Founded in 1842 for "Permanent Indian Frontier" peacekeeping, its soldiers fought in the U.S.-Mexican War (1846–1848), provided armed escort along the Santa Fe and Oregon trails, surveyed unmapped country, and maintained contact with Plains Indians. The post closed in 1853 and when its structures sold at public auction in 1855, the civilian town of Fort Scott became a center of "Bleeding Kansas" intrigue (1855-1860). Union troops fortified the town during the Civil War and the first black regiment to serve in combat was organized here. Post-war disputes over railroad expansion caused the army to return, with headquarters located in town. African American schools were established onsite and included George Washington Carver and Gordon Parks as students.
Authorized Oct. 19, 1978.
Acreage—16.69, all Federal.

Nicodemus
National Historic Site
304 Washington Avenue
Nicodemus, KS 67625-9719
785-839-4233
www.nps.gov/nico

Nicodemus, Kans., is the only remaining western town established by African Americans during the reconstruction period following the Civil War. The town is symbolic of the pioneer spirit of African Americans seeking personal freedom and the opportunity to develop their talents and capabilities. Established Nov. 12, 1996.
Acreage—4.59 Federal: 1.64 Nonfederal: 2.95.

Tallgrass Prairie
National Preserve
PO Box 585
226 Broadway
Cottonwood Falls, KS 66845-9728
620-273-6034
www.nps.gov/tapr

This nationally significant example of the once vast tallgrass prairie ecosystem includes historic buildings and cultural resources of the Spring Hill Ranch in the Flint Hills region of Kansas. The federal government will own up to 180 acres, with The Nature Conservancy—the purchaser of the property in 2005—retaining ownership of the rest of the preserve. Established November 12, 1996.
Acreage—10,893.14 Federal: 43.59 Nonfederal: 10,849.55.

Kentucky

Abraham Lincoln
Birthplace
National Historical Park
2995 Lincoln Farm Road
Hodgenville, KY 42748-9707
270-358-3137
www.nps.gov/abli

A cabin, symbolic of the one in which Lincoln was born, is preserved in a memorial building at the site of his birth. Established as Abraham Lincoln National Park July 17, 1916; transferred from War Dept. Aug. 10, 1933; redesignated Aug. 11, 1939; renamed and redesignated Sept. 8, 1959; redesignated a national historical park March 30, 2009. Boundary changes: May 27, 1949; April 11, 1972; Nov. 6, 1998.
Acreage—344.50, all Federal.

Big South Fork
National River and
Recreation Area
(See Tennessee)

Cumberland Gap
National Historical Park
91 Bartlett Park Road
Middlesboro, KY 40965
606-248-2817
www.nps.gov/cuga
(Also in Tennessee and Virginia)

This mountain pass on the Wilderness Road, explored by Daniel Boone, developed into a main artery of the great trans-Allegheny migration for settlement of the west and was an important military objective in the Civil War. Authorized June 11, 1940. Boundary changes: July 26, 1961; Oct. 26, 1974; Jan. 23, 2004.
Acreage—24,546.83 Federal: 24,530.56 Nonfederal: 16.27.

Fort Donelson National
Battlefield
(See Tennessee)

Mammoth Cave
National Park
PO Box 7
Mammoth Cave, KY 42259-0007
270-758-2328
www.nps.gov/maca

The park was established to preserve the cave system, including Mammoth Cave, the scenic river valleys of the Green and Nolin rivers, and a section of the hilly country of south central Kentucky. This is the longest recorded cave system in the world, with over 350 miles explored and mapped. Organized tours began in 1816. Authorized May 25, 1926; established July 1, 1941. Boundary changes: May 14, 1934; Aug. 28, 1937; Dec. 3, 1940; June 5, 1942. Designated a World Heritage Site Oct. 27, 1981. Designated a Biosphere Reserve 1990.
Acreage—52,830.19 Federal: 52,003.24 Nonfederal: 826.95.

Louisiana

Cane River Creole
National Historical Park
400 Rapides Drive
Natchitoches, LA 71457
318-352-0383
www.nps.gov/cari

This park is part of the 116,000-acre Cane River National Heritage Area. It consists of Oakland Plantation and portions of Magnolia Plantation. Both demonstrate the history of colonization, frontier influences, Creole architecture and culture, cotton agriculture, slavery, and social practices over 200 years.
Authorized Nov. 2, 1994.
Acreage—205.50 Federal: 62.39 Nonfederal: 143.11.

Jean Lafitte
National Historical Park
and Preserve
419 Decatur Street
New Orleans, LA 70130
504-589-3882
www.nps.gov/jela

This park incorporates representative examples of southern Louisiana resources and culture. The Acadian Cultural Center in Lafayette, the Prairie Acadian Cultural Center in Eunice, and the Wetlands Acadian Cultural Center in Thibodaux interpret Cajun culture and history. The Barataria Preserve, south of New Orleans, offers trails and waterways through bottomland forests, swamp, and marsh. The Chalmette unit, east of New Orleans, was the site of the Battle of New Orleans during the War of 1812, and contains the Chalmette National Cemetery. The French Quarter unit interprets the diverse cultures of New Orleans.
Chalmette Unit established as Chalmette Monument and Grounds March 4, 1907; transferred from War Dept. Aug. 10, 1933; reestablished as Chalmette National Historical Park Aug. 10, 1939; incorporation in new park authorized Nov. 10, 1978.
Acreage—22,420.86 Federal: 17,797.60 Nonfederal: 4,623.26.

New Orleans Jazz
National Historical Park
419 Decatur Street
New Orleans, LA 70130
504-589-4806
www.nps.gov/jazz

The park preserves and perpetuates knowledge and understanding of jazz from its origins in New Orleans through its continued evolution. The park provides education and interpretation with an emphasis on jazz performance, and assists organizations involved with jazz and its history.
Authorized Oct. 31, 1994.
Acreage—5.13, all Nonfederal.

Poverty Point
National Monument
c/o Poverty Point State
Commemorative Area
PO Box 248
Epps, LA 71237
318-926-5492
www.nps.gov/popo

This park in northeastern Louisiana, recently inscribed as a World Heritage Site, commemorates a culture that thrived from 4,000 to 3,000 years ago. The site, which has some of the largest prehistoric earthworks in North America, is managed by the state of Louisiana. State park facilities are open to the public. NO FEDERAL FACILITIES.
Authorized Oct. 31, 1988.
Acreage—910.85, all Nonfederal.

Vicksburg
National Military Park
(See Mississippi)

Maine

Acadia National Park

PO Box 177
Bar Harbor, ME 04609-0177
207-288-3338
www.nps.gov/acad

From rocky shorelines to granite mountaintops, Acadia protects the glacially sculpted landscape and diverse natural habitats of Mount Desert Island, Schoodic Peninsula, Isle au Haut, and other islands along Maine's central coast. At 1,530 feet, Cadillac Mountain is the highest point on the east coast of the United States. The park offers exceptional scenery and recreational opportunities through a network of historic carriage roads, hiking trails, and motor roads.Proclaimed Sieur de Monts National Monument July 8, 1916; established as Lafayette National Park Feb. 26, 1919; renamed Acadia National Park Jan. 19, 1929. Boundary changes: Jan. 19, 1929; May 23, 1930; May 29, 1935; Aug. 24, 1935; June 6, 1942; Dec. 22, 1944; July 30, 1947; Sept. 7, 1949; Aug. 1, 1950; July 24, 1956; Oct. 3, 1966; March 4, 1968; March 12, 1968; Oct. 15, 1982. Permanent boundary established Sept. 25, 1986.
Acreage—48,995.91 Federal: 47,998.44 Nonfederal: 997.47.

Appalachian National Scenic Trail

National Park Service
PO Box 50
Harpers Ferry, WV 25425
304-535-6278
www.nps.gov/appa
(Also in Connecticut, Georgia, Maryland, Massachusetts, New Hampshire, New Jersey, New York, North Carolina, Pennsylvania, Tennessee, Vermont, Virginia, and West Virginia)

For public inquiries:
Appalachian Trail
Conservancy
PO Box 807
Harpers Ferry, WV 25425
304-535-6331

The Appalachian Trail is a long public footpath that traverses the scenic, wooded, pastoral, wild, and culturally resonant lands of the Appalachian Mountains. Conceived in 1921, built by private citizens, and completed in 1937, today the trail is managed by the National Park Service, U.S. Forest Service, Appalachian Trail Conservancy, numerous state agencies and thousands of volunteers.
Established Oct. 2, 1968. Length: 2,189 miles
Acreage—235,972.92 Federal: 179,276.29 Nonfederal: 56,696.63.

Saint Croix Island International Historic Site

PO Box 247
Calais, ME 04619-0247
207-454-3871
www.nps.gov/sacn

The attempted French settlement of 1604, which led to an enduring French presence in North America, is commemorated on Saint Croix Island in the Saint Croix River on the Canadian border. Visitor facilities and interpretive trail exhibits are provided on the mainland.
Authorized as a national monument June 8, 1949; redesignated an international historic site Sept. 25, 1984.
Acreage—6.50, all Federal.

Maryland

Antietam National Battlefield

PO Box 158
Sharpsburg, MD 21782-0158
301-432-5124
www.nps.gov/anti

Gen. Robert E. Lee's first invasion of the North was ended on this battlefield in 1862. Antietam (Sharpsburg) National Cemetery—5,032 interments, 1,836 unidentified—adjoins the park; grave space is not available.
Established as a national battlefield site Aug. 30, 1890; transferred from War Dept. Aug. 10, 1933; redesignated as a na

tional battlefield Nov. 10, 1978. Boundary changes: May 14, 1940; April 22, 1960; May 31, 1962; Nov. 10, 1978. Cemetery: Probable date of Civil War interments: 1866. Placed under War Dept. July 14, 1870; transferred from War Dept. Aug. 10, 1933.
Park acreage—3,230.37 Federal: 2742.76 Nonfederal: 487.61. Cemetery acreage: 11.36, all Federal.

Appalachian National Scenic Trail
(See Maine)

Assateague Island National Seashore
7206 National Seashore Lane
Berlin, MD 21811-2540
410-641-1441
www.nps.gov/asis
(Also in Virginia)

The National Seashore protects 37 miles of beach, dunes, maritime forest and marsh habitats, surrounding ocean and bay waters and the dynamic barrier island processes upon which these coastal resources depend. Visitors may enjoy wildlife and wild horse viewing along with many nature-based recreational opportunities. The VA portion of Assateague Island includes the 9,021 acre Chincoteague National Wildlife Refuge, administered by the U.S. Fish and Wildlife Service.
Authorized Sept. 21, 1965. Boundary change: July 10, 1992.
Acreage—41,346.50 Federal: 18,928.27 Nonfederal: 22,418.23. Land area: 15,977.67. Water area: 22,079.

Catoctin Mountain Park
6602 Foxville Road
Thurmont, MD 21788-0158
301-663-9388
www.nps.gov/cato

Part of the forested ridge that forms the eastern rampart of the Appalachian Mountains in Maryland, this mountain park has sparkling streams and panoramic vistas of the Monocacy Valley.
Catoctin Recreation Demonstration Area transferred from Resettlement Administration Nov. 14, 1936; renamed July 12, 1954. Boundary change: July 12, 1954.
Acreage—5,891.49 Federal: 5,890.36 Nonfederal: 1.13.

Chesapeake and Ohio Canal National Historical Park
1850 Dual Highway, Ste. 100
Hagerstown, MD 21740
301-714-2201
www.nps.gov/choh
(Also in the District of Columbia and West Virginia)

The park follows the route of the 184.5-mile canal along the Potomac River between Washington, D.C., and Cumberland, Md. The canal was built between 1828 and 1850.
Placed under National Park Service Sept. 23, 1938; upper canal proclaimed a national monument Jan. 18, 1961; established as a national historical park Jan. 8, 1971. Boundary change: Nov. 10, 1978.
Acreage—19,612.37 Federal: 14,465.19 Nonfederal: 5,147.18

Clara Barton National Historic Site
5801 Oxford Road
Glen Echo, MD 20812-1201
301-320-1410
www.nps.gov/clba

This 38-room home of the founder of the American Red Cross was headquarters of that organization for seven years.
Authorized Oct. 26, 1974.
Acreage—8.59, all Federal.

Fort McHenry National Monument and Historic Shrine
2400 East Fort Avenue
Baltimore, MD 21230-5393
410-962-4290
www.nps.gov/fomc

Successful defense of this fort in the War of 1812, Sept. 13–14, 1814, inspired Francis Scott Key to write "The Star Spangled Banner."
Authorized as a national park March 3, 1925; transferred from War Dept. Aug. 10, 1933; redesignated Aug. 11, 1939. Boundary change: June 5, 1936.
Acreage—43.26, all Federal.

Fort Washington Park
13551 Fort Washington Road
Fort Washington, MD 20744
301-763-4600
www.nps.gov/fowa

This fort across the Potomac River from Mount Vernon was built to protect Washington, D.C. Construction was begun in 1814 to replace an 1809 fort destroyed during the War of 1812. The park also has recreational facilities.
Transfer from War Dept. authorized May 29, 1930, effective Aug. 12, 1940.
Acreage—341.00, all Federal.

**George Washington
Memorial Parkway**
(See Virginia)

Greenbelt Park
6565 Greenbelt Road
Greenbelt, MD 20770-3207
301-344-3948
www.nps.gov/gree

Just 12 miles from Washington, D.C., this woodland park offers urban dwellers access to many forms of outdoor recreation, including camping year-round.
Transferred from Public Housing Authority Aug. 3, 1950.
Acreage—1,175.42 Federal: 1,105.79 Nonfederal: 69.63.

**Hampton
National Historic Site**
535 Hampton Lane
Towson, MD 21286-1397
410-823-1309
www.nps.gov/hamp

This remnant of a vast landholding includes a Georgian mansion, gardens and grounds, and original stone slave quarters.
Designated June 22, 1948. Boundary changes: Dec. 23, 1953; Nov. 10, 1978.
Acreage—62.04, all Federal.

**Harpers Ferry
National Historical Park**
(See West Virginia)

Harriet Tubman Underground Railroad National Historical Park
c/o Blackwater National Wildlife Refuge
2145 Key Wallace Drive
Cambridge, MD 21613
267-838-2376
www.nps.gov/hatu

Maryland's Eastern Shore was home to Harriet Tubman known for her extraordinary work with abolitionist causes and as the Underground Railroad's most famous conductor. The park encompasses a mosaic of state and federal lands in Dorchester County, Maryland that are significant to Tubman's early years and evoke her life while enslaved and as a conductor on the Underground Railroad.
Proclaimed a national monument on March 25, 2013; redesignated a national historical park on Dec. 19, 2014
Acreage—480.00, all Federal.

Monocacy National Battlefield
4632 Araby Church Road
Frederick, MD 21704-7307
301-662-3515
www.nps.gov/mono

In a battle here on July 9, 1864, Confederate Gen. Jubal A. Early defeated Union forces commanded by Maj. Gen. Lew Wallace. Wallace's troops delayed Early's advance on Washington, D.C., however, enabling Union forces to marshal a successful defense of the capital.
Authorized as Monocacy National Military Park, June 21, 1934. Reauthorized and redesignated Oct. 21, 1976. Boundary change: Nov. 10, 1978; Dec. 28, 1980.
Acreage—1,647.01 Federal: 1,550.24 Nonfederal: 96.77.

National Capital Parks - East
1900 Anacostia Drive, SE
Washington, DC 20020
202-690-5185
www.nps.gov/nace
(See District of Columbia)

Piscataway Park
c/o Fort Washington Park
13551 Fort Washington Road
Fort Washington, MD 20744
301-763-4600
www.nps.gov/pisc

The tranquil view from Mount Vernon of the Maryland shore of the Potomac River is preserved by this park, a pilot project in the use of easements to protect significant places from obtrusive urban expansion.
Authorized Oct. 4, 1961. Boundary changes: July 19, 1966; Oct. 21, 1976.
Acreage—4,626.37 Federal: 4,590.57 Nonfederal: 35.80.

**Potomac Heritage
National Scenic Trail**
National Park Service
PO Box B
Harpers Ferry, WV 25425
304-535-4014
www.nps.gov/pohe
(Also in District of
Columbia, Pennsylvania, and
Virginia)

Between the mouth of the Potomac River and the Allegheny Highlands, this evolving Trail network provides access to the beauty and heritage of the Potomac and Youghiogheny river corridors. The network includes the Laurel Highlands Hiking Trail, the Chesapeake & Ohio Canal Towpath and part of the Great Allegheny Passage, named Potomac Heritage Trails segments, the Mount Vernon Trail, bicycling routes on the Northern Neck of Virginia and in southern Maryland, and many parks, historic sites and natural areas.
Established March 28, 1983. Length: 710 miles.

**Thomas Stone
National Historic Site**
6655 Rosehill Road
Port Tobacco, MD 20677-
3400
301-934-6027
www.nps.gov/thst

Haberdeventure, a Georgian mansion built in 1771 near Port Tobacco, Md., was the home of Thomas Stone (1743–87). A signer of the Declaration of Independence, Stone was a delegate to the Continental Congress, 1775–78 and 1783–84. Authorized Nov. 10, 1978.
Acreage—328.25, all Federal.

Massachusetts

**Adams
National Historical Park**
135 Adams Street
Quincy, MA 02169
617-773-1177
www.nps.gov/adam

The park includes the home of Presidents John Adams and John Quincy Adams, of U.S. Minister to Great Britain Charles Francis Adams, and of the writers and historians Henry Adams and Brooks Adams; and the birthplaces of both presidents and United First Parish Church, location of the Adams Crypt. The library contains over 14,000 historic volumes. Designated Adams Mansion National Historic Site Dec. 9, 1946; renamed Nov. 26, 1952; redesignated Adams National Historic Site Nov. 2, 1998; redesignated Adams National Historical Park Nov. 2, 1998. Boundary changes: Nov. 26, 1952; April 11, 1972; Nov. 10, 1978; Oct. 10, 1980; Nov. 2, 1998.
Acreage—23.82 Federal: 9.17 Nonfederal: 14.65.

**Appalachian
National Scenic Trail**
(See Maine)

**Boston African American
National Historic Site**
15 State Street, 9th Floor
Boston, MA 02109
617-742-5415
www.nps.gov/boaf

The site promotes, preserves, and interprets the history of Boston's free African American community on Beacon Hill the 1800s, in partnership with the Museum of African American History, the City of Boston, and private property owners. The 15 pre-Civil War structures along the 1.6 mile Black Heritage Trail were the homes, businesses, schools, and churches of people who fought slavery and injustice
Authorized Oct. 10, 1980.
Acreage—0.59, all Nonfederal.

**Boston Harbor Islands
National Recreation Area**
Boston Harbor Islands
Partnership
408 Atlantic Avenue, Ste. 228
Boston MA 02110-3349
617-223-8667
www.nps.gov/boha

Thirty islands in Boston Harbor make up this treasure of natural and cultural resources and recreational amenities at the doorstep of a major Northeast urban area. The park is managed by a partnership of federal, state, municipal, and non-profit agencies, including the National Park Service. Authorized Nov. 12, 1996.
Acreage—1,482.31 Federal: 245.57 Nonfederal: 1,236.74.

Boston
National Historical Park
Charlestown Navy Yard
Visitor Center
Boston, MA 02129-4543
617-242-5601
www.nps.gov/bost

The events and ideas associated with the American Revolution and the founding and growth of the United States provide the common thread linking the sites that compose this park, among them Bunker Hill, Old North Church, Paul Revere House, Faneuil Hall, Old State House, Old South Meeting House, and a portion of the Charlestown Navy Yard, including the USS Constitution.
Authorized Oct. 1, 1974. Boundary changes: Nov. 10, 1978; Sept. 8, 1980.
Acreage—43.82 Federal: 37.96 Nonfederal: 5.86.

Cape Cod
National Seashore
99 Marconi Site Road
Wellfleet, MA 02667-0250
508-771-2144
www.nps.gov/caco

Ocean beaches, dunes, woodlands, freshwater ponds, and marshes make up this park on outer Cape Cod. It stretches 40 miles from Chatham to Provincetown. Its many cultural remnants include archeological sites, lighthouses, a life-saving station, cultural landscapes, and the Marconi Station Site, where transatlantic wireless communication was achieved in 1903.
Authorized Aug. 7, 1961; established June 1, 1966. Boundary changes: Nov. 10, 1978; Oct. 26, 1998.
Acreage—43,607.14 Federal: 27,548.99 Nonfederal: 16,058.15. Land area: 27,700.

Frederick Law Olmsted
National Historic Site
99 Warren Street
Brookline, MA 02445-5930
617-566-1689
www.nps.gov/frla

This was the first large-scale landscape architecture office in the United States, founded by Frederick Law Olmsted Sr. and continued by his sons and successors. The site includes the Olmsted Archives, which documents over 5,000 projects undertaken by the Olmsted firm.
Authorized Oct. 12, 1979. Boundary change: Nov. 12, 1998.
Acreage—7.21, all Federal.

John Fitzgerald Kennedy
National Historic Site
83 Beals Street
Brookline, MA 02446-6010
617-566-7937
www.nps.gov/jofi

This is the birthplace and early childhood home of the 35th president. It was here, in their first home, that Joseph and Rose Kennedy began to cultivate and instill in their children the family's ideals, aspirations and ambitions. The Kennedy family repurchased the home in 1966 and Rose Kennedy carefully recreated the birthplace as a gift to the American people in the lingering wake of the president's assassination.
Authorized May 26, 1967.
Acreage—0.09, all Federal.

Longfellow - Washington's Headquarters
National Historic Site
105 Brattle Street
Cambridge, MA 02138-3407
617-876-4491
www.nps.gov/long

The Vassall-Craigie-Longfellow House, George Washington's headquarters during the siege of Boston (1775–1776) was later home to poet Henry Wadsworth Longfellow and family (1837–1950). As the first major headquarters used by George Washington as Commander-in-Chief of the Continental Army, the house saw the implementation of important organizational initiatives and planning for the Siege of Boston. While here, General Washington experienced many things that profoundly shaped him for the rest of his life and career. Years later, the Longfellow family, drawn to the house for its historic connection, hosted writers, artists, and statesmen who took part in the flowering of American literature and culture in the 19th century and advocated for the extension of freedom to all Americans. The site is home to a vast collection of decorative and fine arts, a library, and a working research archive.
Authorized Oct. 9, 1972. Redesignated Dec. 22, 2010.
Acreage—1.98, all Federal.

Lowell
National Historical Park
67 Kirk Street
Lowell, MA 01852-1029
978-970-5000
www.nps.gov/lowe

The history and legacy of America's Industrial Revolution is commemorated in downtown Lowell. The Boott Cotton Mills Museum with its weave room of 88 operating looms, a "mill girl" boarding house, the Suffolk Mill turbine, 5.6 miles of power canals, and guided walking, boat, and trolley tours tell the story of the transition from farm to factory, chronicle immigrant and labor history and heritage, and trace industrial technology.
Authorized June 5, 1978. Boundary changes: June 4, 1980; March 27, 1987; May 8, 2008.
Acreage—141.29 Federal: 31.66 Nonfederal: 109.63.

Minute Man
National Historical Park
174 Liberty Street
Concord, MA 01742
978-369-6993
www.nps.gov/mima

Scene of the "shot heard round the world" that began the Revolutionary War on April 19, 1775, the park includes restored sections of Battle Road between Lexington and Concord; the North Bridge; the Minute Man Statue; historic monuments and structures; and the Wayside, home of American authors.
Designated a national historic site April 14, 1959; established Sept. 21, 1959. Boundary changes: Oct. 24, 1992, Mar.30, 2009.
Acreage—1,026.81 Federal: 800.93 Nonfederal: 225.88.

New Bedford Whaling
National Historical Park
33 William Street
New Bedford, MA 02740
508-996-4095
www.nps.gov/nebe

This is the only National Park Service site to commemorate whaling and its contribution to American history. The park includes a 34-acre National Historic Landmark District, the schooner *Ernestina*, and many cultural institutions, including the New Bedford Whaling Museum.
Authorized Nov. 12, 1996.
Acreage—34.00 Federal: 0.34 Nonfederal: 33.66.

Salem Maritime
National Historic Site
160 Derby Street
Salem, MA 01970-5186
978-740-1650
www.nps.gov/sama

The maritime history of New England and the early United States is preserved among the historic buildings, colonial wharves, and a reconstructed tall ship. The site shares the stories of the sailors, privateers, and merchants who brought the riches of the world to America. Established as the first National Historic Site in the United States.
Designated March 17, 1938. Boundary changes: Dec. 12, 1963; Nov. 10, 1978; June 27, 1988; Nov. 28, 1990.
Acreage—9.02 Federal: 8.93 Nonfederal: 0.09.

Saugus Iron Works
National Historic Site
244 Central Street
Saugus, MA 01906-2107
781-233-0050
www.nps.gov/sair

As the location of the first fully-integrated ironworks in North America (1646–68), the site interprets the beginning of the storied American iron and steel industry. It includes a reconstructed blast furnace, forge, rolling and slitting mill, a lush river basin and a restored house from the 1600s.
Established April 5, 1968.
Acreage—8.51, all Federal.

Springfield Armory
National Historic Site
1 Armory Square
Springfield, MA 01105-1299
413-734-8551
www.nps.gov/spar

From 1794 to 1968, Springfield Armory was a center for the manufacture of U.S. military small arms and the scene of important technological advances. The Armory Museum protects one of the world's most extensive firearms collections.
Authorized Oct. 26, 1974; established March 21, 1978.
Acreage—54.93 Federal: 20.60 Nonfederal: 34.33.

Michigan

Isle Royale National Park
800 East Lakeshore Drive
Houghton, MI 49931-1895
906-482-0984
www.nps.gov/isro

This forested island, the largest in Lake Superior, is distinguished by its wilderness character, timber wolves, moose herd, and pre-Columbian copper mines.
Authorized March 3, 1931. Boundary changes: May 28, 1934; June 20, 1938; March 6, 1942; Aug. 14, 1958; April 11, 1972; Oct. 20, 1976. Wilderness designated Oct. 20, 1976. Designated a Biosphere Reserve 1980.
Acreage—571,790.11 Federal: 539,281.87 Nonfederal: 32,508.24. Land area: 133,781.87. Wilderness area: 132,018.

Keweenaw National Historical Park
25970 Red Jacket Road
Calumet, MI 49913-0471
906-337-3168
www.nps.gov/kewe

The park preserves and interprets the history of the Keweenaw Peninsula beginning with prehistoric activity nearly 7,000 years ago through large-scale industrial mining in the 1800s and 1900s. The park's Keweenaw Heritage Sites partners operate most visitor facilities, providing diverse experiences and views of the industry and its participants. LIMITED FEDERAL FACILITIES.
Established Oct. 27, 1992.
Acreage— 1,869.40 Federal: 135.58 Nonfederal: 1,733.82.

Pictured Rocks National Lakeshore
PO Box 40
Munising, MI 49862-0040
906-387-3700
www.nps.gov/piro

Multicolored sandstone cliffs, long beach strands, towering sand dunes, waterfalls, inland lakes, wetlands, hardwood and coniferous forests, and a variety of wildlife compose this scenic area on Lake Superior.
Authorized Oct. 15, 1966; established Oct. 5, 1972. Boundary changes: Nov. 12, 1996; Nov. 25, 2002.
Acreage—73,235.83 Federal: 35,728.86 Nonfederal: 37,506.97. Land area: 63,122.08.

River Raisin National Battlefield Park
1403 East Elm Avenue
Monroe, MI 48162
734-243-7136
www.nps.gov/rira

River Raisin National Battlefield Park preserves, commemorates, and interprets the January 1813 battles of the War of 1812 and their aftermath in Monroe and Wayne counties in Southeast Michigan. The Battles of the River Raisin resulted in the greatest victory for Tecumseh's Confederation and the greatest defeat for the United States during the War of 1812. Although American forces were victorious in the first battle, the second ended in what was described as a "national calamity" by then General William Henry Harrison, and later President of the United States. The battle cry, "Remember the Raisin!" inspired a massive U.S. victory at the Battle of the Thames, which sealed the War of 1812 in the western theater for the U.S., claimed the life of the great Shawnee leader Tecumseh, and resulted in the end the American Indian Confederation. The aftermath of the battles resulted in the implementation of Indian removal from the Northwest Territory at the conclusion of the War of 1812, an aftermath that continues to influence the United States today.
Authorized Mar. 30, 2009. Established Oct. 22, 2010.
Acreage – 42.18, all Federal.

**Sleeping Bear Dunes
National Lakeshore**
9922 Front Street
Empire, MI 49630-9797
231-326-5134
www.nps.gov/slbe

This is a diverse landscape with quiet rivers, sandy beaches, beech-maple forests, clear lakes, and massive "perched" sand dunes towering up to 460 feet above Lake Michigan. Two off-shore wilderness islands offer tranquility and seclusion. The many historic sites include a lighthouse, life-saving service stations, and agricultural landscapes.
Established Oct. 21, 1970. Boundary change: May 28, 2004.
Acreage—71,210.15 Federal: 57,472.53 Nonfederal: 13,737.62. Land area: 59,471.

Minnesota

**Grand Portage
National Monument**
PO Box 426
170 Mile Creek Road
Portage, MN 55605
218-475-0123
www.nps.gov/grpo

This 9-mile portage was a vital link on one of the principal routes for Indians, explorers, missionaries, and fur traders heading for the Northwest. The Grand Portage post of the North West Company has been reconstructed at the eastern terminus of the Grand Portage on Lake Superior
Designated a national historic site Sept. 15, 1951; redesignated Sept. 2, 1958.
Acreage—709.97, all Federal.

**Mississippi National River
and Recreation Area**
111 E. Kellogg Boulevard
Suite 105
St. Paul, MN 55101-1256
651-290-4160
www.nps.gov/miss

Encompassing 72 miles of the Mississippi River corridor through the Twin Cities metropolitan region, the area features a wealth of nationally significant natural, cultural, historic, scenic, economic, and scientific resources, complemented by diverse recreational activities.
Established Nov. 18, 1988.
Acreage—53,775.00 Federal: 62.42 Nonfederal: 53,712.58.

**Pipestone
National Monument**
36 Reservation Avenue
Pipestone, MN 56164-1269
507-825-5464
www.nps.gov/pipe

For centuries American Indians have quarried pipestone from these ancient quarries. Pipes made from this stone are considered sacred and are important spiritual objects for American Indians. Recognizing this cultural activity, the monument's enabling legislation allows quarrying to continue today.
Established Aug. 25, 1937. Boundary change: June 18, 1956.
Acreage—281.78, all Federal.

**Saint Croix
National Scenic Riverway**
(See Wisconsin)

Voyageurs National Park
360 Highway 11
International Falls, MN
56649-8904
218-283-6600
www.nps.gov/voya

This waterway of four large lakes connected by narrows was once the route of the French-Canadian voyageurs. With over 500 islands, the lakes surround a peninsula of boreal forest.
Authorized Jan. 8, 1971; established April 8, 1975. Boundary change: Jan. 3, 1983.
Acreage—218,200.15 Federal: 133,247.72 Nonfederal: 84,952.43 Land area: 134,246. Water area: 83,808.

Mississippi

**Brices Cross Roads
National Battlefield Site**
c/o Natchez Trace Parkway
2680 Natchez Trace Parkway
Tupelo, MS 38804-9718
662-680-4025
www.nps.gov/brcr

Despite a decisive tactical victory over a larger Union force on June 10, 1864, Major General N. B. Forrest's Confederates ultimately failed to disrupt Union supply lines critical to Brigadier General W.T. Sherman's Atlanta campaign. United States Colored Troops (USCT) played a crucial role in the Federals' retreat. Established Feb. 21, 1929; transferred from War Dept. Aug. 10, 1933.
Acreage—1.00, all Federal.

**Gulf Islands
National Seashore**
3500 Park Road
Ocean Springs, MS 39564-9709
228-230-4100
www.nps.gov/guis
(Also in Florida)

Sparkling beaches, historic sites, a wilderness island, islands accessible only by boat, mainland bayous, nature trails, picnic areas, and campgrounds make up this park.
Authorized Jan. 8, 1971. Boundary change: Nov. 10, 1978. Wilderness designated Nov. 10, 1978.
Acreage—138,305.52 Federal: 99,779.27 Nonfederal: 38,562.25. Land area: 19,445.46. Wilderness area: 1,800. (Acreage figures are for entire park, Mississippi and Florida units.)

**Natchez
National Historical Park**
PO Box 1208
Natchez, MS 39121-1208
601-446-5790
www.nps.gov/natc

Before the Civil War, Natchez became a commercial, cultural, and social center of the South's cotton belt. The city today represents one of the best preserved concentrations of significant antebellum properties in the United States. Within the park are Melrose, an excellent example of a planter's home, and the home of William Johnson, a prominent free black man.
Authorized Oct. 7, 1988.
Acreage—108.30 Federal: 85.98 Nonfederal: 22.32.

**Natchez Trace
National Scenic Trail**
c/o Natchez Trace Parkway
2680 Natchez Trace Parkway
Tupelo, MS 38804-9718
662-680-4025
www.nps.gov/natt
(Also in Alabama and
Tennessee)

The Natchez Trace National Scenic Trail traverses the states of Mississippi, Alabama, and Tennessee, and provides visitors an opportunity to experience the unique cultural and natural aspects of the Natchez Trace. The trail parallels the 444-mile corridor of the Natchez Trace Parkway (NPS unit). Five completed sections of this trail are found alongside the Natchez Trace Parkway near Natchez, Port Gibson, Ridgeland and Tupelo, Mississippi and Leipers Fork, Tennessee. Established March 28, 1983. Length: 64 miles.
Acreage—10,995.00, all Nonfederal.

Natchez Trace Parkway
2680 Natchez Trace Parkway
Tupelo, MS 38804-9718
662-680-4025
www.nps.gov/natr
(Also in Alabama and
Tennessee)

The 444-mile Parkway, completed in 2005, roughly follows the route of the Old Natchez Trace, a trail and eventual postal road, which traveled from Natchez, Mississippi to Nashville, Tennessee through Natchez, Choctaw, and Chickasaw territory. Human history dates back 10,000 years; peak use was approximately 1790 – 1830 during the "boatman" period. Established as a parkway under National Park Service by act of May 18, 1938. The Ackia Battleground (authorized as a national monument Aug. 27, 1935) and the Meriwether Lewis Park (proclaimed a monument Feb. 6, 1925 and transferred from War Dept. Aug.10, 1933) were added to the parkway by act of Aug. 10, 1961.
Acreage—52,302.00 Federal: 52,207.30 Nonfederal: 94.70.

Shiloh
National Military Park
(See Tennessee)

Tupelo
National Battlefield
c/o Natchez Trace Parkway
2680 Natchez Trace Parkway
Tupelo, MS 38804-9718
662-680-4025
www.nps.gov/tupe

Disorganized Confederates under Major General Nathan Bedford Forrest fought fiercely but could not overpower Union forces in the Battle of Tupelo, July 13-14, 1864. Critical Union supply lines remained open to support Brigadier General William Tecumseh Sherman's Atlanta campaign.
Established as a national battlefield site Feb. 21, 1929; transferred from War Dept. Aug. 10, 1933; redesignated and boundary changed Aug. 10, 1961.
Acreage—1.00, all Federal.

Vicksburg
National Military Park
3201 Clay Street
Vicksburg, MS 39183
601-636-0583
www.nps.gov/vick
(Also in Louisiana)

Reconstructed forts and trenches evoke memories of the 47-day siege that ended in the surrender of the city on July 4, 1863. Victory gave the North control of the Mississippi River. The Civil War ironclad gunboat USS *Cairo* is on display. Vicksburg National Cemetery—18,244 interments, including 12,954 unidentified—is within the park; grave space is not available.
Park: Established Feb. 21, 1899; transferred from War Dept. Aug. 10, 1933. Boundary changes: June 4, 1963; Oct. 18, 1990. Cemetery: Date of Civil War interments, 1866–1874. Transferred from War Dept. Aug. 10, 1933. Boundary change: March 2, 1955.
Park acreage—1,802.18 Federal: 1,746.73 Nonfederal: 55.45. Cemetery acreage—116.28, all Federal.

Missouri

George Washington Carver
National Monument
5646 Carver Road
Diamond, MO 64840
417-325-4151
www.nps.gov/gwca

Birthplace and childhood home of George Washington Carver, African American agronomist, educator, and humanitarian. The visitor center has a museum, interactive exhibits, a theater, and a store. A ¾-mile trail passes the birthplace site, the Boy Carver statue, the restored 1881 Moses Carver House, and the cemetery.
Authorized July 14, 1943.
Acreage—210.00, all Federal.

Harry S Truman
National Historic Site
223 North Main Street
Independence, MO 64050-2804
816-254-9929
www.nps.gov/hstr

The site preserves the homes of Harry S Truman, 33rd president. The Truman Home, his residence from 1919 to 1972, was called the Summer White House during his administration. The site has four other homes that were part of the family compound: his Uncle and Aunt Noland's home, the Wallace homes owned by Bess Truman's brothers, and the Truman Farm Home in Grandview, Mo., at one time a 600-acre farm.
Designated Dec. 8, 1982; National Park Service administration authorized May 23, 1983. Boundary changes: Oct. 2, 1989, Dec. 14, 1993; Oct. 30, 2004.
Acreage—12.59, all Federal.

Jefferson
National Expansion
Memorial
11 North 4th Street
St. Louis, MO 63102-1882
314-655-1600
www.nps.gov/jeff

Eero Saarinen's soaring stainless steel Gateway Arch on St. Louis' riverfront memorializes the city's role in westward expansion. Visitors can ascend the 630-foot arch and see exhibits on American Indians, Thomas Jefferson, Lewis and Clark, and others in the underground Museum of Westward Expansion. In the nearby Old Courthouse, enslaved Dred Scott sued for his freedom in 1846.
Designated Dec. 21, 1935; Gateway Arch authorized May 17, 1954. Boundary changes: Aug. 29, 1969; Aug. 26, 1992.
Acreage—192.83 Federal: 90.96 Nonfederal: 101.87.

Ozark
National Scenic
Riverways
404 Watercress Drive
Van Buren, MO 63965-0490
573-323-4236
www.nps.gov/ozar

The 134 miles of the Current and Jacks Fork rivers provide canoeing, tubing, fishing, and swimming opportunities. Over 300 springs pour thousands of gallons of clear, cold water into the streams. Ozark culture is preserved throughout the area. This is the first national scenic river.
Authorized Aug. 27, 1964; established June 10, 1972.
Acreage—80,785.04 Federal: 61,368.42 Nonfederal: 19,416.62.

Ulysses S. Grant
National Historic Site
7400 Grant Road
St. Louis, MO 63123-1801
314-842-1867
www.nps.gov/ulsg

Former Army Captain Ulysses S. Grant; his wife, Julia Dent Grant; and their four children lived at the historic White Haven slave plantation from 1854 to 1860, before he became General of all Union Armies during the Civil War and later, the 18th President of the United States.
Authorized Oct. 2, 1989.
Acreage—9.60, all Federal.

Wilson's Creek
National Battlefield
6424 W. Farm Road 182
Republic, MO 65738-9514
417-732-2662
www.nps.gov/wicr

The battle was fought on Aug. 10, 1861, and was the first major battle west of the Mississippi. It was a Confederate victory, but Missouri remained in the Union. Major features include a 5-mile vehicle tour road, the restored 1852 Ray House, Bloody Hill, and the Trans Mississippi museum and library. Authorized as a national battlefield park April 22, 1960; redesignated Dec. 16, 1970. Boundary change: Oct. 30, 2014.
Acreage—2,368.10 Federal: 1,975.20 Nonfederal: 392.90

Montana

Big Hole
National Battlefield
PO Box 273
Wisdom, MT 59761
406-689-3155
www.nps.gov/biho

The site pays tribute to the battle between the Nez Perce Indians and the 7th U.S. Infantry forces with civilian volunteers on August 9–10, 1877. Ninety Nez Perce men, women, and children and 31 soldiers lost their lives.
Established as a military preserve in 1883, designated a national monument June 23, 1910; redesignated a national battlefield May 17, 1963. Added legislatively as a unit of Nez Perce National Historical Park in 1992.
Acreage—1,010.61 Federal: 655.61 Nonfederal: 355.

**Bighorn Canyon
National Recreation Area**
PO Box 7458
Fort Smith, MT 59035-7458
406-666-2412
www.nps.gov/bica
(Also in Wyoming)

Bighorn Lake extends 71 miles behind Yellowtail Dam on the Bighorn River. Archeological and historical resources complement the natural scene. About one third of the area is within the Crow Indian Reservation.
Established Oct. 15, 1966.
Acreage—120,296.22 Federal: 68,490.87 Nonfederal: 51,805.35.

**Fort Union Trading Post
National Historic Site**
(See North Dakota)

Glacier National Park
PO Box 128
West Glacier, MT 59936-0128
406-888-7800
www.nps.gov/glac

Known as the Backbone of the World to the Blackfeet Nation, Glacier is renowned for its spectacular glacier-carved landscapes, sparkling fjord-like lakes, and a diverse array of plant and animal species, created by the overlap of five different ecoregions. Bisecting the park, the national Historic Landmark Going-to-the-Sun road provides access to this remote wild land for over 2 million visitors per year.
Established May 11, 1910. Boundary changes: Feb. 10, 1912; Feb. 27, 1915; July 31, 1939; Dec. 13, 1944; April 11, 1972; Jan. 26, 1978. Authorized as part of Waterton-Glacier International Peace Park May 2, 1932; proclaimed June 30, 1932. Designated a Biosphere Reserve 1976; designated Waterton-Glacier International Peace Park World Heritage Site Dec. 9, 1995.
Acreage—1,013,324.23 Federal: 1,013,027.25 Nonfederal: 296.98.

**Grant-Kohrs Ranch
National Historic Site**
266 Warren Lane
Deer Lodge, MT 59722-0790
406-846-2070
www.nps.gov/grko

Grant-Kohrs Ranch National Historic Site provides an understanding of the nation's frontier cattle era commemorating cowboys and cattlemen through the preservation, interpretation, and operation of an intact ranch with more than 150 years of unbroken history.
Authorized Aug. 25, 1972. Boundary changes: Aug. 31, 1981; Nov. 10, 1998.
Acreage—1,618.38 Federal: 1,491.46 Nonfederal: 126.92.

**Little Bighorn Battlefield
National Monument**
PO Box 39
Crow Agency, MT 59022-0039
406-638-2621
www.nps.gov/libi

This area memorializes one of the last armed efforts of the Northern Plains Indians to preserve their way of life. Here in 1876, 263 soldiers and attached personnel of the U.S. Army, including Lt. Col. George A. Custer, met death at the hands of several thousand Lakota, Arapaho, and Cheyenne warriors.
Established as a national cemetery by the Secretary of War Jan. 29, 1879, to protect graves of 7th Cavalry troopers buried there; proclaimed National Cemetery of Custer's Battlefield Reservation to include burials of other campaigns and wars Dec. 7, 1886; Reno-Benteen Battlefield added April 14, 1926; transferred from War Dept. July 1, 1940; redesignated Custer Battlefield National Monument March 22, 1946; renamed Dec. 10, 1991.
Acreage—765.34, all Federal.

**Nez Perce
National Historical Park**
(See Idaho)

Yellowstone National Park
(See Wyoming)

Nebraska

**Agate Fossil Beds
National Monument**
301 River Road
PO Box 27
Harrison, NE 69346-2734
308-668-2211
www.nps.gov/agfo

This park was originally a working cattle ranch owned by Capt. James Cook and known as Agate Springs Ranch. The park features renowned quarries that contain many well-preserved mammal fossils from the Miocene Epoch; these represent an important chapter in the evolution of mammals. The park's museum collection also contains over 500 Plains indian artifacts from the Cook Family.
Authorized June 5, 1965; established June 14, 1997.
Acreage—3,057.87 Federal: 2,730.08 Nonfederal: 327.79.

**Homestead
National Monument of
America**
8523 West State Highway 4
Beatrice, NE 68310
402-223-3514
www.nps.gov/home

FREE LAND!! Was the cry! The Homestead Act of 1862 had an immediate and enduring effect upon America and the world that is still felt today. This park includes the 160-acre Daniel Freeman Claim, the National Museum on Homesteading, historic buildings and agricultural equipment, genealogy research opportunities, an education center, hiking trails through 100 acres of restored tallgrass prairie and a burr oak forest.
Authorized March 19, 1936. Boundary changes: Sept. 25, 1970; Dec. 16, 2002.
Acreage—211.09 Federal: 205.18 Nonfederal: 5.91.

**Missouri
National Recreational
River**
508 East Second Street
Yankton, SD 57078
402-336-3970
www.nps.gov/mnrr
(Also in South Dakota)

Two reaches of the Missouri River are protected here. The portion originally set aside, from Gavins Point Dam near Yankton, South Dakota, to Ponca, Nebraska, still exhibits the river's dynamic character in its islands, bars, chutes, and snags. An upper reach between Lewis and Clark Lake and Fort Randall Dam has native floodplain forest, tallgrass and mixed-grass prairies, and habitats for several endangered species. The river was designated for remarkable fish, and scenic, recreational, cultural, and ecological values.
Authorized Nov. 10, 1978; expanded May 24, 1991. Length: 59 miles (original segment); 67 miles (1991 addition).
Acreage—48,456.55 Federal: 308.78 Nonfederal: 48,147.77.

**Niobrara
National Scenic River**
214 W. Hwy 20
Valentine, NE 69201
402-376-1901
www.nps.gov/niob

This Great Plains river is rated as one of America's top canoeing adventures, with kayaking and tubing also quite popular. In addition, this 104-mile section of the Niobrara protects an unusual area where many species and ecosystems overlap. The Niobrara supports Boreal, Eastern Woodland, and Rocky Mountain forest types, and multiple prairie ecosystems including Tallgrass, Sandhills, and Mixed-Grass Prairies. The river was designated for outstandingly remarkable fish, wildlife, and scenic, recreational, geological, cultural, ecological and palentological values. Public and private facilities are available.
Authorized May 24, 1991. Length: 104 miles.
Acreage—29,101.02 Federal: 1,030.40 Nonfederal: 28,070.62.

Scotts Bluff
National Monument
190276 Old Oregon Trail
PO Box 27
Gering, NE 69341-9700
308-436-4340
www.nps.gov/scbl

Rising 800 feet above the valley floor, this massive promontory was a landmark on the Oregon and California trails, associated with overland migration across the Great Plains between 1843 and 1869.
Proclaimed Dec. 12, 1919. Boundary changes: May 9, 1924; June 1, 1932; March 29, 1940; June 30, 1961.
Acreage—3,004.73 Federal: 2,954.21 Nonfederal: 50.52.

Nevada

Death Valley
National Park
(See California)

Great Basin
National Park
100 Great Basin
National Park
Baker, NV 89311-9700
775-234-7331
www.nps.gov/grba

Preserves an outstanding segment of the Great Basin, including 5,000-year-old bristlecone pines, 13,063-foot Wheeler Peak, remnant rock glaciers, 75-foot Lexington Arch, the darkest of night skies, and the decorated galleries of Lehman Caves.
Proclaimed as Lehman Caves National Monument Jan. 24, 1922; transferred from the U.S. Forest Service, Aug. 10, 1933; made part of Great Basin National Park when established Oct. 27, 1986
Acreage—77,180.00, all Federal.

Lake Mead
National Recreation Area
601 Nevada Way
Boulder City, NV 89005-2426
702-293-8990
www.nps.gov/lake
(Also in Arizona)

A premier inland water recreation area in the west and the first national recreation area established by an act of Congress. Lake Mead, formed by Hoover Dam, and Lake Mohave, by Davis Dam, provide 290 square miles of water on which to boat, fish, swim, ski, sail and sun. Nearly 87 percent of the 1.5-million-acre park is land, containing a wealth of natural and cultural resources, including nine wilderness areas, the convergence of three of America's deserts and 1,347 recorded archaeological sites. Administered under cooperative agreements with the Bureau of Reclamation, Oct. 13, 1936, and July 18, 1947. Name changed from Boulder Dam Recreation Area Aug. 11, 1947. Established Oct. 8, 1964. Boundary change: Jan. 3, 1975.
Acreage—1,495,805.53 Federal: 1,470,913.26 (of which 4,488.47 are administered by the Bureau of Reclamation) Nonfederal: 24,892.27 Land area: 1,314,516.39 Water area: 186,700.

Tule Springs Fossil Beds
National Monument
601 Nevada Way
Boulder City, NV 89005
702-293-8853
www.nps.gov/tusk

Columbian Mammoths, sloths, American lions, and camels once roamed along wetlands just north of what is now known as Las Vegas, Nevada. The history of the Pleistocene Epoch is preserved at Tule Springs Fossil Beds National Monument and may hold clues about climate change over the past 200,000-plus years. It was listed on the National Register of Historic Places in 1979 for its importance in understanding paleoenvironments and for its association with important advances in archeological methods and analysis, including radiocarbon dating.
Authorized Dec. 19, 2014.
Acreage – 22,650.00, all Federal.

New Hampshire

**Appalachian
National Scenic Trail**
(See Maine)

**Saint-Gaudens
National Historic Site**
139 Saint-Gaudens Road
Cornish, NH 03745-9704
603-675-2175
www.nps.gov/saga

The park includes the home, studios, and gardens of Augustus Saint-Gaudens (1848–1907), America's foremost sculptor of the late 1800s and early 1900s. Six historic buildings are open to the public with over 120 original sculptures on exhibit. Authorized Aug. 31, 1964; established May 30, 1977. Boundary changes: Oct. 31, 1976, Nov. 9, 2000.
Acreage—190.75, all Federal.

New Jersey

**Appalachian
National Scenic Trail**
(See Maine)

**Delaware Water Gap
National Recreation Area**
(See Pennsylvania)

**Gateway
National Recreation Area**
(See New York)

**Great Egg Harbor
Scenic and
Recreational River**
National Park Service Northeast Region
200 Chestnut Street
Philadelphia, PA 19106-2818
215-597-5823
www.nps.gov/greg

For public inquiries:
Great Egg Harbor Watershed Association
P.O. Box 109
Newtonville, NJ 08346-0109
856-697-3479

Running through or along the famous Pinelands National Reserve (Pine Barrens) of southern New Jersey, this river includes many of the Great Egg Harbor River's tributaries. The river's proximity to millions of people, together with it being the largest canoeing river in the Pine Barrens, makes the Great Egg an important recreation destination. The river was designated for outstandingly remarkable wildlife and recreational, historical, hydrological, and traditional cultural use values.
Authorized Oct. 27, 1992. Length: 129 miles.
Acreage—43,311.42, all Nonfederal.

**Middle Delaware
National Scenic River**
(See Pennsylvania)

**Morristown
National Historical Park**
30 Washington Place
Morristown, NJ 07960-4242
973-539-2016
www.nps.gov/morr

Morristown National Historical Park preserves, protects and maintains the landscapes, structures, features, archeological resources and collections of the Continental Army winter encampments of 1777 and 1779-80, the headquarters of General George Washington, and related Revolutionary War sites at Morristown for the benefit and inspiration of the public. The park interprets the history and subsequent commemoration of these encampments and the extraordinary fortitude of the officers and enlisted men under Washington's leadership. The park is comprised of four separate areas – Washington's Headquarters, Fort Nonsense, Jockey Hollow and the New Jersey Brigade/Cross Estate area. The park was established as the nation's first designated National Historical Park.

Authorized March 2, 1933. Boundary changes: June 6, 1953; Sept. 18, 1964; Oct. 26, 1974; Oct. 21, 1976; Oct. 4, 1991; Nov. 6, 1998.
Acreage—1,710.72 Federal: 1,705.69 Nonfederal: 5.03.

**Paterson Great Falls
National Historical Park**
72 McBride Avenue
Paterson, NJ 07501
973-523-0370
www.nps.gov/pagr

Founded by Alexander Hamilton in 1792 as America's first planned industrial city, built around the Great Falls of the Passaic River. The industrial center attracted entrepreneurs, laborers and immigrants with diverse talents. Paterson's mills, powered by a raceway system, produced everything from textiles and Colt firearms to locomotives and aircraft engines.

Authorized March 30, 2009. Established Nov. 7, 2011. Boundary Adjustment: Dec.19, 2014.
Acreage—51.37 Federal: 0.39 Nonfederal: 50.98.

**Statue of Liberty
National Monument**
(See New York)

**Thomas Edison
National Historical Park**
211 Main Street
West Orange, NJ 07052-5515
973-736-0550
www.nps.gov/edis

Thomas Edison's laboratory and his residence were home to the inventor from 1886 until 1931. At his Invention Factory he developed the phonograph and invented the movie camera and nickel-iron-alkaline storage battery. He was awarded 1,093 patents. The site includes his chemistry lab, machine shop, library, the world's first motion picture studio and his 29-room Victorian mansion.

Designated as Edison Home National Historic Site Dec. 6, 1955; Edison Laboratory National Monument proclaimed July 14, 1956; areas combined as Edison National Historic Site Sept. 5, 1962; renamed and redesignated Thomas Edison National Historical Park March 30, 2009.
Boundary changes: Sept. 5, 1962; Oct. 21, 1976.
Acreage—21.25, all Federal.

Paterson Great Falls National Historical Park

New Mexico

Aztec Ruins National Monument
725 Ruins Road
Aztec, NM 87410-9715
505-334-6174
www.nps.gov/azru

Building remains of this large Pueblo Indian community from the 1100s have been partially excavated and stabilized. Proclaimed Aztec Ruin National Monument Jan. 24, 1923; renamed July 2, 1928. Boundary changes: July 2, 1928; Dec. 19, 1930; May 27, 1948; Oct. 28, 1988. Designated a World Heritage Site Dec. 8, 1987.
Acreage—318.40 Federal: 266.78 Nonfederal: 51.62.

Bandelier National Monument
15 Entrance Road
Los Alamos, NM 87544-9701
505-672-3861
www.nps.gov/band

On the mesa tops and canyon walls of the Pajarito Plateau are the remains of Pueblo Indians' cliff houses and villages dating from the 1200s. Proclaimed Feb. 11, 1916; transferred from U.S. Forest Service, Feb. 25, 1932. Boundary changes: Feb. 25, 1932; Jan. 9, 1961; May 27, 1963; Oct. 21, 1976; Feb. 8, 1977; Nov. 18, 1997; Nov. 12, 1998. Wilderness designated Oct. 20, 1976.
Acreage—33,676.67 Federal: 33,654.44 Nonfederal: 22.23. Wilderness area: 23,267.

Capulin Volcano National Monument
PO Box 40
Capulin, NM 88414-0040
505-278-2201
www.nps.gov/cavo

This symmetrical cinder cone is an example of a geologically recent, inactive volcano. Proclaimed Capulin Mountain National Monument Aug. 9, 1916; renamed Dec. 31, 1987. Boundary change: Sept. 3, 1962.
Acreage—792.84, all Federal.

Carlsbad Caverns National Park
3225 National Parks Highway
Carlsbad, NM 88220-5354
505-785-2232
www.nps.gov/cave

Countless formations decorate huge chambers, including the easily accessible Big Room, covering eight acres with a 250-foot-high ceiling. The park contains at least 120 separate caves, including the nation's deepest limestone cave, over 1600 feet, and fourth longest. Proclaimed Carlsbad Cave National Monument Oct. 25, 1923; established as Carlsbad Caverns National Park May 14, 1930. Boundary changes: Feb. 21, 1933; May 4, 1934; Feb. 3, 1939; Dec. 30, 1963. Wilderness designated Nov. 10, 1978. Designated a World Heritage Site Dec. 9, 1995.
Acreage—46,766.45 Federal: 46,427.26 Nonfederal: 339.19. Wilderness area: 33,125.

Chaco Culture
National Historical Park
PO Box 220
Nageezi, NM 87037
505-786-7014
www.nps.gov/chcu

The canyon contains 13 major prehistoric sites and hundreds of smaller ones, built by the Ancestral Puebloan people.
Proclaimed Chaco Canyon National Monument March 11, 1907; renamed and redesignated Dec. 19, 1980. Boundary changes: Jan. 10, 1928; Dec. 19, 1980. Designated a World Heritage Site Dec. 8, 1987.
Acreage—33,960.19 Federal: 32,840.14 Nonfederal: 1,120.05.

El Malpais
National Monument
123 East Roosevelt Avenue
Grants, NM 87020
505-285-4641
www.nps.gov/elma

El Malpais is a spectacular volcanic area, featuring cinder cones, a 17-mile-long lava tube system, and ice caves. The area is rich in ancient Pueblo and Navajo history.
Established Dec. 31, 1987.
Acreage—114,313.87 Federal: 109,946.76 Nonfederal: 4,367.11.

El Morro
National Monument
HC-61, Box 43
Ramah, NM 87321-9603
505-783-4226
www.nps.gov/elmo

Inscription Rock is a 200-foot sandstone monolith on which are carved thousands of inscriptions from early travelers. The monument includes pre-Columbian petroglyphs and the remains of Pueblo Indian dwellings.
Proclaimed Dec. 8, 1906. Boundary changes: June 18, 1917; June 14, 1950.
Acreage—1,278.72 Federal: 1,039.92 Nonfederal: 238.80.

Fort Union
National Monument
PO Box 127
Watrous, NM 87753-0127
505-425-8025
www.nps.gov/foun

Remnants of the Southwest's largest frontier fort, which played a key role in the Indian Wars and the Confederate defeat at Glorieta Pass, are preserved here. A large network of Santa Fe Trail ruts is still visible on the prairie.
Established June 28, 1954.
Acreage—720.60, all Federal.

Gila Cliff Dwellings
National Monument
HC 68, Box 100
Silver City, NM 88061-9352
575-536-9461
www.nps.gov/gicl

These well-preserved cliff dwellings were inhabited from about 1280 to the early 1300s.
Proclaimed Nov. 16, 1907; transferred from U.S. Forest Service, Aug. 10, 1933. Boundary change: April 17, 1962.
Acreage—533.13, all Federal.

Manhattan Project
National Historical Park
(Also in Tennessee and Washington)

This park will be jointly operated with the U.S. Department of Energy and was created "to improve the understanding of the Manhattan Project and the legacy of the Manhattan Project through interpretation of the historic resources." This park, located in Oak Ridge, TN, Hanford, WA, and Los Alamos, NM, is an opportunity for people from around the world to visit these historic sites and gain a deeper understanding of history and world-changing events that happened as part of the Manhattan Project.
Authorized Dec. 19, 2014. Established Nov. 10, 2015.
Boundaries not yet established.

Pecos
National Historical Park
PO Box 418
Pecos, NM 87552-0418
505-757-7200
www.nps.gov/peco

The park preserves 12,000 years of human history, including the remains of the Pecos Pueblo and many other American Indian structures, Spanish colonial missions, homesteads of the Mexican era, a section of the Santa Fe Trail, sites related to the Civil War Battle of Glorieta Pass, and a 1900s ranch.
Authorized as a national monument June 28, 1965; redesignated a national historical park June 27, 1990. Boundary changes: Oct. 21, 1976; June 27, 1990; Nov. 8, 1990.
Acreage—6,694.18 Federal: 6,361.24 Nonfederal: 332.94.

Petroglyph
National Monument
6001 Unser Blvd., NW
Albuquerque, NM 87120-2033
505-899-0205
www.nps.gov/petr

Over 50,000 prehistoric and historic American Indian and Hispanic petroglyphs (images carved into rock) stretch 17 miles along Albuquerque's West Mesa escarpment.
Authorized June 27, 1990. Owned and managed jointly by the National Park Service, the City of Albuquerque, and the State of New Mexico.
Acreage—7,209.30 Federal: 2,936.37 Nonfederal: 4,272.93.

Salinas Pueblo Missions
National Monument
PO Box 517
Mountainair, NM 87036-0496
505-847-2585
www.nps.gov/sapu

This park preserves and interprets the best examples of Spanish Franciscan mission churches and convents of the 1600s remaining in the United States and three large Pueblo Indian villages.
Proclaimed Gran Quivira National Monument Nov. 1, 1909. On Dec. 19, 1980, two state monuments, Quarai and Abo were donated to the National Park Service and joined Gran Quivira in forming Salinas National Monument. Renamed Salinas Pueblo Missions National Monument Oct. 28, 1988. Boundary changes: Nov. 25, 1919; Dec. 19, 1980.
Acreage—1,071.42 Federal: 985.13 Nonfederal: 86.29.

Valles Caldera National
Preserve
39201 New Mexico
Highway 4
Jemez Springs, NM 87025
866-382-5537
www.nps.gov/vall

About 1.25 million years ago, a spectacular volcanic eruption created the 13-mile wide crater-shaped landscape now known as Valles Caldera in the Jemez Mountains of north-central New Mexico. One of only three supervolcanoes in the U.S., the preserve is known for its huge mountain meadows, abundant wildlife, meandering streams, and extensive history of indigenous and Hispanic land use. Hunting and fishing are permitted. LIMITED FEDERAL FACILITIES.
Established July 25, 2000, as a national preserve within the National Forest System managed by the Valles Caldera Trust, a wholly-owned government corporation; transferred from Valles Caldera Trust, U.S. Dept. of Agriculture, Dec. 19, 2014.
Acreage–89,000.00, all Federal.

White Sands
National Monument
PO Box 1086
Holloman AFB, NM 88330-1086
505-679-2599
www.nps.gov/whsa

The park contains a significant portion of the world's largest gypsum dunefield. Glistening white dunes rise 60 feet and cover 275 square miles. Small animals and plants have adapted to this harsh environment.
Proclaimed Jan. 18, 1933. Boundary changes: Nov. 28, 1934; Aug. 29, 1938; June 6, 1942; June 24, 1953; Nov. 10, 1978; Sept. 23, 1996.
Acreage—143,733.25, all Federal.

New York

**African Burial Ground
National Monument**
290 Broadway, First Floor
New York, NY 10007-1823
212-637-2019
www.nps.gov/afbg

From the 1690s until the 1790s, both free and enslaved Africans were buried in 6.6 acres in Lower Manhattan. Lost to history due to landfill and development, the grounds were rediscovered in 1991 because of the planned construction of a federal office building. An outdoor memorial in the form of an Ancestral Libation Chamber provides a place to honor this sacred area.
Proclaimed Feb. 27, 2006.
Acreage—0.35, all Federal.

**Appalachian
National Scenic Trail**
(See Maine)

**Castle Clinton
National Monument**
c/o Federal Hall National
Memorial
26 Wall Street
New York, NY 10005-1907
212-344-7220
www.nps.gov/cacl

Built between 1808–11, this structure served as a defense for New York harbor, an entertainment center, and an immigration depot through which over 8 million people entered the United States from 1855 to 1890. It is located in Battery Park.
Authorized Aug. 12, 1946. Established June 20, 1950.
Acreage—1.00, all Federal.

**Eleanor Roosevelt
National Historic Site**
4097 Albany Post Road
Hyde Park, NY 12538-1997
845-229-9115
www.nps.gov/elro

Eleanor Roosevelt chose Val-Kill for her retreat, her office, her home, and her "laboratory" for social change during the prominent and influential period of her life from 1924 until her death in 1962. Here she formulated and put into practice her social and political beliefs. Val-Kill Cottage is the focal point of the historic site. It was originally built as a factory building for Val-Kill Industries and was converted to a home in 1937.
Authorized May 26, 1977.
Acreage—180.50, all Federal.

**Federal Hall
National Memorial**
26 Wall Street
New York, NY 10005-1907
212-825-6990
www.nps.gov/feha

This building is on the site of the original Federal Hall where the 1735 trial of John Peter Zenger, involving freedom of the press, was held. Here the Stamp Act Congress convened, 1765; Congress under the Articles of Confederation met, 1785–1789; the first U.S. Congress met, 1789; Washington took the oath as first U.S. president and the Bill of Rights was adopted, 1789. Present building was completed in 1842. Designated as Federal Hall Memorial National Historic Site May 26, 1939; redesignated Aug. 11, 1955.
Acreage—0.45, all Federal.

**Fire Island
National Seashore**
120 Laurel Street
Patchogue, NY 11772-3596
516-687-4750
www.nps.gov/fiis

Far from the pressure of nearby big-city life, dynamic barrier island beaches and the estate of William Floyd, signer of the Declaration of Independence, offer an escape. Ocean beaches, dunes, Fire Island Light, and the Floyd estate make this park a blend of recreation, preservation, and conservation.
Authorized Sept. 11, 1964. Boundary changes: Oct. 9, 1965; Nov. 10, 1978. Established Sept. 11, 1984. Wilderness designated Dec. 23, 1980.
Acreage—19,580.42 Federal: 6,241.95 Nonfederal: 13,338.47 Land area: 16,486.43 Wilderness area: 1,363.

Fort Stanwix
National Monument
112 E. Park Street
Rome, NY 13440-5816
315-338-7730
www.nps.gov/fost

The American stand here in August 1777 was a major factor in repulsing the British invasion from Canada. The fort was also the site of the treaties with the Iroquois, Nov. 5, 1768. Known as "the fort that never surrendered," Fort Stanwix, under the command of Col. Peter Gansevoort, successfully repelled a prolonged siege, in August 1777, by British, German, Loyalist, Canadian, and American Indian troops and warriors commanded by British Gen. Barry St. Leger. The failed siege, combined with the battles at Oriskany, Bennington, and Saratoga, thwarted a coordinated effort by the British in 1777, under the leadership of Gen. John Burgoyne, to take the northern colonies, and led to American alliances with France and the Netherlands. The fort was also the site of the 1768 Boundary Line Treaty of Fort Stanwix. The current fort is a reconstruction.
Authorized Aug. 21, 1935; acquisition completed 1973.
Acreage—15.52, all Federal.

Gateway
National Recreation Area
Public Affairs Office
210 New York Avenue
Staten Island, NY 10305
718-354-4606
www.nps.gov/gate
(Also in New Jersey)

A large diverse park spanning two states, Gateway combines recreational activities with natural beauty, wildlife preservation, military history and more. Visitors can hike, picnic, swim, sunbathe, bike, visit the oldest working lighthouse in the nation, visit NYC's first municipal airport, see a historic airplane collection, and camp overnight, all in the New York metropolitan area. With over 26,000 acres of marshes, wildlife sanctuaries, and recreational and athletic facilities; miles of sandy beaches; indoor and outdoor classrooms; picnicking and camping; historic structures, old military installations, airfields, a light- house, and waters around New York Harbor, this park offers urban residents in two states a wide range of recreational opportunities and educational perspectives year-round.
Established Oct. 27, 1972.
Acreage—26,606.63 Federal: 20,444.40 Nonfederal: 6,162.23.

General Grant
National Memorial
122nd Street and
Riverside Drive
New York, NY 10027-3703
212-666-1640
www.nps.gov/gegr

This memorial to Ulysses S. Grant, the Union commander who brought the Civil War to an end, includes the tombs of General and Mrs. Grant. As President of the United States (1869–77), Grant signed the act establishing the first national park, Yellowstone, on March 1, 1872.
Dedicated April 27, 1897. National Park Service administration authorized Aug. 14, 1958. Established May 1, 1959.
Acreage—0.76, all Federal.

Governors Island
National Monument
10 South Street
New York, NY 10004-1900
212-825-3045
www.nps.gov/gois

Governors Island is one-half mile off the southern tip of Manhattan, between the confluence of the Hudson and East rivers. The national monument is within a National Historic Landmark District and includes two early 1800s fortifications—Fort Jay and Castle Williams—that played strategic roles in defending New York City and were key parts of a larger harbor defense system. Open late may through late September.
Proclaimed Jan. 19, 2001; established Feb. 7, 2003.
Acreage—22.91 Federal: 22.41 Nonfederal: 0.50.

**Hamilton Grange
National Memorial**
414 West 141st Street
New York, NY 10031
646-548-2319/2320
www.nps.gov/hagr

The Grange, named after his grandfather's estate in Scotland, was the home of Alexander Hamilton, American statesman and first Secretary of the Treasury.
Authorized April 27, 1962. Established Nov. 19, 1988. Boundary changes: Nov. 9, 2000; moved to St. Nicholas Park June, 7, 2008.
Acreage—1.04, all Federal.

**Home of Franklin D.
Roosevelt
National Historic Site**
4097 Albany Post Road
Hyde Park, NY 12538-1997
845-229-9115
www.nps.gov/hofr

This was the birthplace and life-long home of the 32nd President of the United States. Known as his summer White House, FDR entertained many visiting heads of state here. He helped design and build the first Presidential Library on the property. He and his wife Eleanor are buried in the Rose Garden on the property.
Designated Jan. 15, 1944. Boundary changes: Oct. 23, 1952; Nov. 2, 1964; Jan. 23, 1974; March 3, 1975; May 31, 1984; March 29, 1989; Nov. 10, 1998.
Acreage—849.74, all Federal

**Martin Van Buren
National Historic Site**
1013 Old Post Road
Kinderhook, NY 12106-3605
518-758-9689
www.nps.gov/mava

Lindenwald was the home and farm of eighth president Martin Van Buren from 1841 until his death in 1862. Van Buren was a primary architect of the American political party system. He was a contender for the Democratic nomination in 1844 and the presidential candidate in 1848 for the Free Soil Party, the first mass anti-slavery party in the United States. Lindenwald allows exploration of the nation's turbulent antebellum period. Authorized Oct. 26, 1974.
Acreage—284.93 Federal: 52.17 Nonfederal: 232.76.

Sagamore Hill
National Historic Site
20 Sagamore Hill Road
Oyster Bay, NY 11771-1899
516-922-4788
www.nps.gov/sahi

Sagamore Hill was Theodore Roosevelt's home from 1886 until his death in 1919. As a boy he spent summers in Oyster Bay with his family. The twenty-three room shingle-style, Queen Anne home was built in 1885 from a plan he sketched. Twenty-one rooms are open to the public, and almost all of the furnishings are original. Roosevelt is buried nearby.
Authorized July 25, 1962. Established July 10,1963.
Acreage—83.02, all Federal.

Saint Paul's Church
National Historic Site
897 South Columbus Avenue
Mount Vernon, NY 10550-5018
914-667-4116
www.nps.gov/sapa

This 1763 church is one of New York's oldest parishes (1665-1980). It adjoins the former village green where an election was held that raised issues of Freedom of Religion and the Press. In 1776 the building served as a hospital following the Battle of Pell's Point. The adjoining cemetery contains burials dating from 1665.
Designated July 5, 1943; National Park Service administration authorized Nov. 10, 1978.
Acreage—6.13, all Federal.

Saratoga
National Historical Park
648 Route 32
Stillwater, NY 12170-1604
518-670-2985
www.nps.gov/sara

The American victory here over the British in 1777 was a turning point of the American Revolution and one of the decisive battles in world history. Maj. Gen. Philip Schuyler's country home, and the 154-foot Saratoga monument, and ADA accessible Victory Woods Trail are nearby.
Authorized June 1, 1938. Boundary change: Jan. 12, 1983.
Acreage—3,409.67 Federal: 2,913.17 Nonfederal: 496.50.

Statue of Liberty
National Monument
Liberty Island
New York, NY 10004-1467
212-363-3200
www.nps.gov/stli
www.nps.gov/elis
(Also in New Jersey)

The 152-foot copper statue bearing the torch of freedom was a gift of the French people in 1886 to commemorate the alliance of the two nations in the American Revolution. Designed by Frederic Auguste Bartholdi, the statue has come to symbolize freedom and democracy. Nearby Ellis Island, through which nearly 12 million immigrants passed, was reopened to the public in 1990 as the country's main museum devoted entirely to immigration.
Proclaimed Oct. 15, 1924; transferred from War Dept. Aug. 10, 1933. Boundary change: Sept. 7, 1937. Ellis Island pro- claimed May 11, 1965. Designated a World Heritage Site Oct. 31, 1984.
Acreage—60.86 Federal: 58.38 Nonfederal: 2.48.

Theodore Roosevelt
Birthplace
National Historic Site
28 E. 20th Street
New York, NY 10003-1399
212-260-1616
www.nps.gov/thrb

The 26th president was born in a brownstone house here on Oct. 27, 1858. Demolished in 1916, it was reconstructed and rededicated in 1923 and furnished by the president's widow and sisters.
Authorized July 25, 1962. Established July 11, 1963
Acreage—0.11, all Federal.

Theodore Roosevelt
Inaugural
National Historic Site
641 Delaware Avenue
Buffalo, NY 14202-1079
716-884-0095
www.nps.gov/thri

On September 14, 1901, an unexpected inauguration changed the nation and ushered in the modern presidency. The Theodore Roosevelt Inaugural National Historic Site, Western New York's only National Park Service facility, preserves the home in Buffalo, NY, where Theodore Roosevelt became the 26th President of the United States. Opened to the public on September 14, 1971, and managed by a volunteer board of trustees who comprise the Theodore Roosevelt Inaugural Site Foundation, the Site provides opportunities for the public to understand the historic events surrounding the inauguration and conveys the lasting significance of Theodore Roosevelt's presidency. Theodore Roosevelt took the oath of office as President of the United States on Sept. 14, 1901, in the Ansley Wilcox House after the assassination of President William McKinley.
Authorized Nov. 2, 1966.
Acreage—1.18, all Federal.

Upper Delaware Scenic
and Recreational River
(See Pennsylvania)

Vanderbilt Mansion
National Historic Site
4097 Albany Post Road
Hyde Park, NY 12538-1997
845-229-9115
www.nps.gov/vama

The Vanderbilt name is synonymous with Gilded Age wealth. The mansion, designed by the influential firm McKim, Mead and White, is an important example of Beaux-Arts architecture and design. The surrounding grounds, gardens and Hudson River views constitute a picturesque landscape. This palatial mansion is a fine example of homes built by millionaires in the 1800s. It was constructed by Frederick W. Vanderbilt, a grandson of Cornelius Vanderbilt.
Designated Dec. 18, 1940.
Acreage—211.65, all Federal.

**Women's Rights
National Historical Park**
136 Fall Street
Seneca Falls, NY 13148-1517
315-568-2991
www.nps.gov/wori

Located in Seneca Falls and Waterloo, this park commemorates women's struggle for equal rights and includes the Wesleyan Methodist Chapel, the site of the first Women's Rights Convention in 1848; the Elizabeth Cady Stanton home; the M'Clintock House where the Declaration of Sentiments was written; and other sites related to notable early women's rights activists.
Authorized Dec. 28, 1980. Boundary change: Nov. 12, 1996.
Acreage—7.44 Federal: 7.12 Nonfederal: 0.32.

North Carolina

**Appalachian
National Scenic Trail**
(See Maine)

Blue Ridge Parkway
199 Hemphill Knob Road
Asheville, NC 28803
828-271-4779
www.nps.gov/blri
(Also in Virginia)

Following the crest of the Blue Ridge Mountains, this scenic 470-mile parkway averages 3,000 feet above sea level and embraces large recreational and natural history areas and Appalachian cultural sites.
Initial construction funds allocated under authority of the National Industrial Recovery Act June 16, 1933; National Park Service administration authorized June 30, 1936. Boundary changes: June 30, 1961; Oct. 9, 1968.
Acreage—95,973.71 Federal: 85,339.99 Nonfederal: 10,633.72.

**Cape Hatteras
National Seashore**
1401 National Park Drive
Manteo, NC 27954-2708
252-473-2111
www.nps.gov/caha

Beaches, migratory waterfowl, fishing, surfing, and points of historical interest are features of the nation's first national seashore. Its lands include the 5,915-acre Pea Island National Wildlife Refuge, administered by the U.S. Fish and Wildlife Service.
Authorized Aug. 17, 1937; established Jan. 12, 1953.
Acreage—30,350.65 Federal: 30,350.10 Nonfederal: 0.55. Land area: 26,326.24.

**Cape Lookout
National Seashore**
131 Charles Street
Harkers Island, NC 28531-9702
252-728-2250
www.nps.gov/calo

These undeveloped barrier islands extend 56 miles along the lower Outer Banks embracing beaches, dunes, two historic villages, and Cape Lookout Lighthouse.
Authorized March 10, 1966. Boundary change: Oct. 26, 1974. Designated a Biosphere Reserve 1986.
Acreage—28,243.36 Federal: 25,173.62 Nonfederal: 3,069.74. Land area: 8,741.

**Carl Sandburg Home
National Historic Site**
81 Carl Sandburg Lane
Flat Rock, NC 28731-8635
828-693-4178
www.nps.gov/carl

Connemara was the farm home of the noted poet, Lincoln biographer, and social advocate for the last 22 years of his life.
Authorized Oct. 17, 1968; established Oct. 27, 1972. Boundary change: May 8, 2008.
Acreage—263.65 Federal: 263.52 Nonfederal: 0.13.

Fort Raleigh National Historic Site
c/o Cape Hatteras National Seashore
1401 National Park Drive
Manteo, NC 27954-2708
252-473-5772
www.nps.gov/fora

Roanoke Island history is interpreted here, including the first attempt at English settlement in North America (1584-1587). The fate of Sir Walter Raleigh's Lost Colony remains a mystery.
Designated April 5, 1941. Boundary changes: Aug. 17, 1961; Nov. 16, 1990.
Acreage—512.93 Federal: 355.45 Nonfederal: 157.48.

Great Smoky Mountains National Park
(See Tennessee)

Guilford Courthouse National Military Park
2331 New Garden Road
Greensboro, NC 27410-2355
336-288-1776
www.nps.gov/guco

The battle fought here on March 15, 1781, opened the campaign that led to American victory in the Revolutionary War. The British lost a substantial number of troops at the battle, a factor in their surrender at Yorktown seven months later.
Established March 2, 1917; transferred from War Dept. Aug. 10, 1933.
Acreage—251.49, all Federal.

Moores Creek National Battlefield
40 Patriots Hall Drive
Currie, NC 28435-0069
910-283-5591
www.nps.gov/mocr

The battle on Feb. 27, 1776, between North Carolina Patriots and Loyalists is commemorated here. The patriot victory notably advanced the revolutionary cause in the South.
Established as a national military park June 2, 1926; transferred from War Dept. Aug. 10, 1933; redesignated Sept. 8, 1980. Boundary changes: Sept. 27, 1944; Oct. 26, 1974.
Acreage—87.75, all Federal.

Wright Brothers National Memorial
1401 National Park Drive
Manteo, NC 27954-2708
252-441-7430
www.nps.gov/wrbr

The first sustained flight in a heavier-than-air machine was made here by Wilbur and Orville Wright on Dec. 17, 1903. Authorized as Kill Devil Hill Monument March 2, 1927; transferred from War Dept. Aug. 10, 1933; renamed and redesignated Dec. 4, 1953. Boundary change: June 23, 1959.
Acreage—428.44 Federal: 421.81 Nonfederal: 6.63.

North Dakota

Fort Union Trading Post National Historic Site
15550 Highway 1804
Williston, ND 58801-8680
701-572-9083
www.nps.gov/foun
(Also in Montana)

The principal fur-trading post of the American Fur Company on the Upper Missouri River, Fort Union served the Assiniboine, Crow, Cree, Ojibway, and Blackfeet tribes.
Authorized June 20, 1966. Boundary change: Nov. 10, 1978.
Acreage—440.14 Federal: 436.74 Nonfederal: 3.40.

Knife River Indian Villages National Historic Site
PO Box 9
Stanton, ND 58571-0009
701-745-3300
www.nps.gov/knri

The park contains archeological and historic remnants of the Plains Indian culture and agricultural way of life. The site features the remains of earthlodge villages of the Hidatsa and Mandan.
Authorized Oct. 26, 1974. Boundary change: Oct. 15, 1990.
Acreage—1,748.80 Federal: 1,593.65 Nonfederal: 155.15.

Theodore Roosevelt National Park
PO Box 7
Medora, ND 58645-0007
701-623-4466
www.nps.gov/thro

The park includes scenic badlands along the Little Missouri River and part of Theodore Roosevelt's Elkhorn Ranch. Established as Theodore Roosevelt National Memorial Park April 25, 1947; redesignated Nov. 10, 1978. Boundary changes: June 10, 1948; June 12, 1948; March 24, 1956; Nov. 6, 1963; Nov. 10, 1978. Wilderness designated Nov. 10, 1978. *Acreage—70,446.89 Federal: 69,702.12 Nonfederal: 744.77. Wilderness area: 29,920.*

Ohio

Charles Young Buffalo Soldiers National Monument
1120 US Route 42 East
Wilberforce, OH 45385
937-503-5614
www.nps.gov/chyo

This site features the home of Colonel Charles Young, a soldier, diplomat, and civil rights leader, who overcame stifling inequality to become a leading figure in the years after the Civil War when the United States emerged as a world power. His work ethic, academic leadership, and devotion to duty provided a strong base for his achievements in the face of racism and oppression. His long and distinguished career as a commissioned officer in the United States Army made him a popular figure of this time and a role model for generations of new leaders. NOT OPEN TO THE PUBLIC.
Proclaimed March 25, 2013.
Acreage—59.66, all Federal.

Cuyahoga Valley National Park
15610 Vaughn Road
Brecksville, OH 44141-3018
216-524-1497
www.nps.gov/cuva

This area preserves rural landscapes along the Cuyahoga River between Cleveland and Akron, Ohio. The 20-mile Ohio & Erie Canal Towpath Trail follows the historic route of the canal. Historic structures and natural features can be seen as the trail continues along the Ohio & Erie National Heritage Canalway.
Authorized Dec. 27, 1974; established June 26, 1975; redesignated Oct. 11, 2000. Boundary changes: Oct. 21, 1976; Nov. 10, 1978; Nov. 6, 1986; Jan. 25, 1999.
Acreage—32,571.48 Federal: 20,399.24 Nonfederal: 12,172.24.

Dayton Aviation Heritage National Historical Park
16 S. Williams Street
Wright Brothers Station
Dayton, OH 45402
937-225-7705
www.nps.gov/daav

This park preserves sites associated with Wilbur and Orville Wright and the early development of aviation. It also honors the life and work of African-American poet Paul Laurence Dunbar, classmate and business associate of Orville Wright. The park includes a bicycle and printing shop, the 1905 Wright Flyer III, the flying field where the brothers perfected their airplane, and the Paul Laurence Dunbar House State Memorial.
Authorized Oct. 16, 1992.
Acreage—110.52 Federal: 85.10 Nonfederal: 25.42.

First Ladies National Historic Site
331 S. Market Avenue
Canton, OH 44702
330-452-0876
www.nps.gov/fila

This site, which includes the former home of Ida Saxton McKinley, preserves and interprets the role, impact, and history of First Ladies and other notable women in American history. There is an electronic virtual library and a complete annotated bibliography of First Ladies—from Martha Washington to Michelle Obama—that is updated each year. Costumed docents conduct tours. The National First Ladies' Library and the National Park Service cooperatively manage the site.
Established Oct. 11, 2000.
Acreage—0.46, all Federal.

**Hopewell Culture
National Historical Park**
16062 State Route 104
Chillicothe, OH 45601-8694
740-774-1126
www.nps.gov/hocu

From about 200 BC to AD 500, the Ohio River Valley was a focal point of the prehistoric Hopewell culture. The term Hopewell describes a broad network of beliefs and practices among different Native American groups over a large portion of eastern North America. The culture is characterized by the construction of enclosures made of earthen walls, often built in geometric patterns, and mounds of various shapes. Visible remnants of Hopewell culture are concentrated in the Scioto River valley near present-day Chillicothe, Ohio. The most striking Hopewell sites contain earthworks in the form of squares, circles, and other geometric shapes. Many of these sites were built to a monumental scale, with earthen walls up to 12 feet high, outlining geometric figures more than 1,000 feet across. Conical and loaf-shaped earthen mounds up to 30 feet high are often found in association with the geometric earthworks. The park contains nationally significant archeological resources including large earthwork and mound complexes that provide an insight into the social, ceremonial, political, and economic life of the Hopewell people.
Proclaimed Mound City Group National Monument March 2, 1923; transferred from War Dept. Aug. 10, 1933; renamed and redesignated a national historical park May 27, 1992. Boundary changes: April 3, 1952; Dec. 28, 1980; June 21, 1983; Jan. 8, 1990; Oct. 31, 1990; May 27, 1992, March 30, 2009.
Acreage—1,1766.16 Federal: 1,146.35 Nonfederal: 619.81.

**James A. Garfield
National Historic Site**
8095 Mentor Avenue
Mentor, OH 44060-5753
440-255-8722
www.nps.gov/jaga

This site preserves the family home and artifacts of the 20th president. Exhibits and tours introduce Garfield's humble upbringing and family life. Garfield launched his "Front Porch" campaign after his selection as the 1879 Republican nominee. Authorized Dec. 28, 1980; established July 15, 1996.
Acreage—7.82, all Federal.

**Perry's Victory
and International Peace
Memorial**
PO Box 549
93 Delaware Avenue
Put-in-Bay, OH 43456-0549
419-285-2184
www.nps.gov/pevi

The memorial is a tribute to both a pivotal U.S. naval victory in the War of 1812 and a lasting peace between former enemies. The memorial consists of a 352-foot high column on South Bass Island in Lake Erie surrounded by 25 acres of landscaped grounds. Visible for miles, it stands as a reminder not only of the events of the War of 1812, but also as a symbol of international peace between Great Britain, Canada, and the United States
Established as a national monument June 2, 1936; redesignated a memorial Oct. 26, 1972. Boundary changes: Oct. 26, 1972; Aug. 16, 1978.
Acreage—25.38 Federal: 23.14 Nonfederal: 2.24.

**William Howard Taft
National Historic Site**
2038 Auburn Avenue
Cincinnati, OH 45219-3025
513-684-3262
www.nps.gov/wiho

Taft, the only person to serve as both president (1909–13) and Chief Justice of the United States (1921–30), was born and raised in this home. The Taft education center offers an orientation video and interactive exhibits on the Taft family. Authorized Dec. 2, 1969. Boundary change: Nov. 10, 1978.
Acreage—3.64 Federal: 1.92 Nonfederal: 1.72.

Oklahoma

Chickasaw
National Recreation Area
901 West 1st Street
Sulphur, OK 73086-4822
580-622-7220
www.nps.gov/chic

The park is named to honor the Chickasaw Nation, original occupants of the land. The partially forested hills of south-central Oklahoma and its natural springs, streams, and lakes offer swimming, boating, fishing, camping and hiking.
Authorized as Sulphur Springs Reservation July 1, 1902; renamed and redesignated Platt National Park June 29, 1906; combined with Arbuckle National Recreation Area and additional lands and renamed and redesignated Chickasaw National Recreation Area March 17, 1976. Boundary changes: April 21, 1904; June 18, 1940; March 17, 1976; Dec. 9, 1991; Oct. 30, 2004.
Acreage—9,898.63 Federal: 9,894.13 Nonfederal: 4.50.
Water area: 2,409.

Fort Smith
National Historic Site
(See Arkansas)

Washita Battlefield
National Historic Site
RR1, Box 55A
Cheyenne, OK 73628-9725
580-497-2742
www.nps.gov/waba

The park commemorates the November 27, 1868, attack where the 7th U.S. Cavalry under Lt. Col. George A. Custer destroyed Peace Chief Black Kettle's Cheyenne village. Black Kettle and over 100 Cheyenne were captured or killed. The controversial attack has been described as both a battle and a massacre.
Authorized Nov. 12, 1996.
Acreage—315.20 Federal: 312.20 Nonfederal: 3.00.

Oregon

Crater Lake
National Park
PO Box 7
Crater Lake, OR 97604-0007
541-594-3000
www.nps.gov/crla

Crater Lake lies within the caldera of Mt. Mazama, a volcano of the Cascade Range that erupted about 7,700 years ago. The mountain collapsed, forming a caldera. Its greatest depth of 1,9431,932 feet makes it the deepest lake in the United States. Established May 22, 1902. Boundary changes: June 7, 1924; May 14, 1932; Dec. 19, 1980; Sept. 8, 1982.
Acreage—183,224.05 Federal: 183,223.77 Nonfederal: 0.28.

John Day Fossil Beds
National Monument
32651 Highway 19
Kimberly, OR 97848-9701
541-987-2333
www.nps.gov/joda

Within the scenic John Day River valley is a well-preserved fossil record of plants and animals. This remarkably complete record, spanning over 50 of the 65 million years of the Age of Mammals, is world-renowned.
Authorized Oct. 26, 1974. Boundary change: Nov. 10, 1978.
Acreage—14,062.02 Federal: 13,456.16 Nonfederal: 605.86.

Lewis and Clark
National Historical Park
92343 Fort Clatsop Road
Astoria, OR 97103-9803
503-861-2471
www.nps.gov/lecl
(Also in Washington)

Lewis and Clark National Historical Park preserves, restores, and interprets key historic, cultural, scenic, and natural resources throughout the lower Columbia River area associated with the Lewis and Clark Expedition's arrival at and exploration of the Pacific coast, and commemorates the 1805–1806 winter encampment at Fort Clatsop.
Fort Clatsop National Memorial established May 29, 1958; redesignated a national historical park Oct. 30, 2004. Boundary changes: Nov. 10, 1978; Aug. 21, 2002.
Acreage—3,410.15 Federal: 2,729.32 Nonfederal: 680.83.

Nez Perce
National Historical Park
(See Idaho)

Oregon Caves
National Monument and
Preserve
19000 Caves Highway
Cave Junction, OR
97523-9716
541-592-2100
www.nps.gov/orca

Violent geologic events spanning millions of years and the dissolving action of acidic water created a marble cave nestled within an unusually diverse array of rock types. The area preserves a remnant of old-growth Douglas fir forest and many glacial features. Surrounding the cave entrance is a National Historic District.
Proclaimed July 12, 1909; transferred from U.S. Forest Service, Aug. 10, 1933. Boundary change: Nov. 10, 1978; Dec. 19, 2014.
Acreage—4,554.03, all Federal.

Pennsylvania

Potomac Heritage
National Scenic Trail
(See Maryland)

Allegheny Portage Railroad
National Historic Site
110 Federal Park Road
Gallitzen, PA 16641
814-886-6100
www.nps.gov/alpo

Traces of the first railroad crossing of the Allegheny Mountains can still be seen here. An inclined-plane railroad, built between 1831 and 1834, permitted transportation of passengers and freight over the mountains, providing a critical link between the Pennsylvania Mainline Canal system and the West.
Authorized Aug. 31, 1964. Boundary changes: Nov. 10, 1978; Dec. 19, 2002.
Acreage—1,284.27 Federal: 1,255.02 Nonfederal: 29.25.

Appalachian
National Scenic Trail
(See Maine)

Delaware Water Gap
National Recreation Area
Bushkill, PA 18324-9410
570-588-2451
www.nps.gov/dewa
(Also in New Jersey)

This scenic and historic area preserves relatively unspoiled land on both the New Jersey and Pennsylvania sides of the Middle Delaware River. The river segment flows through the famous gap in the Appalachian Mountains.
Authorized Sept. 1, 1965. Boundary changes: Nov. 10, 1978; April 15, 1981; May 15, 1985; July 16, 1987; July 10, 1991.
Acreage—67,580.61 Federal: 57,203.90 Nonfederal: 10,376.71.

Edgar Allan Poe
National Historic Site
532 North Seventh Street
Philadelphia, PA 19123-3502
215-597-7130
www.nps.gov/edal

The life and work of this gifted American author are portrayed in the three-building complex at North Seventh Street where Poe lived 1843–44.
Authorized Nov. 10, 1978; established Aug. 14, 1980.
Acreage—0.52, all Federal.

Eisenhower
National Historic Site
1195 Baltimore Pike, Suite 100
Gettysburg, PA 17325-7034
717-338-9114
www.nps.gov/eise

This was the only home ever owned by Gen. Dwight D. Eisenhower and his wife, Mamie. It served as a refuge when he was president and as a retirement home after he left office.
Designated Nov. 27, 1967; authorized by act of Congress Dec. 2, 1969. Boundary change: Nov. 10, 1978.
Acreage—690.46, all Federal.

**First State National
Historical Park**
(See Delaware)

**Flight 93
National Memorial**
P.O Box 911
Shanksville, PA 15560
814-893-6322
www.nps.gov/flni

The memorial protects the crash site of Flight 93, which is the final resting place of the passengers and crew. Due to their actions, Flight 93, the fourth plane hijacked as part of the Sept. 11, 2001 attack, did not reach its intended target, thwarting the final part of the terrorists' plan. More than just one feature, the memorial is an entire memorial landscape. Current elements include the Memorial Plaza at the crash site, the Visitor Center, the Learning Center, the Tower of Voice (completion date 2017) and trails.
Authorized Sept. 24, 2002.
Acreage—2,319.96 Federal: 1,642.01 Nonfederal: 677.95.

**Fort Necessity
National Battlefield**
One Washington Parkway
Farmington, PA 15437-9514
724-329-5512
www.nps.gov/fone

Colonial troops commanded by Col. George Washington, then 22 years old, were defeated here in the opening battle of the French and Indian War on July 3, 1754.
Established as a national battlefield site March 4, 1931; transferred from War Dept. Aug. 10, 1933; redesignated Aug. 10, 1961. Boundary change: Oct. 26, 1974.
Acreage—902.80 Federal: 894.47 Nonfederal: 8.33.

**Friendship Hill
National Historic Site**
c/o Fort Necessity
National Battlefield
One Washington Parkway
Farmington, PA 15437-9514
724-329-2501
www.nps.gov/frhi

This home on the Monongahela River near Point Marion, Pa., belonged to Albert Gallatin, Secretary of the Treasury from 1801 to 1813 under Presidents Jefferson and Madison.
Authorized Nov. 10, 1978.
Acreage—674.56 Federal: 661.44 Nonfederal: 13.12.

**Gettysburg
National Military Park**
1195 Baltimore Pike, Suite 100
Gettysburg, PA 17325-7034
717-334-1124
www.nps.gov/gett

The Civil War battle fought here July 1–3, 1863, repulsed the second Confederate invasion of the North. Soldiers' National Cemetery—over 7,000 interments, 1,668 unidentified—adjoins the park. At the dedication of the cemetery, Nov. 19, 1863, President Abraham Lincoln delivered his timeless Gettysburg Address.
Park: Established Feb. 11, 1895; transferred from War Dept. Aug. 10, 1933. Boundary changes: May 12, 1917; Jan. 31, 1948; July 31, 1953; Dec. 2, 1969; Oct. 16, 1987; Aug. 17, 1990; Oct. 10, 2000; Dec. 19, 2014.
Cemetery: Beginning of Civil War interments, Oct. 1863. Placed under War Dept. July 14, 1870. Transferred from War Dept. Aug. 10, 1933.
Park acreage—6,032.54 Federal: 5,032.48 Nonfederal: 1,000.06. Cemetery acreage—20.58, all Federal.

**Hopewell Furnace
National Historic Site**
2 Mark Bird Lane
Elverson, PA 19520-9505
610-582-8773
www.nps.gov/hofu

This is one of the finest examples of a rural American iron plantation of the 1800s. The buildings include a blast furnace, the ironmaster's mansion, and auxiliary structures. Hopewell Furnace was founded in 1771 by Mark Bird, the first ironmaster. The furnace operated until 1883.
Designated Hopewell Village National Historic Site Aug. 3, 1938; renamed Sept. 19, 1985. Boundary changes: June 6, 1942; July 24, 1946.
Acreage—848.06, all Federal.

**Independence
National Historical Park**
143 S. Third Street
Philadelphia, PA 19106-2778
215-597-8787
www.nps.gov/inde

This park is the birthplace of the United States of America; home of the creation of the Declaration of Independence and the U.S. Constitution. The park includes structures, sites, and accredited museum collections in central Philadelphia associated with the American Revolution and the founding and growth of the United States: Independence Hall, Congress Hall, Old City Hall, the Liberty Bell, the First and Second Banks of the United States, Franklin Court, Germantown White House, and others.

Authorized June 28, 1948; established July 4, 1956. On March 16, 1959, incorporated Old Philadelphia Custom House (Second Bank of the United States), which had been designated a national historic site May 26, 1939. Other boundary changes: Aug. 21, 1958; Aug. 27, 1958; March 7, 1959; June 23, 1959; Sept. 14, 1959; Aug. 21, 1964; Oct. 26, 1974; Nov. 12, 1996. Independence Hall designated a World Heritage Site Oct. 24, 1979. Partnership Visitor Center established Dec 7, 1999. National Constitution Center Sept. 16, 1988.
Acreage—44.85 Federal: 33.87 Nonfederal: 10.98.

**Johnstown Flood
National Memorial**
733 Lake Road
South Fork, PA 15956
814-495-4643
www.nps.gov/jofl

The South Fork dam failed on Friday, May 31, 1889, and unleashed 20,000,000 tons of water that devastated Johnstown, Pennsylvania. The flood killed 2,209 people but it brought the nation and the world together to aid the "Johnstown sufferers". Clara Barton successfully led the Red Cross in its first disaster relief effort.

Authorized Aug. 31, 1964. Boundary changes: April 11, 1972; Nov. 10, 1978; Oct. 5, 2004.
Acreage—177.76 Federal: 169.01 Nonfederal: 8.75.

**Middle Delaware
National Scenic River**
c/o Delaware Water Gap
National Recreation Area
Bushkill, PA 18324-9410
570-588-2435
www.nps.gov/dewa
(Also in New Jersey)

This river flows 40 miles through the Delaware Water Gap National Recreation Area. Swimming, boating, and fishing opportunities are available. Here, the river is calm, passing cliffs, fields, and forest with a majority of it designated a National Wild and Scenic River. The river was designated for outstandingly remarkable cultural, recreational, scenic, and ecological values.

Established Nov. 10, 1978. Length: 40 miles.
Acreage—1,973.33, all Nonfederal.

**Potomac Heritage
National Scenic Trail**
(See Maryland)

**Steamtown
National Historic Site**
150 South Washington Avenue
Scranton, PA 18503-2018
570-340-5200
www.nps.gov/stea

The former Delaware, Lackawanna & Western Railroad yard—including remains of the roundhouse, the switchyard, and other buildings, was transformed into an interpretive museum complex. This complex includes a theater showing the park film, locomotive repair/restoration shops, and a collection of steam locomotives and railroad cars that tell the story of steam railroading in America. Park Entrance: Lackawanna Avenue at Cliff Street, Scranton, PA 18503.

Authorized Oct. 30, 1986.
Acreage—62.48 Federal: 51.29 Nonfederal: 11.19.

Thaddeus Kosciuszko National Memorial
c/o Independence National Historical Park
143 S. Third Street
Philadelphia, PA 19106-2818
215-597-7130
www.nps.gov/thko

The life and work of this Polish patriot and hero of the American Revolution are commemorated at 301 Pine Street, Philadelphia.
Established Oct. 21, 1972.
Acreage—0.02, all Federal.

Upper Delaware Scenic and Recreational River
274 River Road
Beach Lake, PA 18405-9737
570-729-7134
www.nps.gov/upde
(Also in New York)

This is a 73.4-mile stretch of river between Hancock and Sparrowbush, N.Y., along the Pennsylvania-New York border. The area includes the Roebling Bridge, believed to be the oldest existing wire-cable suspension bridge, and the Zane Grey home. The river was designated for outstandingly remarkable cultural, recreational, scenic, and ecological values.
Authorized Nov. 10, 1978. Length: 73.4 miles.
Acreage—74,999.56 Federal: 30.75 Nonfederal: 74,968.81.

Valley Forge National Historical Park
1400 N. Outer Line Drive
King of Prussia, PA 19406-1009
610-783-1000
www.nps.gov/vafo

Site of the Continental Army winter encampment, 1777–78. The park preserves historic landscapes, earthworks, archeological sites, historic structures including Washington's Headquarters, and a collection of objects illustrating the life of the continental soldier. The park also protects significant natural resources.
Authorized July 4, 1976. Boundary change: June 28, 1980.
Acreage—3,467.70 Federal: 3,174.86 Nonfederal: 292.84.

Puerto Rico

San Juan National Historic Site
Fort San Cristobal
501 Calle Norzagaray
San Juan, PR 00901
787-729-6777
www.nps.gov/saju

These massive masonry fortifications, oldest in the territorial limits of the United States, were begun by Spaniards in the 1500s to protect a strategic harbor guarding the sea lanes to the Americas.
Designated Feb. 14, 1949. Boundary change: Sept. 29, 1976. Designated a World Heritage Site Dec. 9, 1983.
Acreage—75.13 Federal: 53.20 Nonfederal: 21.93.

Rhode Island

Blackstone River Valley National Historical Park
One Depot Square
Woonsocket, RI 02895
401-762-0250
www.nps.gov/blac

The Blackstone River Valley National Historical Park was established to help preserve, protect, and interpret the nationally significant resources that exemplify the industrial heritage of the Blackstone River Valley. The park also supports the preservation, protection, and interpretation of the urban, rural and agricultural landscape features of the region.
Authorized Dec. 19, 2014.
Acreage—1,489.00, all Nonfederal.

Roger Williams National Memorial
282 North Main Street
Providence, RI 02903-1240
401-521-7266
www.nps.gov/rowi

This memorial commemorates the "outstanding contributions to the development of the principles of freedom in this country." The memorial is a landscaped urban park on the site of the freshwater spring that was the center of the original settlement of Providence, founded by Roger Williams in 1636. Williams fought for the ideal of guaranteed religious freedom to all faiths.
Authorized Oct. 22, 1965.
Acreage—4.56, all Federal.

South Carolina

Charles Pinckney National Historic Site
c/o Fort Sumter
National Monument
1214 Middle Street
Sullivans Island, SC
29482-9748
843-883-3123
www.nps.gov/chpi

Charles Pinckney NHS commemorates Pinckney's contribution as a principal author and signer of the U.S. Constitution. The 28-acre park, a remnant of Pinckney's coastal plantation, is preserved to tell the story of a "forgotten founder," his life of public service, the lives of enslaved African Americans on South Carolina Lowcountry plantations and their influences on Charles Pinckney.
Authorized Sept. 8, 1988.
Acreage—28.45, all Federal.

Congaree National Park
100 National Park Road
Hopkins, SC 29061-9118
803-776-4396
www.nps.gov/cong

This park protects the last significant tract of southern bottomland hardwood forest in the United States. It is home to a rich diversity of plant and animal species associated with an alluvial floodplain. Several national and state record trees are in the park.
Authorized Oct. 18, 1976 as Congaree Swamp National Monument; redesignated Nov. 10, 2003. Boundary changes: Oct. 24, 1988; Nov. 10, 2003. Wilderness designated Oct. 24, 1988. Designated a Biosphere Reserve 1983.
Acreage—26,275.82 Federal: 26,020.66 Nonfederal: 255.16. Wilderness area: 15,000.

Cowpens National Battlefield
338 New Pleasant Road
Gaffney, SC 29341
864-461-2828
www.nps.gov/cowp

Brig. Gen. Daniel Morgan won a decisive Revolutionary War victory here over British Lt. Col. Banastre Tarleton on Jan. 17, 1781.
Established as a national battlefield site March 4, 1929; transferred from War Dept. Aug. 10, 1933; redesignated a national battlefield April 11, 1972. Boundary changes: July 18, 1958; April 11, 1972.
Acreage—841.56 Federal: 790.90 Nonfederal: 50.66.

Fort Sumter National Monument
1214 Middle Street
Sullivans Island, SC
29482-9748
843-883-3123
www.nps.gov/fosu

The first engagement of the Civil War took place here on April 12, 1861. The park includes Fort Moultrie, scene of the patriot victory of June 28, 1776—one of the early defeats of the British in the American Revolution. Together the forts reflect 171 years of seacoast defense.
Authorized April 28, 1948.
Acreage—234.74 Federal: 230.63 Nonfederal: 4.11.

Kings Mountain National Military Park
2625 Park Road
Blacksburg, SC 29702
864-936-7921
www.nps.gov/kimo

American frontiersmen defeated the British here on Oct. 7, 1780, at a critical point during the American Revolution.
Established March 3, 1931; transferred from War Dept. Aug. 10, 1933. Boundary change: June 23, 1959.
Acreage—3,945.29, all Federal.

Ninety Six National Historic Site
1103 Hwy. 248 South
Ninety Six, SC 29666
864-543-4068
www.nps.gov/nisi

This important colonial backcountry trading village was the scene of Nathanael Greene's siege in 1781. The site contains earthwork embankments of a 1781 fortification, remains of two historic villages, a colonial plantation complex, and many prehistoric sites.
Authorized Aug. 19, 1976.
Acreage—1,021.94, all Federal.

South Dakota

Badlands National Park
PO Box 6
Interior, SD 57750-0006
605-433-5361
www.nps.gov/badl

Carved by erosion, this scenic landscape contains animal fossils from 26 to 37 million years ago. Prairie grasslands support bison, bighorn sheep, deer, pronghorn antelope, swift fox, and black-footed ferrets. Approximately half of the park (133,300 acres) is on the Pine Ridge Indian reservation, home of the Oglala Sioux (Lakota) Tribe.
Authorized as a national monument March 4, 1929; established Jan. 24, 1939; redesignated a national park Nov. 10, 1978. Boundary changes: June 26, 1936; May 7, 1952; March 22, 1957; Aug. 8, 1968. Wilderness designated Oct. 20, 1976.
Acreage—242,755.94 Federal: 233,809.13 Nonfederal: 8,946.81.

Jewel Cave
National Monument
R.R. 1, Box 60AA
Custer, SD 57730-9608
605-673-8300
www.nps.gov/jeca

Limestone cave system consisting of a three-dimensional maze of passages, with a layer of calcite spar covering most of the cave surfaces. The cave is the third longest in the world, with over 177 miles of mapped passages (August 2015).
Proclaimed Feb. 7, 1908; transferred from U.S. Forest Service, Aug. 10, 1933. Boundary change: Oct. 9, 1965.
Acreage—1,273.51, all Federal.

Minuteman Missile
National Historic Site
21280 SD Highway 240
Philip, SD 57567
605-433-5552
www.nps.gov/mimi

Preserving elements of the Minuteman II Intercontinental Ballistic Missile System, the park interprets the deterrent value of the land-based portion of America's nuclear defense during the Cold War era and commemorates the people and events associated with this recent period of American history. Resources feature the Delta-09 Launch Facility, where a Minuteman missile is housed in its underground silo, and the Delta-01 Launch Control Facility, where Air Force personnel controlled and maintained ten of the 150 nuclear missiles located in South Dakota.
Authorized Nov. 29, 1999.
Acreage—43.80 Federal: 40.15 Nonfederal: 3.65.

Missouri
National Recreational River
(See Nebraska)

Mount Rushmore
National Memorial
Highway 244
Bldg. 31, Suite 1
Keystone, SD 57751
605-574-2523
www.nps.gov/moru

Colossal heads of Presidents George Washington, Thomas Jefferson, Abraham Lincoln, and Theodore Roosevelt were sculpted by Gutzon Borglum on the face of a granite mountain.
Authorized March 3, 1925; transferred from Mount Rushmore National Memorial Commission July 1, 1939. Boundary changes: May 22, 1940; Oct. 6, 1949.
Acreage—1,278.45 Federal: 1,239.52 Nonfederal: 38.93.

Wind Cave National Park
26611 U.S. Hwy. 385
Hot Springs, SD 57747-9430
605-745-4600
www.nps.gov/wica

This limestone cave in the scenic Black Hills is decorated by beautiful boxwork and calcite crystal formations. The park's mixed grass prairie displays an impressive array of wildlife.
Established Jan. 9, 1903. Boundary changes: March 4, 1931; Aug. 9, 1946; Nov. 10, 1978; Sept. 21, 2005. Wind Cave National Game Preserve, established Aug. 10, 1912, added to park June 15, 1935.
Acreage—33,923.68, all Federal.

Tennessee

**Andrew Johnson
National Historic Site**
12 Monument Avenue
Greeneville, TN 37744-1088
423-639-3711
www.nps.gov/anjo

The site includes two homes, a tailor shop, and the burial place of the 17th president.
Authorized as a national monument Aug. 29, 1935; redesignated Dec. 11, 1963. Boundary change: Dec. 11, 1963.
Acreage—16.68, all federal.

**Appalachian
National Scenic Trail**
(See Maine)

**Big South Fork
National River and
Recreation Area**
4564 Leatherwood Road
Oneida, TN 37841-9544
423-569-9778
www.nps.gov/biso
(Also in Kentucky)

The free-flowing Big South Fork of the Cumberland River is protected here. This was the first park designated as both a national river and a national recreation area, reflecting the decision to preserve the area and offer recreational opportunities. Planning and development by U.S. Army Corps of Engineers authorized May 7, 1974; interim management by National Park Service authorized Oct. 22, 1976; complete transfer of jurisdiction from Secretary of the Army to Secretary of the Interior, including responsibility for completion and planning, acquisition, and development, settled Aug. 25, 1991.
Acreage—123,679.05 Federal: 114,813.02 Nonfederal: 8,866.03.

**Chickamauga and
Chattanooga
National Military Park**
(See Georgia)

**Cumberland Gap
National Historical Park**
(See Kentucky)

**Fort Donelson
National Battlefield**
PO Box 434
Dover, TN 37058-0434
931-232-5706
www.nps.gov/fodo
(Also in Kentucy)

Union General U.S. Grant captured three forts, opened two rivers, and received national recognition for victories here in February 1862.
Park: Established as a national military park March 26, 1928; transferred from War Dept. Aug. 10, 1933. Boundary changes: Sept. 8, 1960; Oct. 25, 2004.
Cemetery: Union dead 670, reinterred in 1867; transferred from War Dept. Aug. 10, 1933.
Park acreage—1,308.91 Federal: 1,243.56 Nonfederal: 65.35. Cemetery acreage—15.34, all federal.

**Great Smoky Mountains
National Park**
107 Park Headquarters Road
Gatlinburg, TN 37738-4102
865-436-1200
www.nps.gov/grsm
(Also in North Carolina)

The Smokies preserve exquisite plants and animals and structures representing southern Appalachian mountain culture.
Authorized May 22, 1926; established for administration and protection only Feb. 6, 1930; established for full development June 15, 1934. Boundary changes: April 19, 1930; July 19, 1932; June 15, 1934; June 11, 1940; Feb. 22, 1944; July 26, 1950; May 16, 1958; Sept. 9, 1963; Aug. 10, 1964; Aug. 9, 1969; Nov. 4, 1969; Nov. 10, 2003; Oct. 18, 2004. Designated a Biosphere Reserve 1976. Designated a World Heritage Site Dec. 6, 1983.
Acreage—522,426.88 Federal: 522,076.73 Nonfederal: 350.15.

X-10 Graphite Reactor, Manhattan Project National Historical Park

Manhattan Project National Historical Park
(Also in New Mexico and Washington)

This park is jointly operated with the U.S. Department of Energy and was created "to improve the understanding of the Manhattan Project and the legacy of the Manhattan Project through interpretation of the historic resources." This park, located in Oak Ridge, TN, Hanford, WA, and Los Alamos, NM, is an opportunity for people from around the world to visit these historic sites and gain a deeper understanding of history and world-changing events that happened as part of the Manhattan Project.
Authorized Dec. 19, 2014. Established Nov. 10, 2015.
Boundaries not yet established.

Natchez Trace National Scenic Trail
(See Mississippi)

Natchez Trace Parkway
(See Mississippi)

Obed Wild and Scenic River
PO Box 429
Wartburg, TN 37887-0429
423-346-6294
www.nps.gov/obed

The park preserves and protects 45 miles of free-flowing streams, the varied wildlife and plant resources, and the rugged character of this area on the Cumberland Plateau. The river was designated for outstandingly remarkable aesthetics, wildlife, fish, and recreational, cultural, ecological, geological, and acquatic values.
Authorized Oct. 12, 1976. Length: 45.3 miles.
Acreage—5,073.35 Federal: 3,713.30 Nonfederal: 1,360.05.

Shiloh National Military Park
1055 Pittsburg Landing Road
Shiloh, TN 38376-9704
731-689-5275
www.nps.gov/shil
(Also in Mississippi)

Shiloh preserves the battlefield where the first major battle in the Western theater of the Civil War occurred. The two-day battle, April 6 and 7, 1862, involved almost 110,000 troops, of which nearly 24,000 were killed, wounded, or missing. The decisive victory enabled Union forces to advance and seize control of the strategic Confederate railway junction at Corinth, Mississippi, on May 30, 1862, then withstand an October Confederate counter-attack
Park: Established Dec. 27, 1894; transferred from War Dept. Aug. 10, 1933. Boundary changes: June 25, 1947; Aug. 22, 1957; May 16, 1958; Dec. 26, 2007.
Cemetery: Union dead reinterred in 1866: 3,584 of whom 2,357 are unknown. Transferred from War Dept. Aug. 10, 1933.
Park acreage—6,720.35 Federal: 4,958.17 Nonfederal: 1,762.18. Cemetery acreage—10.05, all Federal.

Stones River National Battlefield
3501 Old Nashville Highway
Murfreesboro, TN
37129-3094
615-893-9501
www.nps.gov/stri

A fierce midwinter battle took place here, Dec. 31, 1862–Jan. 2, 1863. The Confederates withdrew after the battle and allowed the Union to control middle Tennessee. Stones River National Cemetery—6,850 interments, 2,562 unidentified—is within the park; no grave space available.
Park: Established as a national military park March 3, 1927; transferred from War Dept. Aug. 10, 1933; redesignated April 22, 1960. Boundary changes: April 22, 1960; Dec. 23, 1987; Dec. 11, 1991.
Cemetery: Probable date of Civil War interments, 1865. Transferred from War Dept. Aug. 10, 1933.
Park acreage—709.46 Federal: 649.15 Nonfederal: 60.31. Cemetery acreage—20.09, all Federal.

Texas

Alibates Flint Quarries
National Monument
c/o Lake Meredith
National Recreation Area
PO Box 1460
Fritch, TX 79036-1460
806-857-3151
www.nps.gov/alfl

For thousands of years, people came to the red bluffs above the Canadian River to dig the colorful agatized dolomite from quarries to make projectile points, knives, and other tools.
Authorized as Alibates Flint Quarries and Texas Panhandle Pueblo Culture National Monument Aug. 21, 1965; renamed Nov. 10, 1978. Boundary change: Nov. 10, 1978.
Acreage—1,370.97 Federal: 1,079.23 Nonfederal: 291.74.

Amistad
National Recreation Area
4121 Veterans Blvd.
Del Rio, TX 78840-9350
830-775-7491
www.nps.gov/amis

Boating, watersports, camping, and fishing highlight activities at the Amistad Reservoir on the Rio Grande.
Initially administered under a cooperative agreement with the International Boundary and Water Commission as Amistad Recreation Area, Nov. 11, 1965; authorized as a national recreation area Nov. 28, 1990.
Acreage—58,500.00 Federal: 57,292.44 Nonfederal: 1,207.56.

Big Bend
National Park
PO Box 129
Big Bend National Park, TX
79834-0129
432-477-2251
www.nps.gov/bibe

Mountains contrast with desert within the great bend of the Rio Grande, as the river waters rush through deep-cut canyons and the open desert for 118 miles.
Authorized June 20, 1935; established June 12, 1944. Boundary changes: Aug. 30, 1949; Nov. 5, 1957; May 27, 1989. Designated a Biosphere Reserve 1976.
Acreage—801,163.21 Federal: 775,273.38 Nonfederal: 25,889.83.

Big Thicket
National Preserve
6044 FM 420
Kountze, TX 77625
409-951-6700
www.nps.gov/bith

A great variety of plant and animal species coexist in this biological crossroads of North America.
Authorized Oct. 11, 1974. Designated a Biosphere Reserve 1981. Boundary change: Nov. 12, 1996.
Acreage—109,091.82 Federal: 107,277.14 Nonfederal: 1,814.68.

Chamizal
National Memorial
800 S. San Marcial Street
El Paso, TX 79905-4123
915-532-7273
www.nps.gov/cham

The memorial commemorates the peaceful settlement of a century-old boundary dispute between the United States and Mexico. This commemoration and multi-cultural understanding are enhanced through the arts in the memorial's 500-seat theater, outdoor stage, and three art galleries.
Authorized June 30, 1966; established Feb. 4, 1974.
Acreage—54.90, all Federal.

Fort Davis
National Historic Site
PO Box 1379
101 Lt. Henry Flipper Drive
Fort Davis, TX 79734-1456
432-426-3225
www.nps.gov/foda

Soldiers from Fort Davis, a key West Texas post, helped open the area to settlement and protected travelers along the San Antonio-El Paso Road from 1854 to 1891.
Authorized Sept. 8, 1961; established July 4, 1963. Boundary change: Nov. 6, 1998; March 30, 2009.
Acreage—523.00, all Federal.

Guadalupe Mountains
National Park
400 Pine Canyon Drive
Salt Flat, TX 79847-9400
915-828-3251
www.nps.gov/gumo

Multiple peaks tower above the Texas and New Mexico landscapes. Guadalupe Peak is the highest point in Texas at 8,751 feet, and is capped by the world's most well-preserved Permian period fossil reef. Canyons, sand dunes, and wilderness include Chihuahuan, Rocky Mountain, and Great Plains plants and animals.
Authorized Oct. 15, 1966; established Sept. 30, 1972. Wilderness designated Nov. 10, 1978.
Acreage—86,367.10, all Federal. Wilderness area: 46,850.

Lake Meredith National Recreation Area
PO Box 1460
Fritch, TX 79036-1460
806-857-3151
www.nps.gov/lamr

Lake Meredith, created by Sanford Dam on the Canadian River in the Texas Panhandle, is the setting for boating, fishing, and watersports. The area's canyons, foothills, and meadows provide opportunities for hiking and other activities.
Administered in cooperation with Bureau of Reclamation, March 15, 1965. Name changed from Sanford National Recreation Area to Lake Meredith Recreation Area Oct. 16, 1972; redesignated a national recreation area Nov. 28, 1990.
Acreage—44,977.63, all Federal.

Lyndon B. Johnson National Historical Park
PO Box 329
Johnson City, TX 78636-0329
830-868-7128
www.nps.gov/lyjo

Providing one of most complete pictures of an American president, this park conserves historic properties related to Lyndon Johnson from his birth to death. The Texas White House on the LBJ Ranch is the primary resource. The President and First Lady are buried on the ranch
Authorized as a national historic site Dec. 2, 1969; redesignated a national historical park Dec. 28, 1980.
Acreage—1,570.15 Federal: 674.32 Nonfederal: 895.83.

Padre Island National Seashore
PO Box 181300
Corpus Christi, TX 78480-1300
361-949-8173
www.nps.gov/pais

Noted for its wide sand beaches, excellent fishing, and abundant bird and marine life, the park stretches along the Gulf Coast for 70 miles.
Authorized Sept. 28, 1962; established April 6, 1968.
Acreage—130,434.27 Federal: 130,355.46 Nonfederal: 78.81.

Palo Alto Battlefield National Historical Park
1623 Central Blvd. #213
Brownsville, TX 78520-8326
956-541-2785
www.nps.gov/paal

Preserving the sites of the first two battles of the U.S.-Mexican War (1846-48), the park portrays those battles, the war, the many causes and the lasting consequences from the perspectives of both the U.S. and Mexico.
Authorized Nov. 10, 1978; redesignated a national historical park March 30, 2009. Boundary change: June 23, 1992.
Acreage—3,441.74 Federal: 1,798.93 Nonfederal: 1,642.81.

Rio Grande Wild and Scenic River
c/o Big Bend National Park
PO Box 129
Big Bend National Park, TX 79834-0129
432-477-2251
www.nps.gov/rigr

A 196-mile strip on the American shore of the Rio Grande in the Chihuahuan Desert protects the river. It begins in Big Bend National Park and continues downstream to the Terrell-Val Verde county line. The river was designated for outstandlingly remarkable scenic, geologic, recreational, and cultural values. NO FEDERAL FACILITIES outside Big Bend National Park.
Authorized Nov. 10, 1978. Length: 259.4 miles.
Acreage—9,600.00, all Nonfederal.

San Antonio Missions National Historical Park
2202 Roosevelt Avenue
San Antonio, TX 78210-4919
210-534-8833
www.nps.gov/saan

Four Spanish frontier missions, part of a colonization system that stretched across the Spanish Southwest in the 1600s, 1700s, and 1800s, are preserved here.
Authorized Nov. 10, 1978; established April 1, 1983. designated World Heritage Site, July 5, 2015
Acreage—947.73 Federal: 532.98 Nonfederal: 414.75.

Waco Mammoth National Monument
6220 Steinbeck Bend Dr.
Waco, TX 76708
254-750-7946
www.nps.gov/waco

The paleontological site is home to the only nursery herd of Columbian mammoths known to exist in U.S. To date 23 mammoths, one saber-toothed cat, a camel, and other Ice Age animals have been uncovered. In-situ fossils are displayed inside a climate-controlled Dig Shelter.
Designated July 10, 2015.
Acreage—107.23 Federal: 7.11 Nonfederal: 100.12.

Utah

Arches National Park
PO Box 907
Moab, UT 84532-0907
435-719-2100
www.nps.gov/arch

The park has extraordinary products of erosion in the form of some 2,000 arches, windows, pinnacles, and pedestals. Proclaimed a national monument April 12, 1929; redesignated Nov. 12, 1971. Boundary changes: Nov. 25, 1938; July 22, 1960; Jan. 20, 1969; Oct. 30, 1998.
Acreage—76,678.98 Federal: 76,545.95 Nonfederal: 133.03.

Bryce Canyon National Park
PO Box 170001
Bryce Canyon, UT 84717-0001
435-834-5322
www.nps.gov/brca

Highly colored and picturesque pinnacles, walls, and spires stand in horseshoe-shaped amphitheaters along the edge of the high plateau country in southern Utah. Proclaimed a national monument June 8, 1923; renamed and redesignated Utah National Park June 7, 1924; renamed Bryce Canyon National Park Feb. 25, 1928. Boundary changes: May 12, 1928; June 13, 1930; Jan. 5, 1931; Feb. 17, 1931; May 4, 1931; March 7, 1942.
Acreage—35,835.08 Federal: 35,832.58 Nonfederal: 2.50.

Canyonlands National Park
2282 S. West Resource Blvd.
Moab, UT 84532
435-719-2100
www.nps.gov/cany

In this geological wonderland, rocks, spires, and mesas dominate the heart of the Colorado Plateau, cut by canyons of the Green and Colorado rivers. Prehistoric American Indian rock art and structures dot the redrock landscape. Established Sept. 12, 1964. Boundary change: Nov. 12, 1971. Designated an International Dark Sky Park 2015. *Acreage—337,597.83 Federal: 337,570.43 Nonfederal: 27.40.*

Capitol Reef National Park
HC 70, Box 15
Torrey, UT 84775-9602
435-425-3791
www.nps.gov/care

Capitol Reef preserves over 70 miles of the Waterpocket Fold, a geologic uplift featuring colorful sedimentary layers formed by erosion into a labyrinth of cliffs and canyons. Towering domes of white sandstone account for the name. Archaeological evidence of prehistoric cultures and a historic Mormon pioneer settlement are also preserved. Proclaimed a national monument Aug. 2, 1937; redesignated a national park Dec. 18, 1971. Boundary changes: July 2, 1958; Jan. 20, 1969; Dec. 18, 1971. Designated an International Dark Sky Park 2015.
Acreage—241,904.26 Federal: 241,234.29 Nonfederal: 669.97.

Cedar Breaks National Monument
2390 W. Highway 56 #11
Cedar City, UT 84720-4151
435-586-9451
www.nps.gov/cebr

Multicolored rock formations fill a vast geologic amphitheater, creating a spectacular scenic landscape. Situated at over 10,000 feet elevation, Cedar Breaks offers a variety of year-round recreational opportunities. Summer offers cool high elevation weather with a yearly show of colorful wildflowers, family friendly hiking along scenic rim trails and overlooks, and backcountry hiking navigating red rock slot canyons and waterfalls. Winter activities include snowshoeing, cross country skiing, and snowmobiling. Fall colors paint the landscape with brilliant yellows, oranges, and reds. The park hosts popular night sky "star parties" in summer and winter. Proclaimed Aug. 22, 1933. Boundary changes: March 7, 1942; June 30, 1961.
Acreage—6,154.60, all Federal.

Dinosaur National Monument
(See Colorado)

Glen Canyon
National Recreation Area
PO Box 1507
Page, AZ 86040-1507
928-608-6200
www.nps.gov/glca
(Also in Arizona)

The area encompasses over a million acres of the most rugged canyon country on the Colorado Plateau. Lake Powell stretches 186 miles behind Glen Canyon Dam; its 1,960 miles of shoreline provide water-recreation activities.
Administered by the National Park Service in collaboration with several agencies. Established Oct. 27, 1972. Boundary changes: Jan. 3, 1975; July 1, 2003.
Acreage—1,254,116.62 Federal: 1,239,763.84 Nonfederal: 14,352.78.

Golden Spike
National Historic Site
PO Box 897
Brigham City, UT
84302-0897
435-471-2209
www.nps.gov/gosp

The first transcontinental railroad in the United States was completed here on May 10, 1869, after the Central Pacific and Union Pacific railroads built 1,776 miles of hand-made line.
Designated April 2, 1957; National Park Service administration authorized July 30, 1965. Boundary changes: July 30, 1965; Sept. 8, 1980.
Acreage—2,735.28 Federal: 2,203.20 Nonfederal: 532.08.

Hovenweep
National Monument
McElmo Route
Cortez, CO 81321-8901
970-562-4282
www.nps.gov/hove
(Also in Colorado)

The park protects Ancestral Puebloan towers, pueblos, and cliff dwellings spread over 26 miles on the Utah-Colorado border.
Proclaimed March 2, 1923. Boundary changes: April 26, 1951; Nov. 20, 1952; April 6, 1956. Designated an International Dark Sky Park 2014.
Acreage—784.93, all Federal.

Natural Bridges
National Monument
HC 60, PO Box 1
Lake Powell, UT 84533-0101
435-692-1234
www.nps.gov/nabr

Three natural bridges carved out of sandstone, including the second and third largest in the world, are protected here. Also present are Ancestral Puebloan rock art and remains of ancient structures.
Proclaimed April 16, 1908. Boundary changes: April 16, 1908; Sept. 25, 1909; Feb. 11, 1916; Aug. 14, 1962. Designated an International Dark Sky Park 2007.
Acreage—7,636.49, all Federal.

Rainbow Bridge
National Monument
c/o Glen Canyon
National Recreation Area
PO Box 1507
Page, AZ 86040-1507
928-608-6200
www.nps.gov/rabr

Rainbow Bridge National Monument protects an extraordinary natural bridge which rises 290 feet above the floor of Bridge Canyon, accessible by boat from Lake Powell. Rainbow Bridge is a sacred site for American Indians.
Proclaimed May 30, 1910.
Acreage—160.00, all Federal.

Timpanogos Cave
National Monument
R.R. 3, Box 200
American Fork, UT 84003
801-756-5239
www.nps.gov/tica

Three fault-controlled limestone caves are notable for their diverse and colorful formations, and abundant helictites—water-created formations that grow in all directions and shapes, regardless of gravity.
Proclaimed Oct. 14, 1922; transferred from U.S. Forest Service, Aug. 10, 1933. Authorized joint visitor center with U.S. Forest Service Dec. 6, 2002.
Acreage—250.00, all Federal.

Zion National Park
Springdale, UT 84767-1099
435-772-3256
www.nps.gov/zion

Colorful canyon and mesa scenery includes erosion and rock-fault patterns that create phenomenal shapes and landscapes. The elevation differences at Zion provide habitat for extremely diverse plant communities.

Mukuntuweap National Monument proclaimed July 31, 1909, incorporated in Zion National Monument by proclamation March 18, 1918. Established as a national park Nov. 19, 1919. Separate Zion National Monument proclaimed Jan. 22, 1937, incorporated in park July 11, 1956. Other boundary changes: June 13, 1930; June 3, 1941; Feb. 20, 1960; Oct. 21, 1976; Nov. 12, 1996. Wilderness designated Mar. 30, 2009.
Acreage—147,237.02 Federal: 143,747.65 Nonfederal: 3,489.37.

Vermont

Appalachian
National Scenic Trail
(See Maine)

Marsh-Billings-Rockefeller
National Historical Park
54 Elm Street
Woodstock, VT 05091
802-457-3368
www.nps.gov/mabi

Home to pioneer conservationist George Perkins Marsh, the park includes a model farm and forest developed by Frederick Billings and continued by granddaughter Mary French Rockefeller and her husband, Laurance S. Rockefeller. In partnership with the Billings Farm and Museum, the park focuses on conservation themes and the stewardship of working landscapes and the agricultural countryside. The park is headquarters for the Conservation Study Institute designed to enhance leadership in the field of conservation.

Established as Marsh-Billings National Historical Park Aug. 26, 1992; renamed Oct. 21, 1998.
Acreage—643.07 Federal: 555.07 Nonfederal: 88.00.

Virginia

Appalachian
National Scenic Trail
(See Maine)

Appomattox Court House
National Historical Park
PO Box 218
Appomattox, VA 24522-0218
434-352-8987
www.nps.gov/apco

Here on April 9, 1865, Gen. Robert E. Lee surrendered the Confederacy's Army of Northern Virginia to Lt. Gen. Ulysses S. Grant, leading to the end of the American Civil War.

Authorized as Appomattox Battlefield Site June 18, 1930; transferred from War Dept. Aug. 10, 1933; authorized as a national historical monument Aug. 13, 1935; redesignated April 15, 1954. Boundary changes: Feb. 23, 1939; Oct. 21, 1976; Dec. 3, 1980; Oct. 27, 1992.
Acreage—1,774.12 Federal: 1,694.81 Nonfederal: 79.31.

Arlington House,
The Robert E. Lee
Memorial
c/o George Washington
Memorial Parkway
Turkey Run Park
McLean, VA 22101-0001
703-235-1530
www.nps.gov/arho

This antebellum home of the Custis and Lee families over-looks the Potomac River and Washington, D.C.
Lee Mansion restoration authorized March 4, 1925; transferred from War Dept. Aug. 10, 1933; designated Custis-Lee Mansion by Congress June 29, 1955; renamed June 30, 1972. Boundary change: Nov. 3, 1959.
Acreage—28.08, all Federal.

Assateague Island
National Seashore
(See Maryland)

Blue Ridge Parkway
(See North Carolina)

Booker T. Washington
National Monument
12130 B.T. Washington Hwy.
Hardy, VA 24101-9688
540-721-2094
www.nps.gov/bowa

In April 1856, Booker T. Washington was born into slavery on this 1800s tobacco plantation; at nine, he was later freed. When he returned to visit in 1908, he was an educator, orator, presidential advisor and one of the most influential African Americans of his time. His crowning achievement was to oversee the development of Tuskegee Institute in Alabama as its first principal.
Authorized April 2, 1956. Boundary change: Aug. 21, 2002.
Acreage—239.01, all Federal.

Cedar Creek and
Belle Grove
National Historical Park
7712 Main Street
PO Box 700
Middletown, VA 22645
540-868-9176
www.nps.gov/cebe

Site of the Battle of Cedar Creek, October 19, 1864, this park contains Belle Grove Plantation, one of the few plantations in the Shenandoah Valley and home of an early Shenandoah Valley settler. The Shenandoah Valley is famous for historical landscapes and views of Massanutten Mountain and the Blue Ridge and Allegheny ranges. The park is in development, although many sites are operated by park partners. The park is managed by the National Park Service, in partnership with several nonprofit and municipal entities. The park is within the Shenandoah Valley Battlefields National Historical District. NO FEDERAL FACILITIES.
Authorized Dec. 19, 2002.
Acreage—3,706.20 Federal: 86.38 Nonfederal: 3619.82.

Colonial
National Historical Park
PO Box 210
Yorktown, VA 23690-0210
757-898-3400
www.nps.gov/colo

This park includes Jamestown, site of America's first permanent English settlement; Yorktown, scene of the culminating battle of the American Revolution in 1781; the 23-mile Colonial Parkway; and the Cape Henry Memorial, which marks the approximate site of the first landing of Jamestown's colonists in 1607. Yorktown National Cemetery, containing Civil War gravesites—2,183 interments, 1,434 unidentified—adjoins the park; grave space is not available.
Park: Colonial National Monument authorized July 3, 1930; established Dec. 30, 1930; redesignated June 5, 1936. Boundary changes: Aug. 22, 1933; June 5, 1936; June 15, 1938; Dec. 24, 1942; April 22, 1944; Dec. 23, 1944; May 12, 1948; Sept. 23, 1950; May 13, 1953; March 29, 1956; Aug. 29, 1967; Nov. 12, 1996.
Cemetery: probable date of Civil War interments, 1866. Transferred from War Dept. Aug. 10, 1933.
Park acreage—8,676.91 Federal: 8,605.29 Nonfederal: 71.62. Cemetery acreage—2.91, all Federal.

**Cumberland Gap
National Historical Park**
(See Kentucky)

**Fort Monroe National
Monument**
41 Bernard Road
Fort Monroe, VA 23651
757-722-3678
www.nps.gov/fomr

Fort Monroe National Monument spans the American story through the 21st century, including the American Indian presence, Captain John Smith's journeys, the place where the arc of slavery can be explored, a safe haven for freedom seekers during the Civil War, a bastion of defense for the Chesapeake Bay, and the site that trained leaders of our nation. A public planning process will determine future public services and programming at this new national park with a centuries-old tradition.
Proclaimed Nov. 12, 2011.
Acreage—327.53 Federal: 262.58 Nonfederal: 64.95.

**Fredericksburg
and Spotsylvania County
Battlefields Memorial
National Military Park**
120 Chatham Lane
Fredericksburg, VA
22405-2508
540-693-3200
www.nps.gov/frsp

This park encompasses four major Civil War battlefields—Fredericksburg, Chancellorsville, Wilderness, and Spotsylvania Court House—and four historic buildings associated with them—Chatham, Salem Church, Ellwood, and the house where Stonewall Jackson died.
Park: Established Feb. 14, 1927; transferred from War Dept. Aug. 10, 1933. Boundary changes: Dec. 11, 1989; Oct. 27, 1992; Dec. 9, 1999.
Cemetery: Probable date of unidentified Civil War interments, 1867. Transferred from War Dept. Aug. 10, 1933.
Park acreage—8,379.63 Federal: 7,544.53 Nonfederal: 835.10. Cemetery acreage—12.00, all Federal.

**George Washington
Birthplace
National Monument**
1732 Popes Creek Road
Colonial Beach, VA
22443-9688
804-224-1732
www.nps.gov/gewa

The birthplace of the preeminent leader of the American Revolutionary War era and the first U.S. president. The park includes the foundation of the house where Washington was born, the archeological remains of outbuildings, a commemorative colonial revival plantation, and the family burial ground.
Established Jan. 23, 1930. Boundary changes: March 30, 1931; April 11, 1972; Nov. 10, 1978; May 3, 1993; Dec. 17, 2002.
Acreage—661.73 Federal: 550.23 Nonfederal: 111.50.

**George Washington
Memorial Parkway**
Turkey Run Park
McLean, VA 22101-0001
703-289-2500
www.nps.gov/gwmp
(Also in the District of
Columbia and Maryland)

The parkway, developed as a memorial to the first U.S. president, preserves the natural scenery along the Potomac River. It connects historic sites from Mount Vernon, where George Washington lived, past the Nation's Capital, which he founded, to the Great Falls of the Potomac, where he demonstrated his skill as an engineer.
Authorized May 29, 1930; transferred from Office of Public Buildings and Public Parks of the National Capital Aug. 10, 1933. On Nov. 28, 1989, the road in Maryland was renamed the Clara Barton Parkway. Boundary changes: May 13, 1947; Oct. 10, 1965; Oct. 21, 1976.
Acreage—7,035.22 Federal: 6,803.99 Nonfederal: 231.23.

**Harpers Ferry
National Historical Park**
(See West Virginia)

**Maggie L. Walker
National Historic Site**
c/o Richmond National
Battlefield Park
3215 East Broad Street
Richmond, VA 23223-7517
804-771-2017
www.nps.gov/mawa

This house at 110½ E. Leigh Street, Richmond, VA, was the home of Maggie L. Walker, a leader in the national African American community in the early 1900s. She was the first African American woman to charter and be president of a bank in the United States.
Authorized Nov. 10, 1978.
Acreage—1.29 Federal: 0.36 Nonfederal: 0.93.

**Manassas
National Battlefield Park**
12521 Lee Highway
Manassas, VA 20109-2005
703-754-1861
www.nps.gov/mana

The First and Second Battles of Manassas were fought here July 21, 1861, and Aug. 28–30, 1862. Here Confederate Brig. Gen. Thomas J. Jackson acquired his nickname "Stonewall." Designated May 10, 1940. Boundary changes: April 17, 1954; Oct. 30, 1980; Nov. 10, 1988.
Acreage—5,072.74 Federal: 4,422.25 Nonfederal: 650.49.

**Petersburg
National Battlefield**
1539 Hickory Hill Road
Petersburg, VA 23803-4721
804-732-3531
www.nps.gov/pete

The Union Army waged a 10-month campaign here from 1864–65 to seize Petersburg. The park includes Grant's Headquarters at City Point in Hopewell, Va. The Five Forks Battlefield, in Dinwiddie County, is where the Confederate collapse led to the fall of the city and ultimately of Richmond. Poplar Grove (Petersburg) National Cemetery—6,315 interments, 4,110 unidentified—is near the park; grave space is not available.
Park: Established as a national military park July 3, 1926; transferred from War Dept. Aug. 10, 1933; redesignated a national battlefield Aug. 24, 1962. Boundary changes: June 5, 1942; Sept. 7, 1949; Aug. 24, 1962; April 11, 1972; Nov. 10, 1978; December 26, 1990.
Cemetery: Probable date of Civil War interments 1866. Transferred from War Dept. Aug. 10, 1933.
Park acreage—2,739.72 Federal: 2,657.43 Nonfederal: 82.29. Cemetery acreage—8.72, all Federal.

**Potomac Heritage
National Scenic Trail**
(See Maryland)

**Prince William Forest
Park**
18100 Park Headquarters
Road.
Triangle, VA 22172-1644
703-221-7181
www.nps.gov/prwi

The Piedmont forests of the Quantico Creek watershed shelter hiking trails and five camps built by the Civilian Conservation Corps (CCC) for group and family camping. The camps were built primarily during the 1930s.
Chopawamsic Recreation Demonstration Area transferred from Resettlement Administration Nov. 14, 1936; renamed June 22, 1948.
Acreage—16,080.82 Federal: 14,589.10 Nonfederal: 1,491.72.

**Richmond
National Battlefield Park**
3215 East Broad Street
Richmond, VA 23223-7517
804-226-1981
www.nps.gov/rich

The park commemorates major Civil War battles around Richmond, including Cold Harbor, Beaver Dam Creek, Totopotomoy Creek, Glendale, Fort Harrison, Drewry's Bluff, Malvern Hill, and Gaines' Mill. The park also includes the site of the Chimborazo Confederate Hospital and part of the Tredegar Iron Works, where the main visitor center is located.
Authorized March 2, 1936. Boundary changes: March 3, 1956; Nov. 13, 2000.
Acreage—8,003.51 Federal: 2,862.16 Nonfederal: 5,141.35.

**Shenandoah
National Park**
3655 US Highway 211 East
Luray, VA 22835-9051
540-999-3500
www.nps.gov/shen

Shenandoah National Park lies along the crest of the Blue Ridge Mountains in north central Virginia. The park consists of more than 197,000 acres of mountains, forests, meadows, and culturally and historically significant areas. Perhaps its most well-known feature is the Skyline Drive, a 105-mile scenic roadway planned and designed in the 1930's to meet the recreational needs of a burgeoning middle class and the political needs of the fledgling National Park Service. Forty percent of the park is designated wilderness. The Park boasts abundant wildlife and diverse plant life, 500 miles of hiking trails, including 101 miles of the famous Appalachian Trail, as well as several historically significant landmarks including Skyland, Rapidan Camp, and structures built by the Civilian Conservation Corps.
Authorized May 22, 1926; fully established Dec. 26, 1935; dedicated July 3, 1936. Boundary changes: Feb. 16, 1928; Feb. 4, 1932; June 13, 1939; June 6, 1942; Sept. 13, 1960; June 30, 1961. Wilderness designated Oct. 20, 1976, and Sept. 1, 1978.
Acreage—199,116.92 Federal: 198,259.24 Nonfederal: 857.68. Wilderness area: 79,579.

**Wolf Trap National Park
for the Performing Arts**
1551 Trap Road
Vienna, VA 22182-1643
703-255-1800
www.nps.gov/wotr

The Filene Center, an open-air performing arts pavilion, can accommodate an audience of 7,000, including 3,000 on the sloping lawn in a setting of rolling hills and woods.
Authorized Oct. 15, 1966; redesignated Aug. 21, 2002.
Acreage—130.28, all Federal.

Virgin Islands

**Buck Island Reef
National Monument**
Danish Customs House
Kings Wharf
2100 Church Street, #100
Christiansted, VI 00820-4611
340-773-1460
www.nps.gov/buis

The park, featuring the finest coral reef gardens in the Caribbean, includes coral grottoes, sea fans, and tropical fish. Its interpretive snorkel trail provides a wonderful opportunity to discover the underwater world. The island's beaches and tropical forests are nesting areas for brown pelicans and endangered sea turtles.
Proclaimed Dec. 28, 1961. Boundary change: Feb. 1, 1975.
Acreage—19,015.47, all Federal. Land area: 143.

**Christiansted
National Historic Site**
Danish Customs House
Kings Wharf
2100 Church Street, #100
Christiansted, VI 00820-4611
340-773-1460
www.nps.gov/chri

Urban colonial development of the Virgin Islands is commemorated by structures from the 1700s and 1800s in the heart of the capital of the former Danish West Indies on St. Croix Island.
Designated Virgin Islands National Historic Site March 4, 1952; renamed Jan. 16, 1961. Boundary change: June 27, 1962.
Acreage—27.15 Federal: 26.24 Nonfederal: 0.91.

Salt River Bay
National Historical Park
and Ecological Preserve
Danish Customs House
Kings Wharf
2100 Church Street, #100
Christiansted, VI 00820-4611
340-773-1460
www.nps.gov/sari

The park contains the only known site where members of the Columbus expedition set foot on what is now U.S. territory. It preserves upland watersheds, mangrove forests, and estuarine and marine environments. The site is marked by Fort Sale, a remaining earthworks fortification from the period of Dutch occupation.
Authorized Feb. 24, 1992.
Acreage—989.42 Federal: 224.67 Nonfederal: 764.75.

Virgin Islands Coral Reef
National Monument
1300 Cruz Bay Creek
St. John, VI 00830
340-776-6201
www.nps.gov/vicr

The monument is next to submerged lands that are part of Virgin Islands National Park. This tropical marine ecosystem includes mangroves, sea grass beds, coral reefs, octocoral hardbottom, sand communities, and algal plains. These extraordinary blue-green waters and submerged lands are habitat for threatened and endangered species like humpback whales, pilot whales, dolphins, green and leatherback sea turtles, reef fish, and 25 species of sea birds.
Authorized Jan. 17, 2001.
Acreage—12,708.07 Federal: 11,608.48 Nonfederal: 1,099.59.

Virgin Islands
National Park
PO Box 710
Cruz Bay, St. John, VI 00831
340-776-6201
www.nps.gov/viis

The park covers 2/3rd's of the island of St. John. Features include coral reefs, quiet coves, blue-green waters, and white sandy beaches fringed by green hills. There are also early Indian sites and the remains of Danish colonial sugar plantations.
Authorized Aug. 2, 1956. Boundary changes: June 29, 1960; Oct. 5, 1962; Aug. 18, 1978. Designated a Biosphere Reserve 1976.
Acreage—14,948.46 Federal: 13,104.98 Nonfederal: 1,843.48.   Water area: 5,650.

Washington

Ebey's Landing
National Historical Reserve
PO Box 774
Coupeville, WA 98239-0774
360-678-6084
www.nps.gov/ebla

This rural historic district preserves and protects an unbroken historical record of Puget Sound exploration and settlement from the 1800s to the present. Historic farms, still under cultivation on the prairies of Whidbey Island, reveal land-use patterns unchanged since settlers claimed the land in the 1850's under the Donation Land Claim Act. The Victorian seaport community of Coupeville is also in the Reserve. A Trust Board representing the Town of Coupeville, Island County, Washington State Parks and the National Park Service manages the Reserve through creative conservation and planned development. LIMITED FEDERAL FACILITIES.
Authorized Nov. 10, 1978.
Acreage—19,333.01 Federal: 2,752.67 Nonfederal: 16,580.34.

Fort Vancouver
National Historic Site
612 E. Reserve Street
Vancouver, WA 98661-3811
360-816-6230
www.nps.gov/fova

Established on the north bank of the Columbia River in 1825, Fort Vancouver served as the headquarters for the Hudson's Bay Company's vast fur trading empire in the Pacific Northwest. The site also preserves and interprets a rich legacy of American history – including emigration over the Oregon Trail, military history at Vancouver Barracks, and aviation history at Pearson Air Museum. The McLoughlin House in Oregon City, OR, is also part of this vibrant and diverse park. Authorized as a national monument June 19, 1948; redesignated a national historic site June 30, 1961. Boundary changes: Jan. 15, 1958; June 30, 1961; April 4, 1972; July 29, 2003. *Acreage—206.72 Federal: 197.41 Nonfederal: 9.31.*

Klondike Gold Rush
National Historical Park
319 Second Avenue S.
Seattle, WA 98104
206-553-7220
www.nps.gov/klgo
(See also Alaska)

News of the gold strike in Canada's Yukon Territory spread from Seattle across the country; from here most prospectors left for the gold fields. The park's visitor center is in the Pioneer Square Historic District, the center of Gold Rush activity. Authorized June 30, 1976.
Acreage—12,996.49 Federal: 3,420.00 Nonfederal: 9,576.49.

Lake Chelan
National Recreation Area
810 State Route 20
Sedro-Woolley, WA 98284
360-856-5700
www.nps.gov/noca

Here the beautiful Stehekin Valley, with a portion of fjordlike Lake Chelan, adjoins North Cascades National Park. Established Oct. 2, 1968.
Acreage—61,949.48 Federal: 59,351.42 Nonfederal: 2,598.06.

Lake Roosevelt
National Recreation Area
1008 Crest Drive
Coulee Dam, WA
99116-0037
509-754-7800
www.nps.gov/laro

Formed by Grand Coulee Dam (part of the Columbia River Basin project), the more than 150-mile-long Franklin D. Roosevelt Lake and historic sites are the principal features. Established as Coulee Dam Recreational Area administered under cooperative agreement among the Bureau of Reclamation, the Bureau of Indian Affairs, and the National Park Service, Dec. 18, 1946; agreement renegotiated among the Bureau of Reclamation, the Bureau of Indian Affairs, the National Park Service, the Confederated Tribes of the Colville Reservation, and the Spokane Tribe of Indians April 20, 1990; area renamed Jan. 1, 1997.
Acreage—100,390.31, all Federal.

Lewis and Clark
National Historical Park
(See Oregon)

Manhattan Project
National Historical Park
www.nps.gov/mapr
(Also in New Mexico and Washington)

This park is jointly operated with the U.S. Department of Energy and was created "to improve the understanding of the Manhattan Project and the legacy of the Manhattan Project through interpretation of the historic resources." This park, located in Oak Ridge, TN, Hanford, WA, and Los Alamos, NM, is an opportunity for people from around the world to visit these historic sites and gain a deeper understanding of history and world-changing events that happened as part of the Manhattan Project.
Authorized Dec. 19, 2014. Established Nov. 10, 2015.
Boundaries not yet established.

Minidoka
National Historic Site
Pritchard Park
4192 Eagle Harbor Drive
Bainbridge Island, WA 98110
www.nps.gov/miin
(Also in Idaho)

The Washington unit is comprised of the Bainbridge Island Japanese American Exclusion Memorial. The history and cultural resources associated with the relocation and internment of Japanese Americans during World War II are interpreted here.
Proclaimed Jan. 17, 2001; redesignated a national historic site May 8, 2008.
Acreage—396.30 Federal: 388.30 Nonfederal: 8.00.

Mount Rainier
National Park
55210 238th Avenue East
Ashford, WA 98304-9751
360-569-2211
www.nps.gov/mora

This greatest single-peak glacial system in the United States radiates from the summit and slopes of an ancient volcano, with subalpine flowered meadows and dense forests below.
Established March 2, 1899. Boundary changes: May 28, 1926; Jan. 31, 1931; June 27, 1960; Nov. 16, 1988; Oct. 5, 2004. Wilderness designated Nov. 16, 1988.
Acreage—236,381.49 Federal: 236,316.12 Nonfederal: 65.37. Wilderness area: 228,480.

Nez Perce
National Historical Park
(See Idaho)

North Cascades
National Park
810 State Route 20
Sedro-Woolley, WA 98284
360-856-5700
www.nps.gov/noca

In this wilderness park, high jagged peaks intercept moisture-laden winds, producing glaciers, waterfalls, rivers, lakes, lush forests, and a great diversity of plants and animals.
Established Oct. 2, 1968. Wilderness designated Nov. 16, 1988. The Stephen Mather Wilderness Area extends into Lake Chelan National Recreation Area and Ross Lake National Recreation Area.
Acreage—504,780.94 Federal: 504,654.18 Nonfederal: 126.76. Wilderness area: 634,614.

Olympic National Park
600 East Park Avenue
Port Angeles, WA
98362-6757
360-565-3000
www.nps.gov/olym

This park is a large wilderness area featuring glacier-capped mountains, deep valleys, meadows, lakes, giant trees, more than 70 miles of unspoiled beaches, wildlife like Roosevelt elk and Olympic marmot, and a spectacular temperate rain forest. Proclaimed Mount Olympus National Monument March 2, 1909; transferred from U.S. Forest Service Aug. 10, 1933; renamed and redesignated national park June 29, 1938. Boundary changes: Jan. 2, 1940; May 29, 1943; Jan. 6, 1953; Oct. 21, 1976; Oct. 10, 1986; Nov. 16, 1988; Sept. 30, 1992; Dec. 22, 2010; Feb. 27, 2012. Wilderness designated Nov. 16, 1988. Designated a Biosphere Reserve 1976. Designated a World Heritage Site Oct. 27, 1981.
Acreage—922,650.10 Federal: 913,547.84 Nonfederal: 9,102.26. Wilderness area: 876,669.

Ross Lake
National Recreation Area
810 State Route 20
Sedro-Woolley, WA 98284
360-856-5700
www.nps.gov/noca

Ringed by mountains, this national recreation area offers outdoor activities along the upper Skagit River, between the north and south units of North Cascades National Park.
Established Oct. 2, 1968.
Acreage—117,574.59 Federal: 115,959.59 Nonfederal: 1,615.00.

San Juan Island
National Historical Park
PO Box 429
Friday Harbor, WA
98250-0429
360-378-2240
www.nps.gov/sajh

With over six miles of shoreline, trails, prairies, and military camps, this park commemorates the peaceful settlement of the San Juan Boundary Dispute between Great Britain and the United States from 1853 to 1872, including the Pig War crisis of 1854.
Authorized Sept. 9, 1966.
Acreage—2,145.56 Federal: 2,119.02 Nonfederal: 26.54.

**Whitman Mission
National Historic Site**
328 Whitman Mission Road
Walla Walla, WA 99362
509-522-6360
www.nps.gov/whmi

Ignorance, racism, and ethnocentrism associated with the American Board of Commissioners for Foreign Missions mission to the Weyí·letpu· resulted in many deaths and the continuing vilification of the Cayuse people. Whitman Mission National Historic Site preserves and explores this history and its continuing impact these losses have on the nation.
Authorized as Whitman National Monument June 29, 1936; renamed and redesignated a national historic site Jan. 1, 1963. Boundary changes: Feb. 7, 1961; Feb. 8, 1963.
Acreage—138.53, all Federal.

West Virginia

**Appalachian
National Scenic Trail**
(See Maine)

**Bluestone
National Scenic River**
c/o New River Gorge
National River
PO Box 246
Glen Jean, WV 25846-0246
304-465-0508
www.nps.gov/blue

This river in southwest West Virginia contains natural and historic features of the Appalachian plateau. In its 10 miles ,the lower Bluestone River offers fishing, hiking, boating, and scenery. Pipestem and Bluestone state parks and Bluestone Wildlife Management Area are located along this segment of the river. The river was designated for remarkable scenery, recreation, fish, and wildlife values. NO FEDERAL FACILITIES.
Authorized Oct. 26, 1988. Boundary change: Nov. 12, 1996.
Acreage—4,309.51 Federal: 3,032.00 Nonfederal: 1,277.51.

**Chesapeake and Ohio
Canal
National Historical Park**
(See Maryland)

**Gauley River
National Recreation Area**
c/o New River Gorge
National River
PO Box 246
Glen Jean, WV 25846-0246
304-465-0508
www.nps.gov/gari

The 25.5 miles of the Gauley River and the 5.5 miles of the Meadow River pass through scenic gorges and valleys containing a wide variety of natural and cultural features. The Gauley River contains several Class V+ rapids, making it one of the most adventurous whitewater boating rivers in the East. Both rivers also provide excellent fishing opportunities. LIMITED FEDERAL FACILITIES.
Authorized Oct. 26, 1988.
Acreage—11,605.53 Federal: 4,578.23 Nonfederal: 7,027.30.

**Harpers Ferry
National Historical Park**
PO Box 65
Harpers Ferry, WV 25425-0065
304-535-6029
www.nps.gov/hafe
(Also in Maryland and Virginia)

The town witnessed the arrival of the first successful American railroad, the first successful application of interchangeable parts, John Brown's attack on slavery, the largest surrender of federal troops during the Civil War, education of former slaves, and the beginning of the modern civil rights movement.
Authorized as a national monument June 30, 1944; redesignated May 29, 1963. Boundary changes: July 14, 1960; Oct. 24, 1974; March 5, 1980; Oct. 6, 1989; Sept. 24, 2004.
Acreage—3,669.19 Federal: 3,547.41 Nonfederal: 121.78.

New River Gorge National River
PO Box 246
Glen Jean, WV 25846-0246
304-465-0508
www.nps.gov/neri

A rugged, whitewater river flowing northward through deep canyons, the New is among the oldest rivers on the continent. The free-flowing, 53-mile section from Hinton to Hawks Nest State Park is abundant in natural, scenic, historic, and recreational features.
Authorized Nov. 10, 1978. Boundary changes: Oct. 26, 1988; Nov. 12, 1996; Dec. 17, 2002.
Acreage—72,185.76 Federal: 53,837.65 Nonfederal: 18,348.11.

Wisconsin

Apostle Islands National Lakeshore
415 Washington Avenue
Bayfield, WI 54814-4809
715-779-3397
www.nps.gov/apis

This wild archipelago park consists of 21 islands, 12 miles of mainland shore, a detached lighthouse, and the beautiful but challenging Lake Superior waters. Its picturesque sea caves, pristine beaches, and remote campsites and docks make it a haven for sailors, boaters, and sea kayakers. The park's rich matrix of human stories includes the homeland of the Ojibwe people and the largest number of historic light stations (7) in the NPS. Old growth forests, black bears, timber wolves, and endangered piping plovers also thrive here.
Established Sept. 26, 1970. Boundary change: Oct. 17, 1986; Dec. 19, 2014. Wilderness designated Dec. 8, 2004.
Acreage—69,377.43 Federal: 42,160.70 Nonfederal: 27,216.73. Land area: 42,265.13. Wilderness area: 33,500.

Saint Croix National Scenic Riverway
401 N. Hamilton Street
St. Croix Falls, WI
54024-0708
715-483-2274
www.nps.gov/sacn
(Also in Minnesota)

For 252 miles, the St. Croix and Namekagon rivers flow through some of the most undeveloped country in the upper midwest. Visitors canoe, boat, camp, fish, hike, and view wildlife in the area, renowned for spectacular scenery. The states of Minnesota and Wisconsin manage the lower 25 miles of the St. Croix River to its confluence with the Mississippi River. The river was designated for outstandingly remarkable aquatic resources and scenic, geologic, recreational, cultural, ecological, and riparian vlaues.
Authorized Oct. 2, 1968. Boundary changes: Oct. 25, 1972; Dec. 23, 1980. Length: 252 miles.
Acreage—67,469.74 Federal: 32,256.82 Nonfederal: 35,212.92.

Wyoming

Bighorn Canyon National Recreation Area
(See Montana)

Devils Tower National Monument
PO Box 10
Devils Tower, WY 82714
307-467-5283
www.nps.gov/deto

Devils Tower, the nation's first national monument, is a high, isolated monolith of igneous rock, set upon a pine-clad pedestal within a bend of the Belle Fourche River.
Proclaimed Sept. 24, 1906. Boundary change: Aug. 9, 1955.
Acreage—1,347.21 Federal: 1,346.91 Nonfederal: 0.30.

Fort Laramie
National Historic Site
965 Gray Rocks Road
Fort Laramie, WY
82212-0086
307-837-2221
www.nps.gov/fola

Fort Laramie NHS, in the high plains prairie of SE Wyoming, was an important fur trading post (1834-1849), then a major U.S. military post until 1890. It was the crossroads of the westward expansion emigration routes, and the site of the Treaty of 1868.
Proclaimed a national monument July 16, 1938; redesignated a national historic site April 29, 1960. Boundary changes: April 29, 1960; Nov. 10, 1978.
Acreage—866.60 Federal: 865.27 Nonfederal: 1.33.

Fossil Butte
National Monument
PO Box 592
Kemmerer, WY 83101-0592
307-877-4455
www.nps.gov/fobu

The monument is noted for its well-preserved Eocene fish. Fossil insects, snails, turtles, birds, bats, and plant remains are also found in the 50-million-year-old rock layers.
Established Oct. 23, 1972.
Acreage—8,198, all Federal.

Grand Teton
National Park
P.O. Drawer 170
Moose, WY 83012-0170
307-739-3300
www.nps.gov/grte

Grand Teton features the rugged, awe-inspiring Teton mountain range; pristine glacial lakes nestled along its flanks; the expansive sage-covered valley of Jackson Hole; and the wild and scenic Snake River. Located in northwestern Wyoming, the park lies within the world's largest intact temperate ecosystem. The Teton landscape is home to diverse wildlife, including grizzly bears, wolves, bison, moose and elk.
Established Feb. 26, 1929. Enlarged by Congress Sept. 14, 1950, through a boundary change that incorporated much of the Jackson Hole National Monument, proclaimed March 15, 1943. Bordered by the National Elk Refuge, managed by the U.S. Fish and Wildlife Service, the Bridger-Teton National Forest and Caribou-Targhee National Forest managed by the U.S. Forest Service, the John D. Rockefeller, Jr. Memorial Parkway and Yellowstone National Park.
Acreage—310,043.96 Federal: 307,830.79 Nonfederal: 2,213.17.

John D. Rockefeller, Jr.
Memorial Parkway
c/o Grand Teton National
Park, P.O. Drawer 170
Moose, WY 83012-0170
307-739-3300
www.nps.gov/grte

Authorized by Congress to recognize Rockefeller's philanthropy and significant contributions for the establishment of several national parks: Grand Teton, Acadia, Great Smoky Mountains, and Virgin Islands. Congress also named the highway from Grand Teton's south boundary to West Thumb in Yellowstone in honor of Rockefeller. The remote and largely uninhabited parkway provides a natural link between Grand Teton and Yellowstone.
Authorized Aug. 25, 1972.
Acreage—23,777.22, all Federal.

Yellowstone National
Park
PO Box 168
Yellowstone National Park,
WY 82190-0168
307-344-7381
www.nps.gov/yell
(Also in Montana and Idaho)

Old Faithful Geyser and some 10,000 other thermal features make this the Earth's greatest geyser area. Here, too, are lakes, waterfalls, high mountain meadows, wildlife, and the Grand Canyon of the Yellowstone—all set apart in 1872 as the world's first national park.
Established March 1, 1872. Boundary changes: May 26, 1926; March 1, 1929; April 19, 1930; Oct. 20, 1932. Designated a Biosphere Reserve 1976. Designated a World Heritage Site Sept. 6, 1978.
Acreage—2,219,790.71 Federal: 2,219,789.13 Nonfederal: 1.58.

Part 3

Related Areas

Touro Synagogue National Historic Site

The units in this section have been authorizeed by Congress and will be added as official System units when they fulfill the requirements of their enabling legislation.

**Samuel Colt Memorial Statue,
Coltsville National Historical Park**

Adams Memorial
Washington, DC

This memorial will honor 2nd President John Adams and his legacy; his wife Abigail Smith Adams; their son 6th President John Quincy Adams; his wife Louisa Catherine Johnson Adams; their son Charles Francis Adams; and his son Henry Adams. They were all members of an illustrious family that enriched the Nation through their profound civic consciousness, abiding belief in the perfectibility of the Nation's democracy, and commitment to service and sacrifice for the common good.
Authorized Nov. 5, 2001.
Acreage—undetermined.

Coltsville National Historical Park
40 Huyshope Avenue, #331
Hartford, CT 06106

The result of the inspirational dreams of Samuel and Elizabeth Colt, Coltsville was an industrial village built both to produce the legendary Colt firearms, and to provide practical, spiritual, and recreational opportunities for armory workers. With Sam Colt's untimely passing in 1862, Elizabeth Colt, a successful business woman and philanthropist, ensured that the industrial empire flourished for 40 more years. Coltsville NHP encompasses the Colt armory complex and Colt estate, including the Colt's home Armsmear, Colt Park, the Church of the Good Shepard, and armory worker houses.
Authorized Dec. 19, 2014.
Acreage—135.00, all Nonfederal.

Dwight D. Eisenhower Memorial
Washington, DC

This will be a memorial to honor the 34th President Dwight D. Eisenhower, and his service as the Supreme Commander of the Allied Forces in Europe in World War II.
Authorized Jan. 10, 2002.
Acreage—3.9, all Federal.

Harriet Tubman National Historical Park
Auburn, NY

Acclaimed abolitionist and suffragist Harriet Tubman acquired this land from U.S. Senator William Henry Seward in 1859 and worked and resided here with her family from 1861 until her death in 1913. In 1903 she donated land to the A.M.E. Zion Church in Auburn for the establishment of a home "for aged and indigent colored people." Resources associated with the park include: the Harriet Tubman Home, the Home for the Aged, and the Thompson Memorial A.M.E. Zion Church and its parsonage.
Authorized Dec. 19, 2014.
Acreage—31.5 as proposed, all Nonfederal.

Ronald Reagan Boyhood Home National Historic Site
Dixon, IL

Born in Tampico, Illinois, on February 6, 1911, Ronald Reagan and his family moved many times during his childhood. In December 1920, when he was 9 years old, they rented a house on Hennepin Avenue in Dixon, Illinois. This modest house was Reagan's home from 1920 to 1924, the site of his earliest childhood memories, and a place he recalled with great fondness. The gable-roofed, two-story white frame house is a typical late 19th-century small-town American home.
Authorized Feb. 6, 2002.
Acreage—1.01, all Nonfederal.

In the Act of August 18, 1970, the National Park System was defined in law as "any area of land and water now or hereafter administered by the Secretary of the Interior through the National Park Service for park, monument, historic, parkway, recreational or other purposes." The same law specifically excludes "miscellaneous areas administered in connection therewith," that is, those properties that are neither federally owned nor directly administered by the National Park Service but that the National Park Service assists.

The Affiliated Areas comprise a variety of locations in the United States and Canada that preserve significant properties outside the National Park System. Some of these have been recognized by Acts of Congress, others have been designated national historic sites by the Secretary of the Interior under authority of the Historic Sites Act of 1935. All draw on technical or financial aid from the National Park Service.

Roosevelt Campobello International Park

Aleutian World War II National Historic Area
Ounalashka Corporation
PO Box 149
Unalaska, AK 99685
www.nps.gov/aleu

This area preserves lands owned by the Ounalashka Corporation on the island of Amaknak. It provides for the interpretation of the unique and significant circumstances involving the history of the Aleut people and the role the Aleut people and the Aleutian Islands played in the defense of the United States in World War II.
Designated Nov. 12, 1996.
Acreage—134.94, all Nonfederal.

American Memorial Park
PO Box 5189 CHRB
Saipan, MP 96950
www.nps.gov/amme

This site on the island of Saipan in the Northern Mariana Islands was created as a living memorial honoring the sacrifices made during the Marianas Campaign of World War II. Recreational facilities, a World War II museum, and a flag monument keep alive the memory of over 4,000 U.S. military personnel and local islanders who died in June 1944.
Authorized Aug. 18, 1978.
Acreage—133.00, all Nonfederal.

Benjamin Franklin National Memorial
c/o The Franklin Institute
222 North 20th Street
Philadelphia, PA 19103

In the rotunda of the Franklin Institute the colossal seated statue of Franklin, by James Earle Fraser, honors the inventor-statesman.
Designated Oct. 25, 1972. Owned and administered by the Franklin Institute.
Acreage—0.00.

Chicago Portage National Historic Site
c/o Forest Preserves of Cook County
536 N. Harlem Avenue
River Forest, IL 60305

A portion of the portage between the Great Lakes and the Mississippi, discovered by French explorers Jacques Marquette and Louis Joliet, is preserved here.
Designated Jan. 3, 1952. Administered by Cook County.
Acreage—91.20, all Nonfederal.

Chimney Rock National Historic Site
PO Box F
Bayard, NE 69334

Pioneers camped near this landmark, which stands 500 feet above the Platte River along the Oregon and California trails.
Designated Aug. 2, 1956. Owned by Nebraska; administered by the city of Bayard, the Nebraska State Historical Society, and the National Park Service under a cooperative agreement of June 21, 1956.
Acreage—83.36, all Nonfederal.

Fallen Timbers Battlefield and Fort Miamis National Historic Site
US 24 & Jerome Road
Toledo, OH 43615-2100
www.nps.gov/fati

The site interprets the Aug. 20, 1794, Battle of Fallen Timbers and the location of Fort Miamis, a British fort built with the Indian Confederation to hold the Maumee Valley. Fallen Timbers is considered to be the last American Indian-battle of the American Revolution. Major General Anthony Wayne defeated the British-supplied Indian Confederation, made up of seven tribes led by war chief Little Turtle of the Miami Indians, near the Maumee River. The battle resulted in the Treaty of Greenville, a peace treaty between the United States and the seven tribes. Fort Miamis, 1794-1813, was also the site of a War of 1812 battle.
Established Dec. 9, 1999.
Acreage: 185.00, all Nonfederal.

**Father Marquette
National Memorial**
Michigan Department of
Natural Resources and
Department of State
Straits State Park
720 Church Street
St. Ignace, MI 49781

The memorial pays tribute to the life and work of Father Jacques Marquette, French priest and explorer, including his establishment of a mission at Saint Ignace in 1671, and his historic exploration, in company with Louis Joliet, of the Mississippi River in 1673. It is located in Straits State Park near St. Ignace, Mich., where Marquette founded a Jesuit mission in 1671 and was buried in 1678.

Authorized Dec. 20, 1975. The memorial is part of the Michigan Department of Natural Resources and jointly administered by the Michigan Historical Center and the Parks and Recreation Divisions.

Acreage—52.00, all Nonfederal.

**Gloria Dei
(Old Swedes') Church
National Historic Site**
916 South Swanson Street
Columbus Boulevard and
Christian Street
Philadelphia, PA 19147
www.nps.gov/glde

This second oldest Swedish church in the United States was founded in 1677. The present structure, a splendid example of 1600s Swedish church architecture, was erected about 1700.

Designated Nov. 17, 1942. Church site owned and administered by Corporation of Gloria Dei (Old Swedes') Church. Boundary change: Aug. 21, 1958.

Acreage—3.71 Federal: 2.08 Nonfederal: 1.63.

**Green Springs
National Historic
Landmark District**
c/o Fredericksburg & Spotsylvania National Military Park
120 Chatham Lane
Fredericksburg, VA 22405
www.nps.gov/grsp

This portion of Louisa County in Virginia's Piedmont is noted for its concentration of architecturally varied manor houses, related buildings, and landscapes in an unmarred setting. NO PUBLIC FACILITIES.

Designated a national historic landmark on May 30, 1974. On Dec. 12, 1977, the Secretary agreed to accept preservation easements for nearly half of the 14,000 acres in the district.

*Acreage—15,645.11 Federal (easements): 7,086.99
Nonfederal: 8,558.12.*

**Historic Camden
Revolutionary War Site**
222 Broad Street
PO Box 710
Camden, SC 29020

This early colonial village was established in the mid-1730s and was known as Fredericksburg Township. In 1768 the village was named Camden in honor of Charles Pratt, Lord Camden, a British Parliamentary champion of colonial rights. The site was occupied by the British under Lord Cornwallis from June 1, 1780, until May 9, 1781. Camden was one of the few frontier settlements where two Revolutionary War battles were fought: Aug. 16, 1780, and April 25, 1781.

Authorized May 24, 1982.

Acreage—107.00, all Nonfederal.

**Ice Age
National Scientific Reserve**
Wisconsin Department of
Natural Resources
PO Box 7921
Madison, WI 53707

This reserve contains nationally significant examples of landforms resulting from continental glaciation. Each of the nine units is state-owned and managed as a park recreational area, natural area, or wildlife area.

Authorized Oct. 13, 1964.

Acreage—32,500.00, all Nonfederal.

120

International Peace Garden
10939 Highway 281
Dunseith, ND 58329

This site is a symbol of the peaceful relations between Canada and the United States. North Dakota holds the 888-acre U.S. portion for International Peace Garden, Inc., which administers the area for North Dakota and Manitoba.
Originated by North Dakota in 1931. Dedicated July 14, 1932. Federal aid authorized in acts of Oct. 25, 1949; June 28, 1954; Aug. 28, 1958; Oct. 26, 1974.
Acreage—2,330.30, all Nonfederal.

Inupiat Heritage Center
PO Box 749
Barrow, AK 99723
www.nps.gov/inup

This center is affiliated with New Bedford Whaling National Historical Park to commemorate over 2,000 whaling trips from New Bedford to the western Arctic in the 1800s. The center collects, preserves, and exhibits historical material, art objects, and scientific displays.
Designated Feb. 3, 1999.
Acreage—0.00.

Jamestown
National Historic Site
c/o Preservation Virginia
204 West Franklin St.
Richmond, VA 23220
www.nps.gov/jame

Part of the site of the first permanent English settlement in North America (1607), on the upper end of Jamestown Island, was the scene of the first representative government on this continent, July 30, 1619.
Designated Dec. 18, 1940. Owned and administered by Association for the Preservation of Virginia. Adjacent areas of the historic Jamestown site and island are part of Colonial National Historical Park.
Acreage—21.99 Federal: 1.74 Nonfederal: 20.25.

Kate Mullany
National Historic Site
c/o American Labor
Studies Center
100 South Swan Street
Albany, NY 12210

Catherine A. (Kate) Mullany was an Irish immigrant laundry worker who organized and led Troy's Collar Laundry Union during the 1860s, one of the first all-female unions in the United States. She lived in this house at 350 8th Street, Troy, N.Y., from 1869 to 1875, inherited the house when her mother died in 1876, moved away, returned in 1903, and died here in 1906. The house is owned by the American Labor Studies Center.
Established Dec. 3, 2004.
Acreage—0.06, all Nonfederal.

Lower East Side Tenement
National Historic Site
103 Orchard Street
New York, NY 10002
www.nps.gov/loea

The heart of the Lower East Side Tenement Museum is its landmark tenement building, home to over 7,000 people from 20 nations between 1863 and 1935. The Tenement Museum preserves and interprets the history of immigration through the personal experiences of the generations of newcomers who settled in and built lives on Manhattan's Lower East Side, America's iconic immigrant neighborhood; forges emotional connections between visitors and immigrants past and present; and enhances appreciation for the profound role immigration has played in shaping America's national identity.
Designated Nov. 12, 1998. Expanded Dec. 19, 2014. The site is privately owned by the Lower East Side Tenement Museum.
Acreage—1.20, all Nonfederal.

Oklahoma City National Memorial
620 N. Harvey Avenue
Oklahoma City, OK 73102
www.nps.gov/okci

The bombing of the Alfred P. Murrah Federal Building on April 19, 1995, killed 168 people and injured over 650. The memorial is owned and operated by a private foundation. The National Park Service provides interpretive services on the Outdoor Symbolic Memorial.
Established Oct. 9, 1997; redesignated as affiliated area Jan. 23, 2004.
Acreage—6.24 Federal: 3.12 Nonfederal: 3.12

Pinelands National Reserve
c/o New Jersey Pinelands Commission
15 Springfield Road
PO Box 7
New Lisbon, NJ 08064
www.nps.gov/pine

The Pinelands (Pine Barrens) is a unique ecosystem of historic villages and berry farms amid vast pine-oak forests, extensive wetlands, and diverse species of plants and animals. It is managed by the New Jersey Pinelands Commission and protected by state and federal legislation through a partnership of management by the local, state, and federal governments and the private sector. The National Park Service is the federal representative on the 15 member commission. Public recreation facilities are provided within state parks and forests. Pinelands was the nation's first designated national reserve.
Authorized Nov. 10, 1978. Designated a U.S. Biosphere Reserve in 1983.
Acreage—1,164,025 Federal: 90,530 Nonfederal: 1,073,495.

Red Hill Patrick Henry National Memorial
Patrick Henry Memorial Foundation
1250 Red Hill Road
Brookneal, VA 24528

The law office and grave of the fiery Virginia legislator and orator are preserved at this small plantation. The site contains a reconstruction of Patrick Henry's last home, several dependencies, and a museum.
Designated May 12, 1986.
Acreage—0.00.

Roosevelt Campobello International Park
c/o Executive Secretary
Roosevelt Campobello International Park Commission
PO Box 97
Lubec, ME 04652
www.nps.gov/roca

President Franklin D. Roosevelt was stricken by poliomyelitis here at his summer home in New Brunswick, Canada, at the age of 39.
Established July 7, 1964. Owned and administered by a U.S.-Canadian commission.
Acreage—2,721.50, all Nonfederal.

Sewall-Belmont House National Historic Site
144 Constitution Avenue, NE
Washington, DC 20002
www.nps.gov/nace

Rebuilt after fire damage from the War of 1812, this red brick house is one of the oldest on Capitol Hill. It has been the National Woman's Party headquarters since 1929 and commemorates the party's founder and women's suffrage leader, Alice Paul, and associates. OPEN ON A LIMITED BASIS.
Authorized Oct. 26, 1974.
Acreage—0.35, all Nonfederal.

Thomas Cole National Historic Site
218 Spring Street
Catskill, NY 12414
www.nps.gov/thco

This is the Hudson River home of the eminent British-American landscape painter Thomas Cole (1801–1848). Recognized as the founder of the Hudson River School, America's first indigenous school of landscape painting, Cole created some of his greatest paintings, including the "Voyage of Life" series, in the small studio on the property.
Authorized Dec. 9, 1999. Owned and operated by the Greene County Historical Society.
Acreage—3.40, all Nonfederal.

**Touro Synagogue
National Historic Site**
85 Touro Street
Newport, RI 02840
www.nps.gov/tosy

One of the finest examples of colonial religious architecture, designed by Peter Harrison, this synagogue is the present-day place of worship of Congregation Jeshuat Israel. Designated March 5, 1946. Owned by Congregation Shearith Israel, New York City.
Acreage—0.23, all Nonfederal.

**Wing Luke Museum of the
Asian Pacific American
Experience**
719 South King Street
Seattle, WA 98104
www.nps.gov/wing

Located in Seattle's Chinatown-International District, the Wing Luke Museum connects visitors to the rich, dynamic cultures and art of Asian Pacific Americans through vivid storytelling and inspiring experiences. The museum was first opened in 1967. Designated Feb. 10, 2013.
Acreage—0.00

National Coal Heritage Area

National Heritage Areas expand on traditional approaches to resource stewardship by supporting large-scale, community centered initiatives that connect local citizens to preservation, conservation, and planning processes. Through the facilitation of a local coordinating entity, such as a private non-profit corporation or a public commission, residents of a region come together to improve regional quality of life by protecting their shared cultural and natural resources.

In National Heritage Areas, businesses, governments, non-profit organizations, and private individuals collaborate to promote sustainable economic development and community revitalization projects. This cooperative approach allows National Heritage Areas to achieve both conservation and economic growth in ways that do not compromise local land use controls. Participation in projects and programs is always voluntary, with zoning and land-use decisions remaining under the jurisdiction of local governments.

National Heritage Areas are designated by Congress. Each National Heritage Area is governed by separate authorizing legislation and operates under provisions unique to its resources and desired goals. The National Park Service provides technical planning and limited financial assistance, serving as a partner and advisor. Decision-making authority is in the hands of local residents and organizations.

Since the first designation in 1984, National Heritage Areas now include 48 areas, ranging from factory towns and city neighborhoods to farmland and battlefields. As part of a living, working, evolving landscape, National Heritage Areas reflect the diverse and evolving histories and cultures of the people who call the region home. Visitors who explore these special places will learn about an innovative approach to resource protection; they will also gain insight into the physical character and cultural legacy of the United States.

Abraham Lincoln National Heritage Area
1 Old State Capitol Plaza
Springfield, IL 62701

The Abraham Lincoln National Heritage Area is home to a significant collection of historic resources related to Lincoln's life. Here, in the 42-county region of central Illinois, are courthouses, log cabins, hotels, and homes where Lincoln argued cases and entertained neighbors and friends for over 30 years.
Authorized May 8, 2009.

America's Agricultural Heritage Partnership
(Silos & Smokestacks National Heritage Area)
604 Lafayette Street,
Suite 202
PO Box 2845
Waterloo, IA 50703

Discover the story of agriculture, agribusiness, and farm life through sites, events, and communities. No other region in the United States shares such a rich agricultural legacy.
Authorized Nov. 12, 1996.

Arabia Mountain National Heritage Area
3350 Klondike Road
Lithonia, GA 30038-4406
www.nps.gov/armo

Located in parts of three counties east of Atlanta, Georgia, the heritage area features active quarries, rolling topography, rural landscapes, and unique granite outcroppings.
Authorized Oct. 12, 2006.

Atchafalaya National Heritage Area
1051 North Third Street
Baton Rouge, LA 70804-5239
www.nps.gov/attr

This treasury of nature, culture, and history in south-central Louisiana encompasses the nation's largest river swamp. While the 14 parishes that compose the heritage area are best-known for the Cajun descendants of French-speaking Acadians, the area's complex racial and ethnic mix is reflected in distinctive architecture, music, language, food, and festivals.
Authorized Oct. 12, 2006.

Augusta Canal National Heritage Area
1450 Green Street, Suite 400
Augusta, GA 30903-2367
www.nps.gov/auca

This corridor in northeastern Georgia interprets a piece of our nation's history that transformed Augusta into an industrial center on the eve of the Civil War.
Authorized Nov. 12, 1996.

Automobile National Heritage Area
(See MotorCities National Heritage Area)

Baltimore National Heritage Area
Baltimore Heritage Area Association
12 W. Madison Street,
Suite 120
Baltimore, MD 21201
www.nps.gov/balt

This heritage area includes Baltimore's oldest neighborhoods and features museums, expansive parks and vibrant neighborhoods shaped by patterns of immigration and architecture. At its center is the Inner Harbor, one of the nation's oldest seaports and today a vibrant destination for tourists and residents.
Authorized March 30, 2009

Blue Ridge National Heritage Area
195 Hemphill Knob Road
(Parkway Milepost 384)
Asheville, NC 28803
www.nps.gov/blrn

This heritage area of 25 counties in the Blue Ridge Mountains of North Carolina contains eastern America's tallest mountain (Mt. Mitchell) and deepest gorge (Linville Gorge). The heritage area preserves Cherokee and Scotch-Irish culture, traditional mountain music, arts and crafts, and associated historic sites.
Authorized Nov. 10, 2003.

Cache La Poudre River National Heritage Area
Poudre Heritage Alliance
Poudre Learning Center
8313 F Street
Greeley, CO 80631
www.nps.gov/cala

The corridor encompasses the river and its flood plain from the Roosevelt National Forest to its confluence with the South Platte River in Colorado. This heritage area commemorates the contributions of the Poudre River to the development of water laws in the western United States and the evolution of complex water delivery systems.
Authorized Oct. 19, 1996.

Cane River National Heritage Area
Cane River National Heritage Area, Inc.
1115 Washington Street
Natchitoches, LA 71457
www.nps.gov/crha

This area in Louisiana is a largely rural landscape known for its historic plantations, distinctive Creole architecture, and multi-cultural legacy. It is home to a blend of cultures, including French, Spanish, African, American Indian, and Creole.
Authorized Nov. 2, 1994.

Champlain Valley National Heritage Partnership
54 West Shore Road
Grand Isle, VT 05458-2005
www.nps.gov/chva

Here are the linked navigable waterways and adjacent lands of Lake Champlain, Lake George, the Champlain Canal, and portions of the Upper Hudson River in Vermont and New York. This region, homeland of Algonquin and Iroquois people, played an important role in the establishment of the United States and Canada.
Authorized Oct. 12, 2006.

Crossroads of the American Revolution National Heritage Area
101 Barrack Street
Trenton, NJ 08608
www.nps.gov/xrds

This area encompasses 213 municipalities and all or parts of 14 counties from Bergen to Gloucester in New Jersey. Gen. George Washington planned and led some of the most decisive military actions of the American Revolution across this landscape.
Authorized Oct. 12, 2006.

Delaware and Lehigh National Heritage Corridor
2750 Hugh Moore Park Road
Easton, PA 18042-7120
www.nps.gov/dele

This 165-mile region, rich in anthracite coal and other natural resources, is a transportation crossroads. Canals and railroads in the Delaware and Lehigh valleys transported lumber, hard coal, slate, iron, and steel from mountain to market, fueling America's Industrial Revolution.
Authorized Nov. 18, 1988.

Erie Canalway National Heritage Corridor
PO Box 219
Waterford, NY 12188
www.nps.gov/erie

This heritage corridor commemorates and celebrates the impacts of the Erie Canal on the expansion of the United States. The 524-mile canal system is an engineering marvel that knitted together New England, New York, and the West, spreading commerce and ideas.
Authorized Dec. 21, 2000.

Essex National Heritage Area
10 Federal Street, Suite 12
Salem, MA 01970
www.nps.gov/esse

The area encompasses 500 square miles of eastern Massachusetts. It includes thousands of historic sites, rivers and marshes, and miles of unspoiled coastline. The heritage area illuminates almost 400 years of our nation's history.
Authorized Nov. 12, 1996.

Freedom's Frontier National Heritage Area
PO Box 526
Lawrence, KS 66044-0526

This area encompasses counties in eastern Kansas and western Missouri. Along this border, before and during the Civil War, a conflict took place between the forces of slavery and freedom. As abolitionists and others fought to keep Kansas a free state and pro-slavery forces gathered in Missouri, the Eastern press began calling the region "Bleeding Kansas."
Authorized Oct. 12, 2006.

Freedom's Way National Heritage Area
94 Jackson Road #311
Devens, MA 01434

Freedom's Way National Heritage Area in Massachusetts and New Hampshire includes 45 communities stretching across the two states. The area has a long history of social and intellectual innovation including the emergence of a democratic vision that led to the American Revolution; a tradition of religious freedom and experimentation; and nationally influential movements for conservation, social justice, abolitionism, and the American Renaissance of the nineteenth century. Authorized March 30, 2009.

Great Basin National Heritage Route
PO Box 78
Baker, NV 89311-0078

The heritage route incorporates the classic landscape of White Pine County, Nevada, Duckwater Shoshone Reservation, Nevada, and Millard County, Utah. This region of biological diversity and fragile ecological communities has cultural sites and American Indian heritage. Highlights include the Nevada Northern Railway Museum and Fillmore Territorial Statehouse, Nevada, and Topaz Japanese Relocation Camp, Utah. Authorized Oct. 12, 2006.

Gullah/Geechee Cultural Heritage Corridor
Gullah Geechee Cultural
Heritage Corridor
Commission
PO Box 1007
Johns Island, SC 29457
www.nps.gov/guge

This area recognizes the important contributions made to American culture and history by Africans and African Americans known as the Gullah/Geechee who settled in the coastal counties of South Carolina and Georgia, the southeast coast of North Carolina, and the northeast coast of Florida. Authorized Oct. 12, 2006.

Hudson River Valley National Heritage Area
Hudson River Valley
Greenway
625 Broadway - 4th Floor
Albany, NY 12207
www.nps.gov/hurv

The heritage area stretches from New York City to Saratoga County, north of Albany. The area promotes and interprets resources that support three corridor-wide themes: the interrelationship of nature and culture, the vital roles of freedom and dignity throughout the valley's history, and the historical and contemporary role of commerce. Authorized Nov. 12, 1996.

Illinois & Michigan Canal National Heritage Corridor
Canal Corridor Association
754 First Street
LaSalle, IL 61301

The corridor commemorates and interprets the 97-mile canal, completed in 1848, that connected Lake Michigan to the Illinois River along an American Indian portage route. By forging the last link in water transport between the Great Lakes and the Mississippi watershed, the canal rapidly transformed Chicago from a small settlement to a critical transportation hub. Authorized Aug. 24, 1984.

John H. Chafee Blackstone River Valley National Heritage Corridor
Blackstone Heritage Corridor,
Inc.
1 Depot Square
Woonsocket, RI 02895

This area is composed of 24 cities and towns on 454 square miles of land in the watershed of the Blackstone River. Beginning in the 1700s, the Blackstone Valley provided the setting for a remarkable transformation from farm to factory, a local story that became the model for a national phenomenon—the Industrial Revolution. Authorized Nov. 10, 1986.

Journey Through Hallowed Ground National Heritage Area
15481 2nd Street
Waterford, VA 20197-0077

The area stretches 175 miles along the U.S. Route 15 corridor. The journey includes Gettysburg, Pennsylvania, Frederick and Washington counties, Maryland, Harpers Ferry, West Virginia, and Thomas Jefferson's Monticello in Charlottesville, Virginia. Its path is a treasure trove of history—American Indian and African American sites, restored architectural gems, presidential homes, and the nation's greatest concentration of Civil War battle sites.
Authorized May 8, 2008.

Kenai Mountains-Turnagain Arm National Heritage Area
PO Box 771054
Eagle River, AK 99577

Kenai Mountains-Turnagain Arm National Heritage Area highlights the experience of the Native Alaskans, Russians, explorers, gold miners, and settlers who traveled through the branching valleys and over the waters of this rugged mountain coordinator. In the heritage area, the isolated historic communities that developed around transportation and the Gold Rush are dwarfed by the sweeping landscapes, by the magnificence of the mountains and the strength and dominance of nature.
Authorized March 30, 2009.

Lackawanna Valley National Heritage Area
538 Spruce Street, Suite 516
Scranton, PA 18503

This region in northeastern Pennsylvania gives residents and visitors a chance to understand the people and industries that made the United States a powerhouse of technology and ingenuity. Visitors can see where anthracite coal was mined, steel forged, and textiles woven—and they can learn about the people who did that back-breaking work.
Authorized Oct. 6, 2000.

Mississippi Delta National Heritage Area
Delta Center for Culture and Learning
Delta State University
PO Box 3152
Cleveland, MS 38733
www.nps.gov/mide

Mississippi Delta National Heritage Area includes counties in the alluvial floodplain of the Mississippi River. This area was cleared for cotton production, and peopled by sharecroppers and landowners, including immigrants from Europe and Asia. Many people from this region became the source of "The Great Migration" north, and thus the family home of many living today in northern cities, like Chicago and Detroit. It is an area known as "The Birthplace of the Blues" and Gospel music as well as many sites that were pivotal in the early civil rights movement.
Authorized March 30, 2009.

Mississippi Gulf Coast National Heritage Area
Mississippi Department of Marine Resources
1141 Bayview Ave., Suite 101
Biloxi, MS 39530
www.nps.gov/migu

The area encompasses the Mississippi Coastal Plain that borders the Gulf of Mexico. The landscape has been shaped by the natural coastal and riverine environment and cultural influences, including early American Indians and Spanish, French, and English settlers.
Authorized Dec. 8, 2004.

Mississippi Hills National Heritage Area
398 East Main Street, Suite 132
Tupelo, MS 38804
www.nps.gov/mihi

Mississippi Hills National Heritage Area represents a distinctive cultural landscape shaped largely by the dynamic intersection of Appalachian and Delta cultures, an intersection that produced a powerful concentration of nationally significant cultural icons. Lasting contributions to our country's musical and literary legacies were forged by Hills' natives Elvis Presley, Howlin' Wolf, and Tammy Wynette. The heritage area seeks to interpret and share the stories of these individuals, as well as the legacies of Civil Rights pioneers James Meredith and Ida B. Wells-Barnett.
Authorized March 30, 2009.

**Mormon Pioneer
National Heritage Area**
115 West Main Street
Mt. Pleasant, UT 84647
www.nps.gov/mopi

The region, stretching through six counties along U.S. Highway 89 in southern Utah, is recognized for its dramatic landscapes. Communities along the corridor reflect the experience of Mormon colonization.
Authorized Oct. 12, 2006.

**MotorCities National
Heritage Area**
(formerly Automobile
National Heritage Area)
200 Renaissance Center
Suite 3148
Detroit, MI 48243
www.nps.gov/auto

The area consists of six corridors representing the region that put the world on wheels. Auto-related museums, historical sites, and natural, cultural, and recreational resources link, protect, preserve, and interpret the automobile's story.
Authorized Nov. 6, 1998. Renamed Dec. 19, 2014.

**Muscle Shoals National
Heritage Area**
University of North Alabama
One Harrison Plaza - UNA
Box 5231
Florence, AL 35632
www.nps.gov/mush

Muscle Shoals National Heritage Area spans across six counties within the Tennessee River basin. The region celebrates its musical legacy, including the booming years of the Muscle Shoals recording studios in the 1960s and 1970s and the creation of the rich heritage that helped shape today's music scene. Authorized March 30, 2009.

**National Aviation
Heritage Area**
Aviation Heritage
Foundation
PO Box 414, Wright Brothers
Station
Dayton, Ohio 45409
www.nps.gov/avia

The National Aviation Heritage Area is recognized as the Birthplace of Aviation and home of the Wright Brothers. This eight-county area in southwest Ohio builds on the Wright brothers' legacy and the aviation history that followed them in the Dayton, Ohio, region. Heritage area partners celebrate and interpret the history of flight, preserve related historic resources, and look to the future with many education programs that focus on science, technology, engineering and math.
Authorized Dec. 8, 2004.

**National Coal
Heritage Area**
Coal Heritage Highway
Authority
PO Box 15
100 Kelly Ave.
Oak Hill, WV 25901
www.nps.gov/coal

In no other place has coal mining so dominated an economy and social structure as the 5,300-square-mile region encompassed by this area in southern West Virginia. Huge amounts of coal, unsurpassed in quality, have been exported, leaving a society and landscape rich in history and culture. Today, the rugged area's communities retain much of their original character as "company towns," reflecting local traditions, immigrant laborers, and the dominance of the coal industry. Authorized Nov. 12, 1996.

**Niagara Falls
National Heritage Area**
PO Box 1932
Timon Hall, Room 125
Niagara University, NY
14109
www.nps.gov/nifa

This area, stretching from the western boundary of Wheatfield, N.Y., to the mouth of the Niagara River on Lake Ontario, includes the communities of Niagara Falls, Youngstown, and Lewiston, N.Y. The region is home to natural wonders, cultural traditions, and nationally significant historical sites. It has associations with American Indians, European exploration, the French and Indian War, the American Revolution, the War of 1812, and the Underground Railroad.
Authorized May 8, 2008.

Northern Plains National Heritage Area
Northern Plains Heritage Foundation
401 W. Main Street
Mandan, ND 58554

The Northern Plains National Heritage Area stretches almost the length of the free-flowing Missouri River, in the homeland of the Mandan and Hidatsa Indians. The area contains Fort Abraham Lincoln State Park, Fort Mandan and the Lewis and Clark Interpretive Center, Knife River Indian Villages National Historic Site, North Dakota Heritage Center and the state Capitol Grounds, and the tall cottonwoods of Cross Ranch State Park.
Authorized March 30, 2009.

Northern Rio Grande National Heritage Area
PO Box 610
Espanola, NM 87532-0610
www.nps.gov/norg

In northern New Mexico, the area stretches from Santa Fe to Taos and includes Santa Fe, Rio Arriba, and Taos counties. It encompasses a mosaic of cultures and history, including eight Pueblos and the descendants of Spanish ancestors who settled here as early as 1598.
Authorized Oct. 12, 2006.

Ohio and Erie National Heritage Canalway
Ohio and Erie Canalway Association
PO Box 609420
Cleveland, OH 44109

This area of northeast Ohio celebrates the canal that enabled shipping between Lake Erie and the Ohio River and vaulted Ohio into commercial prominence in the early 1830s. The canal and Towpath Trail pass through agricultural lands and rural villages into industrial communities like Akron, Canton, and Cleveland that trace their prosperity to the canal.
Authorized Nov. 12, 1996.

Oil Region National Heritage Area
217 Elm Street
Oil City, PA 16301
www.nps.gov/oire

This area in northwestern Pennsylvania tells the story of Col. Edwin Drake's drilling of the world's first successful oil well in 1859. Visitors learn about the legacy of the petroleum industry, which continues to shape the economy, society, politics, and daily life.
Authorized Dec. 8, 2004.

Quinebaug and Shetucket Rivers Valley National Heritage Corridor
(See The Last Green Valley National Heritage Corridor)

Rivers of Steel National Heritage Area
The Bost Building
623 E. Eighth Avenue
Homestead, PA 15120
www.nps.gov/rist

The area celebrates the industrial history of Pittsburgh and the surrounding region, which for over a century was the "Steel Making Capital of the World." The area documents and shares the stories of immigrants who worked in the steel industry.
Authorized Nov. 12, 1996.

Sangre de Cristo National Heritage Area
PO Box 844
Antonito, CO 81101

Sangre de Cristo National Heritage Area in the San Luis Valley is the cradle of Colorado's earliest settlement, and is recognized as a confluence of Hispano, Anglo, and American Indian cultures. Spanning more than 3,000 square miles, the area includes the counties of Conejos, Costilla, and Alamosa, the Monte Vista National Wildlife Refuge, the Baca National Wildlife Refuge, the Alamosa National Wildlife Refuge, and the Great Sand Dunes National Park and Preserve, containing the largest sand dunes in North America.
Authorized March 30, 2009.

Schuylkill River Valley National Heritage Area
Schuylkill River Greenway Association
140 College Drive
Pottstown, PA 19464
www.nps.gov/scrv

For generations, people of southeastern Pennsylvania have viewed the Schuylkill River as integral to their way of life. They built homes, raised families, and shaped the course of history along its banks. The 125-mile river is central to the story of colonization and industrialization of America. Authorized Oct. 6, 2000.

Shenandoah Valley Battlefields National Historic District
Battlefields Foundation
PO Box 897
New Market, VA 22844-0897
www.nps.gov/shvb

Here are the stories of the soldiers and civilians who shaped a critical period in American history. During the American Civil War, Virginia's Shenandoah Valley was in the crossfire between the North and South. This agricultural valley was militarily significant due to its ability to feed armies and its location close to the capitals of the opposing sides, Richmond, Va., and Washington, D.C. Authorized Nov. 12, 1996.

Silos & Smokestacks National Heritage Area
(See America's Agricultural Heritage Partnership)

South Carolina National Heritage Corridor
PO Box 477
Belton, SC 29627
www.nps.gov/soca

Bounded at one end by the historic port city of Charleston and at the other by the Blue Ridge mountains, the corridor has historical, cultural, and natural resources that tell the vibrant story of South Carolina's centuries-old history. Authorized Nov. 12, 1996.

South Park National Heritage Area
Park County Department of Heritage, Tourism and Community Development
501 Main Street
PO Box 1373
Fairplay, CO 80440

South Park National Heritage Area commemorates the rich mining and ranching history of the American West, and includes 19 working ranches, some of which were founded as early as the 1860s along headwaters of the South Platte River. It also includes a number of mines, including the world's highest mine, at 14,157 feet, on Mt. Lincoln near Alma, Colorado. Authorized March 30, 2009.

Tennessee Civil War National Heritage Area
Center for Historic Preservation, Middle Tennessee State University
1421 East Main Street
Murfreesboro, TN 37132
www.nps.gov/tecw

A number of sites interpret and preserve the legacies of the Civil War and Reconstruction in Tennessee. The heritage area provides technical assistance with historical documentation and interpretation projects across the state. Authorized Nov. 12, 1996.

The Last Green Valley National Heritage Corridor
(Formerly the Quinebaug and Shetucket Rivers Valley National Heritage Corridor)
PO Box 29
203 B Main Street
Danielson, CT 06239
www.nps.gov/qush

This region in northeast Connecticut and south central Massachusetts is one of the last primarily rural areas in the northeastern U.S. It includes archeological sites, excellent water quality, rural landscapes, architecturally significant mill structures and villages, several National Historic Landmarks and historic districts, and large parks and open spaces. Authorized Nov. 2, 1994. Renamed Dec. 19, 2014.

Upper Housatonic Valley National Heritage Area
PO Box 493
Salisbury, CT 06068-0493
www.nps.gov/uphv

This region in northwestern Connecticut and western Massachusetts is noted for its picturesque landscape, the meandering Housatonic River, and traditional New England towns. The area's early history was marked by the American Revolution, early industrialization, and deforestation followed by a long history of reclamation and conservation.
Authorized Oct. 12, 2006.

Wheeling National Heritage Area
1400 Main Street, 3rd Floor
Wheeling, WV 26003
www.nps.gov/whee

The area commemorates the 1849 suspension bridge that extended the National Road (U.S. Route 40) into Ohio. The bridge brought people and goods to the city and enabled eastern settlers to migrate to the western frontier. The heritage area preserves and celebrates Wheeling's dramatic setting, resources, and history, including its role as birthplace of the state of West Virginia during the Civil War.
Authorized Oct. 11, 2000.

Yuma Crossing National Heritage Area
180 West First Street, Suite E
Yuma, AZ 85364
www.nps.gov/yucr

This heritage area celebrates the pivotal role Yuma, Arizona, played as a Colorado River crossing point in the 1800s and the city's innovative role in water management in the 1900s.
Authorized Oct. 19, 2000.

Public Law 90-542, of October 2, 1968, provides for the establishment of a system of rivers to be preserved as free-flowing streams accessible for public use and enjoyment. Components of the system, which may include only a portion of a river, are classified as wild, scenic, or recreational rivers. They are classified according to the degree of development on the river, shoreline, and adjacent lands. Thus a wild river shows little evidence of human activity, the river is free of dams, and it is generally inaccessible except by trail. A scenic river is one with relatively primitive shorelines but accessible in places by road. A recreational river has more development, is accessible, and may have been dammed or diverted in the past.

Once a river is designated a component of the National Wild and Scenic Rivers System, the objective of the managing agency is to preserve or enhance the features that qualified the river for inclusion within the system; any recreational use must be compatible with preservation. The rivers listed here are administered by the National Park Service. Those administered by the U.S. Fish and Wildlife Service are components of the National Wildlife Refuge System.

Rivers and streams that are in state-protected systems may become units of the national system if the state's governor asks for such inclusion. The Secretary of the Interior may then designate the river, if it is appropriate, as a unit of the system. Federally managed components of the system are designated by acts of Congress. Usually Congress first authorizes a detailed study to determine the qualification of a river area for the system.

Saint Croix National Scenic Riverway

Alagnak Wild River
1000 Silver Street, Bldg.603
PO Box 245
King Salmon, AK 99613
907-246-3305
www.nps.gov/alag

See Alagnak Wild River, Alaska, a unit of the National Park System.

Alatna Wild River
Gates of the Arctic
National Park and Preserve
201 First Avenue
Doyon Bldg.
Fairbanks, AK 99701-4848

The stream lies wholly within Gates of the Arctic National Park and Preserve, Alaska, in the Central Brooks Range. Wildlife, scenery, and interesting geologic features abound in the river corridor. The River was designated for outstandingly remarkable scenic and recreational values.
Authorized Dec. 2, 1980. Length: 83 miles.

Aniakchak Wild River
Katmai National Park
and Preserve, PO Box 7
King Salmon, AK 99613-0007

The river, which lies within Aniakchak National Monument and Preserve, Alaska, flows out of Surprise Lake in the Aniakchak caldera and plunges spectacularly through The Gates, a great cleft in the caldera wall. The designation includes the mainstem and major tributaries, Hidden Creek, mystery Creek, albert Johnson Creek, and the North Fork Aniakchak River. The river was designated for outstandingly remarkable fish and geological, recreational, scenic, and ecological values.
Authorized Dec. 2, 1980. Length: 63 miles.

Bluestone
National Scenic River
c/o New River Gorge
National River
PO Box 246
Glen Jean, WV 25846-0246
www.nps.gov/blue

See Bluestone National Scenic River, West Virginia, a unit of the National Park System.

Cache la Poudre Wild and
Scenic River
2150 Centre Avenue
Building E
Fort Collins, CO 80526

The Cache la Poudre River is located east of the Continental Divide, in the northern Front Range of Colorado. The contributions of the river to the development of water law in the western United States, the evolution of water delivery systems, and the shaping of the region's cultural heritage are all commemorated along the flood plain of this working river through programs and activities that combine the area's rich history, beautiful scenery and many opportunities for recreation. The Cache la Poudre and South Fork Cache la Poudre are designated for 12 miles within Rocky Mountain National Park. The designation continues downstream for an additional 64 miles, managed by the U.S. Forest Service. The river was designated for outstandingly remarkable scenic, recreational, cultural, and ecological values.
Authorized Oct. 30, 1986. Length: 76 miles.

Charley Wild River
Yukon-Charley Rivers
National Preserve
201 First Avenue
Doyon Bldg.
Fairbanks, AK 99701-4848

Lying within Yukon-Charley Rivers National Preserve, Alaska, this stream is known for the exceptional clarity of its water. For the experienced canoeist or kayaker, it offers many miles of whitewater challenges. The designation includes the entire river, and its major tributaries: Copper Creek, Bonanza Creek, Hosford Creek, Derwent Creek, Flat-Orthmer Creek, Crescent Creek, and Moraine Creek. The river was designated for outstandingly remarkable recreational, cultural, and natural values.
Authorized Dec. 2, 1980. Length: 208 miles.

Chilikadrotna Wild River
Lake Clark National Park
and Preserve
4230 University Drive
Suite 311
Anchorage, AK 99508-4626

The river lies within Lake Clark National Park and Preserve, Alaska. Long stretches of swift water and outstanding fishing are exceptional features. The river was designated for outstandingly remarkable fish and scenic, recreational, and historical values.
Authorized Dec. 2, 1980. Length: 11 miles.

Eightmile National Wild and Scenic River
c/o National Park Service
Northeast Region
National Wild and Scenic
Rivers Division
200 Chestnut Street
Philadelphia, PA 19106-2818

Located in Connecticut, this is a 62-square-mile watershed of rolling forested landscape with over 150 miles of pristine rivers and streams and a variety of historic features. Most notable is that the overall ecosystem is healthy and intact throughout essentially all of its range. The river was designated for outstandingly remarkable fish, wildlife, and scenic, recreational, geological, historical, botanical, ecological, hydrological, and traditionally cultural values.
Authorized: May 8, 2008. Length: 25.3 miles.

Farmington National Wild and Scenic River
c/o National Park Service
Northeast Region
National Wild and Scenic
Rivers Division
200 Chestnut Street
Philadelphia, PA 19106-2818

The Farmington River Valley is an important habitat for wildlife and is currently the only place in Connecticut with nesting bald eagles. The West Branch is recognized as one of the most valuable trout fisheries in Connecticut and the northeast region, and it is also essential to the Atlantic salmon recovery plans for the Connecticut River. The river was designated for outstandingly remarkable fish, wildlife, and scenic, recreational, geological, historical, ecological, hydrological, and traditionally cultural use values.
Authorized Aug. 26, 1994. Length: 14 miles.

Flathead River
Flathead National Forest
1935 3rd Avenue E.
Kalispell, MT 59901

Glacier National Park
PO Box 128
West Glacier, MT 59936-0128

Coursing the western boundary of Glacier National Park, Montana, this is a noted spawning stream. The designation includes portions of the North, Middle, and South Fork Flathead Rivers, and Bear Creek. The river was designated for outstandingly remarkable fish, wildlife, and scenic, recreational, geological, historical, botanical, and ethnographical values.
Authorized Oct. 12, 1976. Length: 219 miles.

Great Egg Harbor Scenic and Recreational River
c/o National Park Service
Northeast Region
National Wild and Scenic
Rivers Division
200 Chestnut Street
Philadelphia, PA 19106-2818
www.nps.gov/greg

See Great Egg Harbor Scenic and Recreational River, New Jersey, a unit of the National Park System.

John Wild River
Gates of the Arctic
National Park and Preserve
201 First Avenue
Doyon Bldg.
Fairbanks, AK 99701-4848

The river flows south through the Anaktuvuk Pass of Alaska's Brooks Range, located within the Gates of the Arctic National Park and Preserve. The river was designated for outstandingly remarkable wildlife and scenic and cultural values.
Authorized Dec. 2, 1980. Length: 52 miles.

Kern River
Sequoia National Park
47050 Generals Highway
Three Rivers, CA 93271-9651

This river includes both the north and south forks of the Kern. The south fork is totally free-flowing. It descends through deep gorges with large granite outcroppings and domes interspersed with open meadows. The river was designated for outstandingly remarkable wildlife and scenic, recreational, and geologicalvalues.
Authorized Nov. 24, 1987. Length: 81 miles.

Kings River
Kings Canyon National Park
47050 Generals Highway
Three Rivers, CA 93271-9651

This river includes the entire middle and south forks, which are largely in Kings Canyon National Park. Beginning in glacial lakes above treeline, the rivers flow through deep, steep-sided canyons, over falls and cataracts, eventually becoming an outstanding whitewater rafting river in its lower reaches. The river was designated for outstandingly remarkable wildlife and scenic, recreational, and geological values.
Authorized Nov. 3, 1987. Length: 81 miles.

Kobuk Wild River
Gates of the Arctic
National Park and Preserve
201 First Ave., Doyon Bldg.
Fairbanks, AK 99701-4848

This river is contained within Gates of the Arctic National Park and Preserve, Alaska. From its headwaters in the Endicott Mountains, the stream courses south through a wide valley and passes through two scenic canyons. The river was designated for outstandingly remarkable fish and scenic, recreational, geological, and cultural values.
Authorized Dec. 2, 1980. Length: 110 miles.

Lamprey
Wild and Scenic River
c/o National Park Service
Northeast Region
National Wild and Scenic
Rivers Division
200 Chestnut Street
Philadelphia, PA 19106-2818

The Lamprey River in southeastern New Hampshire has the largest quantity of anadromous fish in the Great Bay watershed, hosts substantial numbers of freshwater mussel species, and includes archeological sites of prehistoric and nineteenth-century culture, which are representative of the early settlement of New Hampshire's seacoast region. The river was designated for outstandingly remarkable fish, wildlife, and historical, cultural, botanical, ecological, and hydrological values.
Authorized Nov. 12, 1996. Length: 23.5 miles.

Lower Delaware
Wild and Scenic River
c/o National Park Service
Northeast Region
National Wild and Scenic
Rivers Division
200 Chestnut Street
Philadelphia, PA 19106-2818
www.nps.gov/lode

This river includes portions of the mainstem Delaware River and 3 tributaries: Tinicum Creek, Tohickon Creek, and Paunacussing Creek. The river valley contains habitats that do not occur elsewhere in the region, including flora and fauna usually found only in arctic-alpine climates. In addition, the river is one of the most significant corridors in the nation, containing buildings used during Washington's famous crossing, historic navigation canals, and Native American and colonial era archaeological sites and mills. The river was designated for outstandingly remarkable scenic, recreational, geological, cultural, and ecological values.
Authorized Nov. 1, 2000. Length: 67.3 miles.

Maurice Scenic and Recreational River
c/o National Park Service
Northeast Region
National Wild and Scenic
Rivers Division
200 Chestnut Street
Philadelphia, PA 19106-2818

This rivers includes portions of the Maurice River and three tributaries: Manumuskin River and Menantico and Muskee Creeks. The Maurice River corridor is an unusually pristine Atlantic Coastal river with nationally and internationally important resources. Serving as a critical link between the Pinelands National Reserve and the Delaware Estuary, it is also part of the Atlantic Flyway, where its clean waters and related habitats are vitally important to the migration of shorebirds, songbirds, waterfowl, raptors, rails, and fish. The river was designated for outstandingly remarkable fish, wildlife, and recreational, cultural, and ecological values. Authorized Dec. 1, 1993. Length: 35.4 miles.

Merced River
Yosemite National Park
PO Box 577
Yosemite National Park, CA
95389-0577

Including the south fork, this segment of the Merced flows through superlative scenery—glaciated peaks, lakes, alpine and subalpine meadows—in alternating pools and cascades. The South Fork possesses one of the few remaining pristine Sierra fisheries with self-sustaining populations of rainbow, eastern brook, and brown trout. The river was designated for outstandingly remarkable scenic, recreational, geological, cultural, biological, and hydrological values. Authorized Nov. 2, 1987. Length: 81 miles.

Middle Delaware River
c/o Delaware Water Gap
National Recreation Area
Bushkill, PA 18324-9410

See Middle Delaware National Scenic River, Pennsylvania, a unit of the National Park System.

Missisquoi and Trout National Wild and Scenic Rivers
2839 VT Route 105
East Berkshire, VT 05447

The designation includes portions of the Missisquoi River, upstream and downstream of the Canadian border, and its major tributary, the Trout River with Big Falls, the largest natural, undammed falls in Vermont. The rivers are renowned for their numerous deep and picturesque bedrock swimming holes. The river was designated for outstandingly remarkable fish, wildlife, and cultural, geological, historical, recreational, and scenic values. Authorized Dec. 19, 2014. Length: 46.1 miles.

Missouri National Recreational River
508 East Second Street
Yankton, SD 57078

See Missouri National Recreational River, Nebraska, a unit of the National Park System.

Mulchatna Wild River
Lake Clark National Park
and Preserve
4230 University Drive
Suite 311
Anchorage, AK 99508-4626

Mulchatna Wild River, which lies within Lake Clark National Park and Preserve, Alaska, is exceptionally scenic as it flows out of Turquoise Lake with the glacier-clad Chigmit Mountains to the east. Moose and caribou inhabit the area. The river was designated for outstandingly remarkable fish and scenic, recreational, and historical values. Authorized Dec. 2, 1980. Length: 24 miles.

Musconetcong National Wild and Scenic River
c/o National Park Service
Northeast Region
National Wild and Scenic
Rivers Division
200 Chestnut Street
Philadelphia, PA 19106-2818

This river, nestled in the heart of the distinctive New Jersey Highlands region, features a remarkably diverse array of natural and cultural resources. It is often referred to as the best trout fishery in New Jersey, where anglers in the region have access to the river from hundreds of acres of publicly owned lands along the river's banks. The river was designated for outstandingly remarkable scenic, recreational, historical, cultural, and ecological values. Authorized: Dec. 22, 2006. Length: 24.2 miles.

Niobrara
National Scenic River
214 W. Hwy 20
Valentine, NE 69201-2104
www.nps.gov/niob

See Niobrara National Scenic Riverway, Nebraska, a unit of the National Park System.

Noatak Wild River
PO Box 1029
Kotzebue, AK 99752-1029

c/o Gates of the Arctic
National Park and Preserve
201 First Avenue
Doyon Bldg.
Fairbanks, AK 99701-4848

Noatak Wild River is situated in Gates of the Arctic National Park and Preserve and Noatak National Preserve in Alaska. The Noatak drains the largest mountain-ringed river basin in America that is still virtually unaffected by human activities. The river was designated for outstandingly remarkable fish, wildlife, and cultural, recreational, and scenic values. Authorized Dec. 2, 1980. Length: 330 miles.

North Fork of the Koyukuk
Wild River
Gates of the Arctic
National Park and Preserve
201 First Ave., Doyon Bldg.
Fairbanks, AK 99701-4848

The river flows from the south flank of the Arctic Divide through broad, glacially-carved valleys beside the rugged Endicott Mountains in Alaska's Central Brooks Range. The river was designated for outstandingly remarkable cultural, historic, recreational, and scenic vlaues. Authorized Dec. 2, 1980. Length: 102 miles.

Obed
Wild and Scenic River
PO Box 429
Wartburg, TN 37887-0429
www.nps.gov/obed

See Obed Wild and Scenic River, Tennessee, a unit of the National Park System.

Rio Grande
Wild and Scenic River
c/o Big Bend National Park
PO Box 129
Big Bend National Park, TX
79834-0129
www.nps.gov/rigr

See Rio Grande Wild and Scenic River, Texas, a unit of the National Park System.

River Styx
Wild and Scenic River
c/o Oregon Caves National
Monument and Preserve
19000 Caves Highway
Cave Junction, OR
97523- 9716

The River Styx is actually the underground segment of Cave Creek as it flows through Oregon Caves National Monument. The river was designated because of its free flow and water quality.
Authorized Dec. 19, 2014. Length: 0.4 miles.

Saint Croix
National Scenic Riverway
401 N. Hamilton Street
St. Croix Falls, WI
54024-0708
www.nps.gov/sacn

See Saint Croix National Scenic Riverway, Wisconsin, a unit of the National Park System.

Salmon Wild River
Kobuk Valley National Park
PO Box 1029
Kotzebue, AK 99752-1029

Salmon Wild River, located within Kobuk Valley National Park, Alaska, is small but exceptionally beautiful, with deep, blue-green pools and many rock outcroppings. The river was designated for outstandingly remarkable recreation, wildlife, and cultural values.
Authorized Dec. 2, 1980. Length: 70 miles.

**Snake River Headwaters
Wild and Scenic River**
c/o Bridger-Teton National
Forest
340 N. Cache
PO Box 1888
Jackson, WY 83001

The Snake River Headwaters flows through parts of Yellowstone and Grand Teton National Parks, the John D. Rockefeller Memorial Parkway, and the Bridger-Teton National Forest in Wyoming. The river was designated for outstandingly remarkable fish, wildlife, and cultural, geological, recreational, scenic, and ecological values.
Authorized March 30, 2009. Length: 387.5 miles.

**Sudbury, Assabet and
Concord National Wild
and Scenic River**
c/o National Park Service
Northeast Region
National Wild and Scenic
Rivers Division
200 Chestnut Street
Philadelphia, PA 19106-2818

The Sudbury and Assabet Rivers join in Concord, Massachusetts, to form the Concord River. The Concord flows through both Great Meadows National Wildlife Refuge and Minute Man National Historical Park. The river played a significant role in early American history as the site of the "shot heard 'round the world" and in the writings of Henry David Thoreau, Ralph Waldo Emerson, and others. The river was designated for outstandingly remarkable ecological, historical, scenic, and recreational values as well as for its place in American literature.
Authorized April 9, 1999. Length: 29 miles.

**Taunton
Wild and Scenic River**
c/o National Park Service
Northeast Region
National Wild and Scenic
Rivers Division
200 Chestnut Street
Philadelphia, PA 19106-2818

The Taunton River is the longest undammed coastal river in New England, supporting 154 species of birds and 45 species of fish, including the bald eagle and the Atlantic sturgeon. The river was designated for outstandingly remarkable fish, estuary, diversity, and historical, archaeological, recreational, scenic, ecological, biological, and agricultural values.
Authorized March 30, 2009. Length: 40 miles.

Tinayguk Wild River
Gates of the Arctic
National Park
201 First Avenue,
Doyon Bldg.
Fairbanks, AK 99701-4848

Alaska's Tinayguk River is the largest tributary of the North Fork of the Koyukuk. Both lie entirely within the pristine environment of Gates of the Arctic National Park and Preserve, Alaska. The river was designted for outstandingly remarkable recreatioanl value.
Authorized Dec. 2, 1980. Length: 44 miles.

Tlikakila Wild River
Lake Clark National Park
and Preserve
4230 University Drive
Suite 311
Anchorage, AK 99508-4626

Located about 100 miles west of Anchorage in Lake Clark National Park, Alaska, Tlikakila Wild River is closely flanked by glaciers, 10,000-foot-high, rock-and-snow-capped mountains, and perpendicular cliffs. The river was designated for outstandingly remarkable fish, wildlife, and geological, historical, recreational, and scenic values.
Authorized Dec. 2, 1980. Length: 51 miles.

Tuolumne River
Yosemite National Park
PO Box 577
Yosemite National Park, CA
95389-0577

The Tuolumne originates from snowmelt off Mounts Dana and Lyell in Yosemite National Park and courses 54 miles before crossing into Stanislaus National Forest. The national forest segment contains some of the most noted whitewater in the High Sierra and is an extremely popular rafting stream. The river was designated for outstandingly remarkable cultural, recreational, scenic, and biological values.
Authorized Sept. 28, 1984. Length: 83 miles.

**Upper Delaware Scenic
and Recreational River**
274 River Road
Beach Lake, PA 18405-9737

See Upper Delaware Scenic and Recreational River, Pennsylvania, a unit of the National Park System.

Virgin
Wild and Scenic River
c/o Zion National Park
Springdale, UT 84767-1099
435-772-3256
www.nps.gov/zion

Over the course of 13 million years, the Virgin River has carved through the red sandstones of Zion National Park, Utah, to create some of the most unforgettable scenery in the National Park System. The erosion from this river created "The Narrows," which is one of the premiere hiking adventures in the park. The river was designated for outstandingly remarkable fish, wildlife, and cultural, geological, recreational, and scenic values.
Authorized March 30, 2009. Length: 169.3 miles.

Wekiva
Wild and Scenic River
c/o National Park Service
Southeast Region
National Wild and Scenic
Rivers Division
100 Alabama Street SW
Atlanta, GA 30303

The Wekiva River Basin is a complex ecological system of rivers, springs, seepage areas, lakes, streams, sinkholes, wetland prairies, hardwood hammocks, pine flatwoods, and sand pine scrub communities. Water qualitiy is exhibited in spring-fed clear streams and blackwater streams receiving most of their flow from precipitation. The river was designated for outstandingly remarkable fish, wildlife, and historical, recreational, and scenic values.
Authorized Oct. 13, 2000. Length: 41.6 miles.

Westfield
Wild and Scenic River
c/o National Park Service
Northeast Region
National Wild and Scenic
Rivers Division
200 Chestnut Street
Philadelphia, PA 19106-2818

The Westfield River provides over 50 miles of the Northeast's finest whitewater, canoeing, and kayaking; contains one of the largest roadless wilderness areas remaining in the state; and is home to several endangered species. The river was designated for outstandingly remarkable fish, wildlife, and geological, historical, recreational, scenic, ecological, biological, and hydrological values.
Authorized Nov. 2, 1993. Lengthened: Oct. 29, 2004. Length: 78.1 miles.

White Clay Creek
Wild and Scenic River
c/o National Park Service
Northeast Region
National Wild and Scenic
Rivers Division
200 Chestnut Street
Philadelphia, PA 19106-2818

White Clay Creek flows through southwestern Chester County, Pennsylvania, and northwestern New Castle County, Delaware. The White Clay Creek watershed is renowned for its scenery, opportunities for birding and trout fishing, and for its historic resources. The watershed is also an important source of drinking water for residents of Pennsylvania and Delaware. The river was designated for outstandingly remarkable fish, wildlife, and geological values.
Authorized Oct. 24, 2000. Lengthened: Dec. 19, 2014. Length: 199 miles.

Wolf River
c/o National Park Service
Midwest Region
National Wild and Scenic
Rivers Division
601 Riverfront Drive
Omaha, NE 68102

Noted as one of the most scenic and rugged rivers in the Midwest, the Wolf flows through the Menominee Reservation. The river is not developed for public use.
Authorized Oct. 2, 1968. Length: 24 miles.

APPALACHIAN TRAIL CONSERVANCY/MICHAEL SCOTT PETTY

Appalachian National Scenic Trail

The National Trails System Act of 1968, as amended, calls for establishing trails in both urban and rural settings for people of all ages, interests, skills, and physical abilities. The act promotes the enjoyment and appreciation of trails while encouraging greater public access. It establishes four classes of trails: national scenic trails, national historic trails, national recreation trails, and side and connecting trails.

National scenic trails are to be continuous, extended routes of outdoor recreation within protected corridors. The first two established under the National Trails System Act were the Appalachian and the Pacific Crest trails. They wind through some of the nation's most striking natural beauty.

National historic trails recognize original trails or routes of travel of national historic significance including past routes of exploration, migration, and military action.

The term national recreation trail is given to an existing local or regional trail when recognized by the federal government, with the consent of any federal, state, local, nonprofit, or private entity having jurisdiction over these lands. Today almost 1,300 of these trails have been designated throughout the country. They are located in all 50 states, the District of Columbia, and Puerto Rico.

Side and connecting trails provide additional access to and between components of the National Trails System. To date, seven have been designated.

Since 1968, 45 long-distance trails have been studied for inclusion in the system, and 30 have been designated. The National Park Service administers 21; the Bureau of Land Management administers one; and the National Park Service and Bureau of Land Management jointly administer two. The U.S. Forest Service administers six.

The National Park Service encourages all public and private agencies to develop, maintain, and protect trails. With the cooperation and support of a nationwide trails community, the vision of an interconnected, cross-country trail system will become a reality. For information about the National Trails System Act visit: www.nps.gov/nts.

Ala Kahakai
National Historic Trail
National Park Service
c/o Kaloko-Honokōhau
National Historical Park
73-4786 Kanalani Street, #14
Kailua Kona, HI 96740-2608
www.nps.gov/alka

Ala Kahakai, "trail by the sea," connects shoreline trails associated with Polynesian settlement, illustrating how Hawaiians flourished as a civilization. Events commemorated along the trail include Captain Cook's historic landing, the rise of Kamehameha I, and changes leading to Hawaii's unique blend of cultures. The trail runs along beaches, passes ancient sites, and goes through natural, urban, and wilderness areas. Established Jan. 24, 2000. Length: 175 miles.

Appalachian
National Scenic Trail
National Park Service
PO Box 50
Harpers Ferry, WV 25425
www.nps.gov/appa

For public inquiries:
Appalachian Trail
Conservancy
PO Box 807
Harpers Ferry, WV 25425

About 2,150 miles of this scenic trail follow the Appalachian Mountains from Katahdin, ME, through New Hampshire, Vermont, Massachusetts, Connecticut, New York, New Jersey, Pennsylvania, Maryland, West Virginia, Virginia, Tennessee, and North Carolina, to Springer Mountain, GA. The trail is one of the two initial components of the National Trails System. It is also a unit of the National Park System. Established Oct. 2, 1968. Length: 2,175 miles.

Arizona
National Scenic Trail
USDA Forest Service
Southwestern Region
Coronado National Forest
300 W. Congress Street
Tucson, AZ 85701

For public inquiries, contact:
Arizona Trail Association
534 N. Stone Avenue
Tucson, Arizona 85705
(602) 252-4794
ata@aztrail.org
www.aztrail.org

The Arizona National Scenic Trail is an 800-mile primitive trail throughout the entire state of Arizona, from the US/Mexico border to the Utah state line. The trail connects deserts, mountains, canyons, forests, communities and people. It is open to all forms of non-motorized recreation and is one of the most biodiverse trails in America.
Administered by the U.S. Forest Service.
Established March 30, 2009. Length: 800 miles

California
National Historic Trail
National Park Service
National Trails
Intermountain Region
PO Box 728
Santa Fe, NM 87504-0728
www.nps.gov/cali

The California Trail is a system of overland routes, with five entry points along the Missouri River and ending at many locations in California and Oregon. From 1831, the trail saw one of America's great mass migrations, seeking the promise of riches and a new life in California.
Established Aug. 3, 1992. Length: 5,600 miles.

Captain John Smith
Chesapeake National
Historic Trail
National Park Service
410 Severn Avenue, Suite 314
Annapolis, MD 21403
www.nps.gov/cajo

This historic trail commemorates the exploratory voyages in 1607-1609 of Captain Smith, interprets the historic and contemporary lifeways of American Indians, and explores the watershed's natural history. Connecting dozens of gateway communities and hundreds of parks, museums, and public access sites, the trail provides land and water-based learning and recreation opportunities along the Chesapeake Bay and its tributaries.
Established: Dec. 19, 2006. Length: 3,000 miles.

**Continental Divide
National Scenic Trail**
USDA Forest Service
Rocky Mountain Region
740 Simms Street
Golden, CO 80401

This trail runs along the Rocky Mountains near the Continental Divide from the US/Canadian border at Waterton Lake in Glacier National Park through Montana, Idaho, Wyoming, Colorado and New Mexico, ending at the US/Mexican border in the Big Hatchets Wilderness Conservation Area. Administered by the U.S. Forest Service
Established Nov. 10, 1978. Length: 3,200 miles.

**El Camino Real de los Tejas
National Historic Trail**
National Park Service
National Trails
Intermountain Region
PO Box 728
Santa Fe, NM 87504-0728
www.nps.gov/elte

Established in the late 1600s as a route connecting missions across the plains of Texas, the route played key roles in securing the Spanish frontier with France, in holding Mexico's northern frontier after independence in 1821, and as the gateway for American settlement of Texas after the Republic period. The route was known as the "Old San Antonio Road." Established Oct. 18, 2004. Length: multiple routes totaling about 2,600 miles.

**El Camino Real
de Tierra Adentro
National Historic Trail**
National Park Service
National Trails
Intermountain Region
PO Box 728
Santa Fe, NM 87504-0728
www.nps.gov/elca

From 1598 to 1882, the 1,600-mile Camino Real de Tierra Adentro joined Mexico City and Santa Fe. It aided exploration, colonization, economic development, and subsequent cultural interactions among Spanish, Anglo, and native peoples. Only the 404 miles in the United States are designated as a National Historic Trail. Co-administered with the Bureau of Land Management.
Established Oct. 13, 2000. Length: 404 miles.

**Florida
National Scenic Trail**
USDA Forest Service
National Forests in Florida
325 John Knox Road, Building F-100
Tallahassee, FL 32303-4106

The trail runs north from Big Cypress National Preserve and the Kissimmee Prairie through various national and state forests to the Gulf Islands National Seashore, all in Florida. Over 1,000 miles have been developed for public use. Administered by the U.S. Forest Service.
Established March 28, 1983. Length: 1,300 miles.

**Ice Age
National Scenic Trail**
National Park Service
700 Rayovac Drive
Suite 100
Madison, WI 53711
www.nps.gov/iatr

Winding over Wisconsin's glacial moraines, the trail links six of the nine units of the Ice Age National Scientific Reserve. It traverses significant features of Wisconsin's glacial heritage. 634 miles are open to public use; additional miles are being developed.
Established Oct. 3, 1980. Length: 1,000 miles.

**Iditarod
National Historic Trail**
Bureau of Land Management
6881 Elmore Road
Anchorage, AK 99507

One of Alaska's preeminent Gold Rush trails, the trail extends from Seward to Nome and is composed of a network of trails and side trails developed in the early 1900s. An annual dog-sled race from Anchorage to Nome brings this trail international attention. Administered by the Bureau of Land Management.
Established Nov. 10, 1978. Length: 2,350 miles.

**Juan Bautista de Anza
National Historic Trail**
National Park Service
c/o NPS Pacific-West Region Office
333 Bush Street, #500
San Francisco, CA 94104-2828
www.nps.gov/juba

The trail commemorates the overland route taken by Spanish colonists in 1775-76 to establish the Presidio and Mission of San Francisco. The Anza Expedition was comprised of 30 families (over 240 individuals) who emigrated from northern Mexico to establish Spain's northernmost colony in Alta California.
Established Aug. 15, 1990. Length in U.S.: 1,200 miles.

Lewis and Clark
National Historic Trail
National Park Service
601 Riverfront Drive
Omaha, NE 68102
www.nps.gov/lecl

The route of the 1804-1806 Lewis and Clark Expedition extends from Wood River, Illinois, to the mouth of the Columbia River near present day Astoria, Oregon. It follows the historic outbound and return routes to connect 11 states (Illinois, Missouri, Kansas, Nebraska, Iowa, South Dakota, North Dakota, Montana, Idaho, Washington, and Oregon) and many tribal lands where public, private, and tribal sites provide for public use and interpretation of the expedition. Established Nov. 10, 1978. Length: 3,700 miles.

Mormon Pioneer
National Historic Trail
National Park Service
324 South State St., Suite 200
Salt Lake City, UT 84111
www.nps.gov/mopi

This trail follows the route over which Brigham Young led the Mormons from Nauvoo, Illinois, to the site of today's Salt Lake City, Utah, in 1846–47. Established Nov. 10, 1978. Length: 1,300 miles.

Natchez Trace
National Scenic Trail
National Park Service
c/o Natchez Trace Parkway
2680 Natchez Trace Parkway
Tupelo, MS 38804-9718
www.nps.gov/natt

The Natchez Trace National Scenic Trail traverses the states of Mississippi, Alabama, and Tennessee and provides visitors an opportunity to experience the unique cultural and natural aspects of the Natchez Trace. The Natchez Trace was a primitive trail stretching some 500 miles through the wilderness from Natchez, Mississippi, to Nashville, Tennessee. The trail parallels the 444-mile corridor of the Natchez Trace Parkway. There are also five developed pedestrian/equestrian sections near the following areas: Nashville, TN; Tupelo, MS; Jackson, MS; Port Gibson, MS; and Natchez, MS. Established March 28, 1983. Length: 64 miles.

New England
National Scenic Trail
National Park Service
Northeast Region
15 State Street
Boston, MA 02109
www.nps.gov/neen

The New England Trail traverses a classic New England landscape: long-distance vistas of rural towns, agrarian lands, forests, and river valleys. The trail also highlights diverse ecosystems, from traprock ridges to vernal pools, lakes, and waterfalls. Established March 30, 2009. Length: 215 miles.

Nez Perce (Nee-Me-Poo)
National Historic Trail
USDA Forest Service
Northern Region
12730 Highway 12
Orofino, ID 83544

The Nez Perce Trail commemorates the war and flight of the non-treaty Nez Perce Indians in 1877. It begins in northeastern Oregon, extends across Idaho to central Montana, bisecting Yellowstone National Park in Wyoming and ending near the Bears Paw Mountains in Montana. Administered by the U.S. Forest Service. Established Oct. 6, 1986. Length: 1,170 miles.

North Country
National Scenic Trail
National Park Service
PO Box 288
Lowell, MI 49331
www.nps.gov/noco

The trail connects outstanding scenic, natural, and cultural sites in seven northern tier states extending from Crown Point, NY, to Lake Sakakawea in North Dakota. Additional miles are being developed. Established March 5, 1980. Length upon completion: approximately 4,600 miles.

Old Spanish
National Historic Trail
National Park Service
National Trails
Intermountain Region
PO Box 728
Santa Fe, NM 87504-0728
www.nps.gov/olsp

Opened by Santa Fe trader Antonio Armijo in 1829, this trail connected Santa Fe to Los Angeles across Mexico's northern frontier. In the following years, Mexicans, Americans, and American Indians traded wool products, horses, mules, and human captives along the trail. Today's route connects natural landmarks, springs, mountain and canyon passes, and historic towns. Co-administered with the Bureau of Land Management.
Established Dec. 4, 2002. Length: about 2,700 miles.

Oregon
National Historic Trail
National Park Service
National Trails
Intermountain Region
PO Box 728
Santa Fe, NM 87504-0728
www.nps.gov/oreg

Between 1841 and 1860, hundreds of thousands of pioneers followed this trail westward from points along the Missouri River to Willamette Valley, Oregon.
Established Nov. 10, 1978. Length: 2,170 miles.

Overmountain Victory
National Historic Trail
National Park Service
2635 Park Road
Blacksburg, SC 29702
www.nps.gov/ovvi

This route follows the path of a band of Revolutionary War patriots who mustered in western Virginia and eastern Tennessee and came across the mountains of North Carolina to Kings Mountain in South Carolina. There they defeated British-led militia in 1780, helping turn the tide for eventual American victory in the war.
Established Sept. 8, 1980. Length: 330 miles.

Pacific Crest
National Scenic Trail
USDA Forest Service
Pacific Southwest Regional Office (Region 5)
1323 Club Drive
Vallejo, CA 94592

Extending from the Mexican border northward along the Sierra and Cascade peaks of California, Oregon, and Washington, the trail reaches the Canadian border near Ross Lake, Washington. The trail is one of the two initial components of the National Trails System. Administered by the U.S. Forest Service.
Established Oct. 2, 1968. Length: 2,638 miles.

Pacific Northwest
National Scenic Trail
USDA Forest Service
c/o Mt. Baker-Snoqualmie NF
2930 Wetmore Avenue
Suite 3A
Everett, WA 98201

This trail begins at the Continental Divide and travels west to the Pacific Ocean. Along the way it passes through wilderness, working landscapes, and downtown Main Streets of the Pacific Northwest. It connects the Pacific Crest and Continental Divide National Scenic Trails.
Administered by the U.S. Forest Service.
Established March 30, 2009. Length: 1,200 miles.

Pony Express
National Historic Trail
National Park Service
National Trails
Intermountain Region
PO Box 728
Santa Fe, NM 87504-0728
www.nps.gov/poex

For about 18 months in 1860–61, horseback riders carried mail between St. Joseph, MO, and Sacramento, CA, in about 10 to 16 days, proving that a regular overland communications link to the Pacific coast was possible. Most of the 185 relay stations no longer exist.
Established Aug. 3, 1992. Length: approximately 2,000 miles.

**Potomac Heritage
National Scenic Trail**
National Park Service
PO Box B
Harpers Ferry, WV 25425
www.nps.gov/pohe

Between the mouth of the Potomac River and the Allegheny Highlands, this evolving trail network provides access to the beauty and heritage of the Potomac and Youghiogheny river corridors. The network includes the Laurel Highlands Hiking Trail, the Chesapeake & Ohio Canal Towpath, part of the Great Allegheny Passage, various named Potomac Heritage Trail segments, the Mount Vernon Trail, bicycling routes on the Northern Neck of Virginia and in southern Maryland, and many parks, historic sites and natural areas.
Authorized: March 28, 1983. Length: approximately 710 miles.

**Santa Fe
National Historic Trail**
National Park Service
National Trails
Intermountain Region
PO Box 728
Santa Fe, NM 87504-0728
www.nps.gov/safe

From 1821 the Santa Fe Trail was an international trade route between Missouri and New Mexico. After the U.S.-Mexican War (1846–1848), it continued to be used for commercial and military freighting, mail delivery, stagecoach lines, and general travel.
Established May 8, 1987. Length: 1,203 miles.

**Selma to Montgomery
National Historic Trail**
National Park Service
7002 US Highway 80 West
PO Box 595
Hayneville, AL 36040-4612
www.nps.gov/semo

This trail commemorates the 1965 voting rights march led by Dr. Martin Luther King, Jr. The marchers walked along U.S. Highway 80 from Brown Chapel A.M.E. Church in Selma, AL, to the State Capitol in Montgomery. The march helped inspire passage of voting rights legislation signed by President Johnson on Aug. 6, 1965.
Established Nov. 12, 1996. Length: 54 miles.

**Star-Spangled Banner
National Historic Trail**
National Park Service
c/o Fort McHenry
National Monument and
Historic Shrine
2400 E. Fort Ave.
Baltimore, MD 21230
www.nps.gov/stsp

This five-pronged set of land and water trails commemorates the movements of British and American forces in the Chesapeake Bay region during the War of 1812. In the summer of 1814, British naval forces occupied the Chesapeake Bay, burned public buildings in Washington, D.C., occupied Alexandria, VA, and laid siege to Fort McHenry in Baltimore, MD. During that unsuccessful siege, Francis Scott Key wrote the poem that became the U.S. national anthem.
Established: May 8, 2008. Length: 290 miles.

**Trail of Tears
National Historic Trail**
National Park Service
National Trails
Intermountain Region
PO Box 728
Santa Fe, NM 87504-0728
www.nps.gov/trte

The Trail of Tears commemorates the primary land and water routes, round-up routes, and disbandment routes used for the forced removal of over 16,000 Cherokee Indians from their ancestral lands in North Carolina, Tennessee, Georgia, and Alabama to Indian Territory (today's Oklahoma) in 1838–39.
Established Dec. 16, 1987; Amended Mar. 30, 2009. Length: approximately 5,045 miles.

**Washington-Rochambeau
Revolutionary Route
National Historic Trail**
National Park Service
200 Chestnut Street,
Philadelphia, PA 19106
www.nps.gov/waro

The Washington-Rochambeau Revolutionary Route commemorates the land and water routes used by the allied forces of the American and French armies and navies leading to the 1781 British surrender at Yorktown, VA, and their victorious return north to Boston, MA. The network of land and water routes traverses nine states and the District of Columbia.
Established March 30, 2009. Length: over 1,000 miles by land and water.

Glacier Bay National Park and Preserve

Alphabetical Listing

HAWAII 50
Hawai'i Volcanoes National Park, Hawaii 50
Herbert Hoover National Historic Site, Iowa 55
Historic Camden Revolutionary War Site, South Carolina 120
Hohokam Pima National Monument, Arizona 25
Home of Franklin D. Roosevelt National Historic Site, New York 82
Homestead National Monument of America, Nebraska 72
Hoover, Herbert (See Herbert Hoover NHS)
Honouliuli National Monument, Hawaii 50
Hopewell Culture National Historical Park, Ohio 88
Hopewell Furnace National Historic Site, Pennsylvania 91
Horseshoe Bend National Military Park, Alabama 18
Hot Springs National Park, Arkansas 30
Hovenweep National Monument, Colorado 39, Utah 102
Hubbell Trading Post National Historic Site, Arizona 25
Hudson River Valley National Heritage Area, New York 127

Ice Age National Scenic Trail, Wisconsin 143
Ice Age National Scientific Reserve, Wisconsin 120
IDAHO 51
Iditarod National Historic Trail, Alaska 143
ILLINOIS 52
Illinois and Michigan Canal National Heritage Corridor, Illinois 127
Independence National Historical Park, Pennsylvania 92
INDIANA 54
Indiana Dunes National Lakeshore, Indiana 54
International Peace Garden, North Dakota 121
Inupiat Heritage Center, Alaska 121
IOWA 54
Isle Royale National Park, Michigan 66

James A. Garfield National Historic Site, Ohio 88
Jamestown National Historic Site, Virginia 121
Jean Lafitte National Historical Park and Preserve, Louisiana 57
Jefferson Memorial (See Thomas Jefferson Memorial)
Jefferson National Expansion Memorial, Missouri 70
Jewel Cave National Monument, South Dakota 95
Jimmy Carter National Historic Site,

Georgia 49
John D. Rockefeller, Jr., Memorial Parkway, Wyoming 113
John Day Fossil Beds National Monument, Oregon 89
John Fitzgerald Kennedy National Historic Site, Massachusetts 63
John H. Chafee Blackstone River Valley National Heritage Corridor, Rhode Island 127
John Muir National Historic Site, California 32
John Wild River, Alaska 135
Johnson, Andrew (See Andrew Johnson NHS)
Johnson, Lyndon B. (See Lyndon B. Johnson NHP and Lyndon Baines Johnson Memorial Grove on the Potomac)
Johnstown Flood National Memorial, Pennsylvania 92
Joshua Tree National Park, California 32
Journey Through Hallowed Ground National Heritage Area, Virginia 128
Juan Bautista de Anza National Historic Trail, California 143

Kalaupapa National Historical Park, Hawaii 50
Kaloko-Honokōhau National Historical Park, Hawaii 50
KANSAS 55
Kate Mullany National Historic Site, New York 121
Katmai National Park and Preserve, Alaska 21
Kenai Fjords National Park, Alaska 21
Kenai Mountains-Turnagain Arm National Heritage Area, Alaska 128
Kennedy, J.F. (See John Fitzgerald Kennedy NHS)
Kennesaw Mountain National Battlefield Park, Georgia 49
KENTUCKY 56
Kern River, California 136
Keweenaw National Historical Park, Michigan 66
King, Martin Luther, Jr. (See Martin Luther King, Jr., NHS and Martin Luther King, Jr. Memorial)
Kings Canyon National Park, California 33
Kings Mountain National Military Park, South Carolina 94
Kings River, California 136
Klondike Gold Rush National Historical Park, Alaska 21, Washington 109
Knife River Indian Villages National Historic Site, North Dakota 86
Kobuk Valley National Park, Alaska 21
Kobuk Wild River, Alaska 136
Korean War Veterans Memorial, District of Columbia 42